THE
HIDDEN
WAYS

Alistair Moffat was born in Kelso, Scotland in 1950. He is an award-winning writer, historian and Director of Programmes at Scottish Television, former Director of the Edinburgh Festival Fringe and former Rector of the University of St Andrews. He is the founder of Borders Book Festival and Co-Chairman of The Great Tapestry of Scotland project.

alistairmoffat.co.uk

Also by Alistair Moffat

Scotland, A History from Earliest Times
Bannockburn: The Battle for a Nation
The British: A Genetic Journey
The Reivers
The Wall: Rome's Greatest Frontier
Before Scotland
The Sea Kingdoms
The Borders: A History
Tyneside: A History of Newcastle and Gateshead from Earliest Times
Tuscany: A History

THE
HIDDEN
WAYS

SCOTLAND'S FORGOTTEN ROADS

ALISTAIR
MOFFAT

CANONGATE

This paperback edition published in Great Britain in 2018 and in the USA and Canada in 2019 by Canongate Books

First published in Great Britain in 2017 and in the USA and Canada in 2018 by Canongate Books Ltd, 14 High Street, Edinburgh EH1 1TE

Distributed in the USA by Publishers Group West and in Canada by Publishers Group Canada

canongate.co.uk

1

British Library Cataloguing-in-Publication Data
A catalogue record for this book is available on
request from the British Library

ISBN 978 1 78689 103 7

Typeset in Dante MT by Palimpsest Book Production Ltd,
Falkirk, Stirlingshire

Printed and bound in Great Britain by Clays Ltd, St Ives plc.

In memory of my father, John Lauder Moffat

Contents

The First Steps

When I am going that way, I often pull in by the side of a single-track road that passes the farm where my grandmother was born. Cliftonhill sits on the south-facing slopes of the valley of the Eden Water, near Kelso in the Scottish border country. And it is beautiful. Near the field entry where I stop, there is a gap in the hedge that lets me look down to the Eden Water winding its lazy way to join the Tweed a mile or two to the east. The contours of the fields are old, and they are moulded to the meander of the little river. On the opposite bank, they climb up to Hendersyde Farm.

Nothing much has changed since 1896, the year my grannie was born. What I see when I lean on the fence a few metres from her farm cottage is what she saw as a child, and it moves me very much. I seem to slip through a crack in time, back to when Bina was a four year old looking for hens' eggs around the stackyard, helping to lead the milker cows into the evening byre, waving a stick and shouting at the bullocks to help her mother and grandfather move them onto new grazing. These were the everyday stories she told me, what Bina called 'the auld life' on the land. To walk to where she once stood and look south over the folded ridges leading up to the dark heads of the Cheviots is to let me walk beside her once more.

Bina lived in a crowded, two-room cottage, full of women and one man, her grandfather, William Moffat. He was First Horseman at Cliftonhill, the old term for the head ploughman. With his wife, Margaret Jaffrey (in Scotland, women often kept their maiden name and it is what is inscribed on her tombstone in the kirkyard at Ednam, the village at the foot of the hill), William had four daughters. My great-grandmother, Annie Moffat, also kept her name – but only because she had no husband. Baby Bina was illegitimate.

Early one summer morning I decided to walk where Annie and my old great-aunts walked. In the nineteenth and early twentieth centuries many women worked in the fields and because of the nature of their contracts with farmers and the men they hired, they were called bondagers. Wearing bonnets with a wide brim around their faces to keep out the rain and the sun, and full skirts to do the same, these women would rise early, pull on their hob-nail boots, shoulder their hoes and walk down the hill to the bottom fields by the Eden to swing open the gate to the turnip field. When I walked where they walked, I fancied I could hear the clatter of their boots and their quiet chatter as the mist lifted off the little river. For a moment I was with them, these people who made me, and through the damp earth and the fresh smell of green I intuited something of the rhythm of their lives.

That walk has stayed with me. It prompted me to begin thinking about this book and the project that goes with it, about how vital it was to stop, get out of the car (or off the train or bus) and not to see the countryside through the glass of a windscreen or a window. Anyone who wants to understand something of the elemental nature of our history should try to walk through it, should listen for the natural sounds our ancestors heard, smell the hedgerow honeysuckle and the pungent, grassy, milky stink of cowshit, look up and know something of shifts in the weather and the transit of the seasons and feel the earth that once was grained into their hands.

This is not a set of romantic, ahistorical notions, or a rash of New Age nonsense, but a necessity for anyone who seriously wishes to understand the texture, the feel of the millions of lives lived on the land of Scotland, lives that are rarely recorded anywhere. To walk in the footsteps of our ancestors is to sense some of that everyday experience come alive under our feet. The cities and large towns where most Scots now live are very recent and the habit of working indoors in well-heated and lit factories or offices, usually sitting down, is also very new, little more than two centuries old. Even as late as 1900, more than 400,000 Scots worked on farms, far more than in heavy industry, or mining or the building trades. And they were out in all weathers, often cold, sometimes wet through, old sacking across their shoulders long since sodden. Before the industrial and agricultural revolutions of a century or more before, almost all Scots worked and lived on the land or had a close link with food production of some kind. For the overwhelming balance of our history, the 11,000 years since the end of the last Ice Age, the Scots have been country people.

And except for the tiny minority who owned horses, we walked everywhere. That habit died much more recently, within the span of my own lifetime. When the age of mass transport arrived in the late nineteenth century, ordinary people sometimes travelled on trains, if they could afford it. But it was not until the early 1960s when car ownership became possible for most (even if it was an old banger) that we stopped walking. My mother, Ellen Irvine, worked in the Hawick mills in the 1930s, and she and her sisters would think nothing of walking seven or eight miles or more to a country dance in a village hall, and then walking seven or eight miles home afterwards. There was no alternative.

Now, we sit and stare blankly out of a car windscreen or train window, and we see the countryside rush past as little more than the space between destinations. We are missing a great deal. Certainly, important moments in Scotland's history happened in (very small) towns such as Edinburgh, St Andrews and Stirling. But in Walter Scott's excellent phrase, that tended to be the big bow-wow stuff. Almost all of us come from generations of ordinary people who worked the land, and to understand something of their lives we should find a pair of boots and a map, and try to walk where they walked.

The Hidden Ways began as a highly personal journey back into the twilight of the past, but I quickly realised that what I was doing might have a wider application, be a good way of connecting with the experience of a hundred generations of Scots, going back 2,000 or 3,000 years, far back into the darkness of the deep past, beyond the reach of genealogy or written records of any kind. Many modern roads overlie much older ways, tracks where people walked from where they lived to towns or villages, or between them. It occurred to me that if the faded map of roads no longer travelled in Scotland could be made vivid once more, then that would allow many people to walk beside the ghosts of an immense past, beside their people.

And so work began, and the first steps were taken. Some of them turned out to be very surprising.

Faltering Steps

The Wet Road

On the night of 6 July 1307, a vast army camped on Burgh Marsh on the southern shore of the Solway Firth, about three miles north-west of the old Roman city of Carlisle and its squat, sturdy castle. Instead of pitching his pavilions, corralling the animals and allowing his men to bivouac in the shelter of the ancient walls in preparation for striking north into Scotland, the army commander had led his host into the low-lying, midge-infested marshes to the west, where both horses and men will have spent an uncomfortable night. But this single-minded king cared little for comfort.

Much given to volcanic rages, relentlessly ambitious, and six foot two inches tall, Edward I of England towered over the medieval history of Britain. On his tomb in Westminster Abbey, the description *Malleus Scotorum*, the Hammer of the Scots, is inscribed. And it was true. Edward almost succeeded in converting Scotland into an English colony, as he had done with Wales. But the conquest was never completed and in 1306 Robert Bruce defied the man who claimed to be his overlord and had himself crowned King of Scots at Scone. A year later Edward led a vast army northwards. With more than 20,000 men, it was enough to crush resistance, once and for all. But the king was very old for the

5

times at 68, and was suffering from persistent dysentery. On 7 July 1307, he died on Burgh Marsh.

In 1685 the Duke of Norfolk paid for the erection of a monument to mark the place where this 'great and terrible king' passed into history. It is a strange sandstone pillar that stands in the midst of the empty marshes, surrounded by iron railings, with the flat horizon of the Solway behind and the green hills of Scotland far beyond. When I first came to the Burgh Marsh, I discovered that no road leads to or from this lonely exclamation mark in the landscape, only a wind and rainswept path. The salty grass was pockmarked with half-concealed sinkholes and in places treacherous. Being careless, not looking where I was going, one leg suddenly slipped down a deep sinkhole right up to my backside and I might have broken it if I hadn't fallen sideways. Surely this was no place to bring a vast medieval army, its ox-carts, the armoured knights and their snorting destriers, and all the rumbling paraphernalia of war. What on earth was Edward I and his huge army doing here?

They were about to take a road no longer travelled, the wet road across the Solway Firth. To the east, where the modern A74 thrums with traffic, there was once a vast, waterlogged, sucking and trackless bog known as the Solway Moss. Marching around it involved a long and dangerous detour, and for many centuries generals preferred to take a direct route and ford the Solway Firth at low tide. On the farther shore stood the mass of the Lochmabenstane, a relic of a prehistoric stone circle, and to keep to the right line those who waded up to their waists across the outfalls of the Rivers Eden and Esk needed to keep their eye fixed on this sea-mark.

It was a bright autumn day and there was no haze over the water. I could see the ancient stone clearly and I had borrowed a pair of waders. I could see the flat expanse of Rockcliffe Sands and that meant the tide was out. Although I couldn't tell if it was ebbing or flooding, I waded out for about a hundred metres until the water was at thigh-level. Before each step, I poked at the sea bed with my old hazel crook, feeling for any sudden shelf or hole – something I should have done earlier on the marsh. Parts of the bed felt gravelly. I knew I was on the southern edge of the outflow of the River Eden and the current seemed strangely weak. But I was alone and it occurred to me, when I was part of the way across, that if I reached the northern shore, my car was parked on the southern. Something I had not thought of until I was standing in the Solway Firth. Would I have enough time to wade back across before the tide came rushing in? Discretion prevailed over daftness and I waded back to the banks of the Burgh Marsh.

The standing stone and the wet road that led to it gave the Solway its name: the Vikings called it the Sulvath Fjordr, the Firth of the Pillar Ford. The Old Scandinavian word *vath* is cognate to the English 'wade', and the term 'wath' is still used for a ford across the Solway. There were three fords used in the Middle Ages and beyond: the Annan Wath, the Dornock or Sandywathe, and the Solewath. Edward I's camp was close to where the Solewath, the Pillar Ford, ran across the river courses and the Rockcliffe Sands to make landfall in Scotland at the Lochmabenstane. In the event, the old king's death meant the English army did not wade into the firth but turned around and made their way back south.

The Solway fords are all but forgotten and certainly no longer crossed. But their use is very surprising to a modern eye, the way we see the landscape now, and wading across the firth is something that would never occur to us. The image of great armies, Roman legions and medieval hosts, splashing across tells a different sort of history, offers a new understanding of how our ancestors saw the landscape and made their way through it. Washed over by the grey waters of the firth, the fords are hidden ways and they tell half-forgotten stories about Scotland.

Step No Further

The Lost Road

On Tiree, where they survive in numbers, corncrakes are heard much more than they are seen. Their grating 'krek-krek' call is loud and very different from the sweeter notes of the blackbird and the thrush. Particularly in the mating season when males mark out their territory, the call needs to be clearly audible because crakes are ground-nesting birds who like to conceal themselves in the long grass of meadows and hayfields. Not only are they signalling to potential mates, they are also warning other males to keep their distance.

As late as the middle of the nineteenth century, corncrakes were common across Britain. In her vast book on household management and cookery, Mrs Beeton recommended roasting them on a skewer and advised that four would make a satisfying dish. But rather than hunting, it was the coming of mechanised hay cutting that made the crakes rare, as their nests were often wrecked before the eggs could hatch. Across Britain their numbers collapsed, shrinking back to the Hebrides, to the meadows and machairs of Tiree and a handful of other islands. Long gone from the Scottish Lowlands, the echo of these noisy little birds survives only in very occasional place names, and one of these is fascinating, exotic – a signpost for a lost road.

Crhachoctrestrete appears in the documents turned out

by the clerks of King David I in the early twelfth century. It was used by them and later royal officials to mark part of the boundaries of Coldinghamshire, the lands belonging to the ancient convent of St Aebbe and its successor, Coldingham Priory. Precision mattered because until the twelfth century the priory belonged to the Prince Bishop of Durham.

Crhachoctrestrete is a strange, complex, lyrical Old English name; it has three elements and read in reverse order they mean 'the paved road by the oak tree where there are crakes'. Strete, or the Latin *strata*, is almost always a reference to Roman roads, as in Watling Street or Ermine Street in England. *Octre* is oak tree and *crhach* is crake. The place name of Crhachoctrestrete, or any recognisable derivative, appears on no modern maps, but it seems that the paved road once ran through eastern Berwickshire. The documents suggest a route that spurred off the arterial Roman road north of modern Berwick upon Tweed, what was known as the Devil's Causeway. It led westward into the undulating fields above Billie and then on to Bunkle Castle before striking north to Oldhamstocks and the East Lothian coastal strip. No large development of any other significant sort has taken place in eastern Berwickshire since the legions tramped north, and armed with a large-scale Ordnance Survey map, a GPS device, a camera and as much common sense as I could muster, I drove deep into the countryside to places where I reckoned the road might still be visible 2,000 years after it was made. I wanted to walk where the Romans had marched, literally making an inroad into unknown territory. Perhaps I could somehow see it as they saw it.

It was a baking, windless July day and the corn, the trees and every other growing thing was at its fullest burst, the June rain having made the hedgerows lush – and impenetrable – and the grass, nettles and willowherb chest-high in places. I parked in the shade next to Bunkle (or Bonkyll) Church, a beautiful, singular site surrounded by mature hardwood trees and reached by a leafy lane. Apart from a substantial manse, there were no other buildings near. Perhaps it was Bonkyll's isolation that made security unnecessary, and it was pleasing to be able to enter what was a foursquare, late Georgian kirk, clearly still used for worship, well kept and welcoming.

Close by the kirk stood a ruined apse, clearly much older. I discovered later that it had been built in the late eleventh century and was testament to an ancient sacred site, and an enduring, even moving, continuity. But where was the community that the old kirk had served and where was Bunkle Castle? The Ordnance Survey marked it lying next to the main road, about 400 metres north of the kirk. But all I could see was a densely wooded copse set on no more than a low mound. Making my way back up the leafy lane, I walked along the roadside, but the hedge was so dense and the woodland so dark that I could make out nothing. When I finally fought my way through the beech branches and skittered down a slope, I saw a fence with a kissing gate, and looming behind it a massive fragment of masonry. Thrashing through the nettles and long grass, I scrambled up onto the low mound and was able to trace a circular tumbledown wall and several other fragments of tremendously thick masonry. It was as though Bunkle Castle was being overwhelmed by greenery, swallowed by the Earth.

Yet it was once a place of great power, commanded by a man who would become the progenitor of kings and queens of Great Britain and Ireland. Sir John Stewart held Bunkle and fought alongside William Wallace in the wars for Scotland. In 1298 he led the company of Scottish archers at the Battle of Falkirk and was killed as Edward I's mounted

knights repeatedly charged the splintering Scottish forma-
tions of spearmen, the schiltrons. But Sir John's end was
also a beginning. Recent research into his ancestral DNA
has shown that the Royal Stewart marker carried down the
male line from Robert II to James VII and II originated with
him, John Stewart, Lord of Bunkle, or Bonkyll. Henry Lord
Darnley, the father of James VI and I, was a direct descendant.

Between the kirk and the castle there is now a wide grass
park where I could see a few horses and cows with calves
at foot, grazing. But once Bunkle had been a village, a place
known for its cottage weavers, the inspiration for disparaging
doggerel verse recorded by a local historian. And yet there
were no signs of the slightest ground disturbance, no humps
and bumps, and aerial photographs showed nothing of note.
The place name is a reference to the church, for *cill* or *kyll*
is a Celtic version of the Latin *cella*, a chapel, and an ancient
one at that. The first element of *bun* is still used in Scots
Gaelic place names and means 'at the foot of'. The sense
of Bunkle or Bonkyll is 'the village by the kirk' and it appears
that the castle took the same name. But there was no indi-
cation of a paved road or Roman road on the ground.

Part of my hypothesis was that if the road ran west off
the Devil's Causeway and its surface had endured centuries
of winter frosts and rains, then it might still have been in
use in the Middle Ages. Many other Roman roads were
regularly travelled long after the legions departed. I drove
over to the site of Billie Castle, but its remains were even
more slight than Bunkle's. There seemed to be nothing to
see. The Ordnance Survey then led me further east to
Causewaybank Farm. A place name with 'causeway' or
'causey' is often a memory of where a paved road crossed
an obstacle and the single-track road through the farm dipped
downhill to cross a burn. Here there might be traces. But

as at Bunkle and Billie, there was nothing to be seen and no obvious route a road might take.

The Romans did not undertake the mighty labour of building a road for no good reason, but I could not work out why they would have wanted to travel through the Berwickshire countryside and then up through the Lammermuirs to Old-hamstocks when they had a perfectly serviceable coast road. And yet there it was in the documents – the Crhachoctrestrete, the paved road by the oak tree where there are crakes. Maybe place names would help.

To reach the site of Billie Castle, I had driven through the pretty village of Auchencrow. Apparently unusual on a map of everyday English, Old English or Scots names such as Sunnyside, Fairlaw, Reston and Preston, it derives from Gaelic. Unfortunately Achaidh na Cra has nothing to do with crakes or even craws: it means 'the Field of the Trees'. In any event, it had been known by an earlier name that began with Alden, probably an Old English personal name. And there was no sign of the line of a paved road, nothing I could see in a hedge line or a boundary of any sort. All I had noted was a very straight road from Billie Castle to Auchencrow.

Even though it had been a long and frustrating day, I decided to drive into the hills above Bunkle. The medieval boundary documents had listed a place called Eiforde after Crhachoctrestrete and all that I had read agreed that this must be a ford across the Eye Water, the little river that reaches the sea at Eyemouth.

Looking more closely at the OS map, I saw that the Drakemire Burn ran into the Eye close to what looked like a very straight track that aimed north-west towards Oldhamstocks. *Drek* or *drake* is an Old Scots name for the crake, an onomatopoeic version of its call. Maybe there was a gossamer trace of the Crhachoctrestrete somewhere nearby. Across the Eye at Butterdean Farm the map showed two intriguing sites: Camp Well and the site of a castle. The combination was very suggestive. But when I stopped to look around I could see nothing of either feature and there was no one to ask.

The Ordnance Survey took me through the farm to a crossroads, one that turned out to be busy. To the north, access was denied by a sequence of very emphatic roadside signs. A contractor was using the very straight road as a means to bring construction materials to a wind farm and I was unequivocally warned to go no further. Or else. In addition, a vast tonnage of aggregate had been thrown down and rolled flat on the track marked on the map. Maybe it really was time to point the car west and go home.

But to the south there stretched a much more promising road. It had been badly rutted by the giant wheels of modern tractors and there was a good deal of standing water of uncertain depth. It had been fouled by the rainbow glint of diesel. I fished out my wellies and decided to splash through and see where it led. Once the track cleared a shelter belt on the west and passed a field entry, and the tractor ruts consequently became much less deep, it slowly dawned on me that this was an ancient road of some kind, even though it appeared to lead from nowhere to nowhere.

At about a hundred metres from the crossroads, the track widened dramatically and it was hard underfoot. Maybe, maybe, maybe. To the east there was clear evidence of a ditch and, where there were bare patches, cobbles about the size of a fist had been rammed down to make an even surface. A great deal of work had gone into the construction of this road, the work of very many hands. It led down to the shallow valley of the Eye Water, perhaps to the place noted as Eiforde in the medieval documents.

The grass and nettles were very high by the waterside and I stumbled several times over invisible piles of stones. Something substantial shot out of the undergrowth and into the burn, perhaps a water rat. I could see that I had come to the point where the Drakemire Burn joined the Eye, making the crossing wider, and the opposite bank looked too steep for walkers or riders, far less carts. Maybe not. Maybe this was an old farm track. But what encouraged me were two parallel lines of mature trees climbing up the opposite side of the Eye towards the main road, the A6112.

Once I had flogged back up the hill and returned to my car at the crossroads, I turned around, crossed the little river at Grantshouse and drove west on the main road, finding a layby near the lines of trees. If I had entertained any doubts about this being a Roman road, the Crhachoctrestrete, they evaporated when I saw this wide avenue. Here it was. Between two fields of pasture, the road – because that was what it undoubtedly was – swept majestically down the slope, at least fifteen to eighteen metres wide in places, and there were clearly worked kerbstones lying amongst the roots of the trees on either side. It was very dramatic and the canopy of the beeches made a tunnel, a time tunnel. They also told me something else. There were about forty or fifty trees, all of them mature and planted by the sides of the road at the same time so that they would create an avenue. The landowner who had this done knew that this was an ancient road and he or she respected it, enhanced it by marking it so clearly in the landscape.

The paved road had become the Roman road by the oak tree where there are crakes, and I had found at least a mile of its length. At last. How much more there might be was for another day. Climbing back into my car, I found a bottle of (warm) water, wrote up my notes and resolved to see if it was possible to walk to Oldhamstocks once the wind farm restrictions had been lifted.

* * *

What follows is a diary, a series of accounts of walks along some of Scotland's hidden ways. I have arranged them not in the order I did them, but chronologically, beginning in the mists of prehistory and ending with a lost road built in the panicky summer of 1940. The ways I walked all had differing uses. Some were military, others commercial and one was done for the love of God. I also tried to walk through different geography, so there are Highland as well as Lowland journeys, and one in the old heart of a city.

Over the last twenty years, I have written a great deal about Scotland's history and most of my research for my books has been done at home or in libraries, latterly with the help of the internet, and also through several visits to sites that seemed important. This book was very different. In my writing life I have never physically exerted myself so much. For the routes I took and those I didn't, I walked about 300 miles, I took thousands of photographs on my phone (this turned out to be a much better way of recording a walk than scribbling in a notebook), and once or twice I very nearly troubled the emergency services – or would have if my phone had had a signal.

Being in my late 60s, what my wife calls the cocktail hour of life, some of these walks were much more tiring than I anticipated, even though my farm work keeps me reasonably fit. But that is the nature of research. Surprises come thick and fast. The shortest of all the walks was in fact the most exhausting and the longest was one of the most easily achieved. All of them are printed indelibly on my memory, usually for the right reasons, and all taught me a great deal, were eye-opening in every way. And as someone who perhaps knows more than most about Scotland's history, I saw parts of it in a completely new light. In Jim Hunter's memorable phrase, I compiled an archive of the feet.

The walks took a year to complete and I made my way through Scotland's past in all weathers, in all four seasons and across all sorts of terrain. When I first began thinking seriously about this book, after several visits to the place where my grandmother was born, I hoped I could walk in the footsteps of many of the ancestors of most Scots. And I feel I did that. I walked where they walked, I saw what they saw, and I felt the wind, the rain and the sun on my face just as they did. And more, I was alone – and alive – in the landscape with nothing but my own resources to sustain me. On my back I carried food, water, spare clothing and a groundsheet, and in my pockets a map and a compass. And I hoped that my body would cope, that I wouldn't fall and break something. I came greatly to value that solitude and self-reliance and was at peace in a landscape that was neither empty nor quiet. All around me I felt the ghosts of an immense past, I heard their whispers and I smiled when they walked by my side through the fields and woods. I relished the companionship of the dead.

This series of journeys may have been exhausting, but it is by no means exhaustive. Many more hidden ways wait to be rediscovered and I hope readers are prompted to help bring a faded map of Scotland back into vivid focus. If you do, you will see our country differently, and perhaps more clearly.

Fortingall
Kenmore
Aberfeldy
Croft Moraig
River Tay
Loch Tay
Cleaven Dyke
Inchtuthil
Dunkeld
Stanley
River Tay
Scone
Perth
Firth of Tay

The River Road ①

I

The River Road

Loch Tay to the Firth of Tay

It seemed right to begin in Perthshire. Not only can it claim to be the heart of Scotland, it is also its essence, encompassing both the wildness of the Highlands and some of our most fertile farmland. And running through Perthshire, from its source in the mountains down to the sea beyond Dundee, is the mighty River Tay. Fed by Loch Tay, it is immediately a big river, and a highway deep enough to allow small craft to be paddled down its length. In volume, it is by far the biggest river in Britain, bigger than the Thames and Trent together. And what all this means is something significant: it is the closest in Scotland we have to a prehistoric routeway.

Some of these survive in England, such as the Ridgeway, the Icknield Way and the Sweet Track. But in Scotland none can be identified for any length. The Tay, however, has been much travelled for millennia and it flows through a richly preserved prehistoric landscape; along its banks there are also monuments to the reach of the Roman Empire, to early medieval sanctity, to the Jacobite convulsions of the late seventeenth century, to the ingenuity of the industrial revolution and to modern sport.

The Tay is not a hidden way in a literal sense, but the ways in which the peoples of the past used it have often been forgotten. And they offer a historical framework, from prehistory to the present day, for the nine other routes that follow.

This journey begins with a tree, the ancient, lustrous and dense yew tree. Its evergreen shade shelters uncounted country churchyards, where many generations of villagers have passed its flaking trunk and looping boughs on their way to Sunday services. Its solidity seems as dependable as the churches it protects. But some yews appear to be very old, decrepit, themselves in need of care. At Hambledon Parish Church in Surrey, the girth of one tree measures thirty-five feet and its creaking branches rest on the heads of handy tombstones. Twelve miles to the south at Stedham in West Sussex the vicar and his parishioners paid for wire hawsers to hold their yew together. As with many of these remarkable trees, it had long ago lost its heartwood and become hollow, the growth continuing through satellite root systems formed at the tree's edge. In Much Marcle churchyard, in Herefordshire, the verger has built benches inside a massive old specimen, using wood from its fallen branches.

The yew tree seems eternal, its glossy dark green foliage fringing the shutter-click of a million baptisms, weddings and funerals. As the generations pass beneath it, the yew lives on and on, nodding its old head in the evening breeze, much loved, protected, even revered.

Perhaps Britain's most famous yew tree stands a long way north of these English country churchyards. The remains of the oldest yew of all are to be found at Fortingall in Highland Perthshire, in the shadow of the mountains, and in 1769 its girth was said to be vast at fifty-two feet. Like the tumbledown megaliths of a wooden henge, fragments of the hollowed trunk used to lie in a wide circle and funeral processions passed through it as they entered the graveyard. The Fortingall yew is believed to have lived for at least 4,500 years – the oldest living organism in Europe. More recent studies have produced a table correlating girth with likely age and the results are startling, prompting a radically different view of the iconic yew. It appears that more than 500 churchyards in Britain, most of them in the south-east of England, have trees which are older than the churches. Some of them much older.

What this means is both obvious and obscure. Clearly yew trees were growing, many of them to maturity, before a church was built beside them and before bodies began to be buried around it. Equally clearly, early churches were not just built anywhere but only on sanctified sites, ground that had been blessed by incoming missionary priests and made holy with the sanction of Almighty God. The Reverend Gilbert White, the author of *The Natural History and Antiquities of Selborne*, in Hampshire, and many other eighteenth-century antiquaries believed that the yews were planted in the early Christian period because a connection was made between the great age, the apparent immortality of the trees and the Christian belief in the resurrection and in eternal life. But if many of the trees predate the arrival of Christianity, then this traditional interpretation cannot stand.

Some other explanation for the prior presence of so many yews must be found, an explanation that travels to the shadowy heart of Scotland's pre-Christian past, an explanation that begins to tell a long, half-forgotten story, the story of Scotland before Scotland. And that is why the ancient yew at Fortingall, standing close to the geographical heart of Scotland, is a good place to begin.

When my journey up the course of the Tay reached Aberfeldy, I turned off the main road and crossed the river by General Wade's elegant bridge. It carried one of the most strategically important of his roads, one that struck deep into the heart of the mountains and the core of Jacobite support. Built in 1730, it runs from Crieff to Dalnacardoch to join the road to Inverness, and its purpose was to move soldiers and artillery quickly to places where trouble flared. A network had been created by the 1750s and, just as Roman roads had done, it allowed a small army to be more effective because it could be highly mobile.

I turned west off the line of General Wade's road to find the mouth of Glen Lyon and signs for Fortingall. On the road, I passed another sign, one for the hamlet of Dull. Under its name ran the line, 'Twinned with Boring of Oregon'.

Beyond Dull, the River Lyon meandered on its narrow flood plain and I noticed what looked like a low mound with a single standing stone planted near its centre. I pulled off the road and found myself outside the splendid Fortingall Hotel, a crow-stepped, foursquare, well-looked-after building. What I had entirely failed to notice was the little church standing to its east, partly hidden by a very bushy yew tree. Ignoring the standing stone, I opened the cast-iron gate into the kirkyard and stepped back more than 4,000 years into pre-history.

The ancient tree is well defended by a stout stone wall and black, spiked iron railings. Behind stand some taller trees and even on a sunny day the imprisoned yew is mostly in shadow, its tangled form difficult to make out clearly. Near the centre of a circle of pale wooden pegs what looked like a partly rotted trunk had sent out substantial limbs at drunken angles, while close to the wall where I stood another trunk had sent out thicker branches also at strange angles. These were supported by blocks of masonry, a little like the headstones at Hambledon Church. Despite the impression of decrepitude and decay, the green foliage of the ancient yew is still abundant and lustrous. In fact, a recent study shows that the tree is still developing and changing. In 2015 a horticulturalist from the Royal Botanic Garden in Edinburgh noticed three ripe red berries on one of its outer branches. It had long been thought of as a masculine tree, one that produced pollen (female yews grow berries), but it seemed that the old tree was undergoing a sex change, late in life.

Apparently the two trunks of the yew need the protection of its wall and railing enclosure. An information board told me that people were in the habit of removing large bits of it, and children used to light fires inside the original hollow trunk.

A more recent event recalled the persistent magic of these ancient trees. On 25 January 1990, a tremendous gale blew down the yew in Selborne churchyard. Almost immediately thousands of people descended on the village, some of them to mourn the tree's passing, most to beg or steal a piece of the wood. Certainly Gilbert White had made it the most famous yew tree in England, but it also seemed that an old power was at work, a power which has lasted for millennia, for when archaeologists arrived to examine the upended root system they found the tangled remains of very many skeletons. Since 1200, and probably long before, people had been buried hard up against the side of the tree. As the centuries passed and it slowly grew over their graves, the roots curled around the skeletons, often moving them from their original positions. Perhaps their souls were drawn up through the old yew's trunk and sent out into the free air.

The word 'yew' is a straight survival from the Old Welsh *ywen* or *pren ywen* for yew tree. And it should be remembered that before the coming of the Anglo-Saxons in the sixth and seventh centuries, dialects of Old Welsh were spoken the length of Celtic Britain. In all these old languages and the habits of mind they articulated, there are glimmers of a deep religious hinterland. It was believed that the sinuous roots and branches (what I saw at Fortingall was typical of the way yews grow) took a unique grip on the earth and the air, curling around the bodies of the dead and drawing out their essence, their dream-souls, then expelling them into the sky through their ever-living branches. Now, that is a crude unpacking of complex, confused and contradictory fragments from a wide variety of Welsh, Irish and Scottish sources, but it has proved to be the core of a persistent belief.

At Fortingall, people still wish to be buried close to the great tree, and perhaps over the centuries many skeletons lie wrapped in its roots, moving slowly closer to its hollow heart. As I walked around the small churchyard, I noticed that John Keddie had been interred on 8 September 2010, and Jenny Kinimonth on 8 July 2015. More continuity stood against the wall of the whitewashed kirk. A very old and hefty font had been filled not with holy water but Perthshire rainwater. In an alcove inside the kirk, itself not old, there was another tangible link with a long past. Cast in iron with a bronze coating was a priest's handbell, what was once used to summon the faithful or the forgetful to worship in a time before clocks and watches. Several have been found in Highland Perthshire. They remind us that when the word of God first came to Scotland there were few churches to shelter adherents. Missionaries preached in the open air and to summon a congregation they walked around settled places ringing a bell. It was the beginning of an ancient practice that much later led to bell towers and wonderful music. And when the priests did this, they called out the name of the meeting place. It had to be somewhere familiar and preferably a place with pre-existing sacred associations. Often a place with a yew tree, and that became the natural place to build a church.

While the dedication of the kirk at Fortingall is very early and very unusual, (to Coeddi, a bishop of Iona who died in 712) the sanctity of the site is clearly much older. The yew stands in a clear context, an area where much has survived from the pre-Christian millennia. What had first caught my attention and made me stop my car was the Càrn nam Marbh, the Cairn of the Dead, a Bronze Age burial mound from the second or first millennium BC that had been reused in the fourteenth century to bury those who died in the pandemic of the Black Death. They were not welcome in the old kirkyard and the sacred yew would not be allowed to wrap its roots around their rotting corpses. The standing stone I had seen planted in the mound turned out to be called Clach a' Phlaigh, the Plague Stone, but archaeologists reckoned that it had been set up 3,000 years before, probably as part of a stone circle. A strange plaque on it reads, 'Here lie the victims of the Great Plague of the fourteenth century, taken here on a sledge drawn by a white horse led by an old woman'. It is a haunting image; the stuff of nightmares.

The Cairn of the Dead clearly had significance beyond the macabre. As the old yew looked on, a great bonfire was built at Samhain, a Celtic festival that marked the end of summer, now Christianised as Halloween. While it crackled and roared in the October wind, the community at Fortingall took hands and made a circle around the fire. Then they danced, first moving sunwise and then widdershins, in modern terms clockwise and anti-clockwise. Known as *deiseal* in Gaelic, sunwise was the lucky, prosperous course, what was most propitious. Anti-clockwise much less so. Insofar as it can be understood or generalised, Celtic belief held that the gods were not like the loving and forgiving Christian God and were likely to be malicious unless they were propitiated. This could mean doing things in the correct ritual manner: funeral processions in the Hebrides still approach the graveside from east to west, or sunwise. These beliefs died hard and the bonfire at Fortingall was lit as late as 1924 before the flames of paganism finally died down.

Having resisted the comforts and scones of the Fortingall Hotel, I drove up Glen Lyon to cross by the pass at Auchtar and find the northern shores of Loch Tay. The autumn sun shimmered off the water and the light flickered through the birches by the side of the loch road to Kenmore. There the River Tay begins, flowing directly out of the loch and immediately becoming a big, navigable waterway. A fascinating statistic illustrates the change from a huge, placid loch to a vibrant, urgent river. From the foot of Ben Lui at the western end, it takes 420 days for a drop of water to reach Kenmore. From there the same drop of water takes only 20 days to reach the estuary of the Firth of Tay and disappear into the North Sea. But before I began to follow the river, a highway through our early history, I wanted to visit the remains and a reconstruction of a prehistoric waterworld.

Along the shorelines of Loch Tay lie the foundations of many crannogs, eighteen between Fearnan and Kenmore, by the short stretch of lochside road I had just driven. Prehistoric builders created small artificial islands from stones and wooden piles driven into the loch bed so that they could carry a platform for roundhouses, the characteristic domestic design in the second and first millennia BC. Some could be reached from the shore by wooden walkways on stilts, all had a place where boats could be tied up.

Near Tayside Marina, on the southern shore of the loch, a crannog has been reconstructed to a superb standard. On the day I visited, the guide gave an excellent, atmospheric tour as a fire was lit in the dark interior and the centuries rolled back. One detail has stuck. When I asked about there being no opening in the roof for smoke and the danger of sparks setting fire to the thatch, the guide explained that the fire created a cone of carbon monoxide that extinguished sparks as soon as they spiralled up to it. Smart prehistoric interior design.

Many historians believe that crannogs were built out on the water so that they could be more easily defended. I think that a questionable analysis since arrows could fire their thatch in moments. There seemed a simpler explanation. Now we think of water as an obstacle to be crossed or moved around because we are conditioned by where cars and other vehicles can reach. But until the middle of the nineteenth century water was the fastest, safest and most reliable means of travel. The crannogs were built on the loch because the loch was a highway. It was much easier to cross from one crannog on the southern shore to another on the northern than it was to walk around. And it is that way of seeing movement through the landscape that made the Tay a river road through Scotland's prehistory, a way of understanding something of how people lived 3,000 years ago.

Not being a boatman, or a canoeist, or a swimmer, I decided to follow the Tay by travelling along its banks, walking where I could, driving where there was no path. From Kenmore, I made my way downriver. So that I could stay on the southern bank, I walked along the fringes of a lovely golf course laid out in the grounds of Taymouth Castle. A massive nineteenth-century grey block, it was of course visited by Queen Victoria as she carried on her love affair with all things Highland. I wanted to stay on the southern bank so that I could go and look at the stone circle at Croft Moraig. It turned out to be very close to the road to Aberfeldy, an accident that somehow seemed to diminish its impact.

There are the remains of three circles of megaliths, all of them the successors of a wooden henge-like structure that appears to have been set up in a horseshoe shape. When these monuments began their mysterious lives, many were made from wood. Woodhenge, near Stonehenge, was vast and is perhaps the best known. While it is extremely difficult to hypothesise – there is simply nothing much to go on – on the nature of the rituals that took place inside the circles, one governing impulse is clear: the tree trunks and the megaliths that replaced them marked off sacred ground. Inside was different, perhaps a place that was closer to the gods, an inner sanctum, and outside was the everyday, temporal world. Some of Croft Moraig's stones stand tall, up to two metres, but the space they enclose is not large, certainly no place for a congregation of worshippers of any size. It may be that the inner sanctum was a hidden place where mystery happened, where rituals were enacted by those who had secret knowledge, who could claim spirituality, authority and were able to commune with the gods. Outside were the laity, possibly the people on whose behalf the mysteries were played out. These are not fanciful, other-worldly theories. For most of the first two millennia of Christianity, priests celebrated the mass on the far side of the rood screens of their churches. And while the laity heard the rituals, they did not see them.

When archaeologists investigated Croft Moraig in 1965, they found fragments of pottery that allowed them to date the setting up of the first stone circle (more like an oval) to c.2,000 BC. It seems that it was surrounded by a stone bank, something that might have acted as a screen. A large recumbent stone carries about twenty cup and ring marks. Also known as prehistoric rock art, these engravings appear to be abstract, not representational in any conventional sense, and enigmatic. Their function has never been fully understood.

To my speculative eye, they looked like receptacles for offerings of some kind, libations or food. Perhaps as celebrants entered the stone circle or the laity approached it, they placed something on the cup and ring marks. They look as though they would hold liquid. Another attractive interpretation is that they held colour – red and yellow ochre decoration that carried some symbolic meaning. There are many examples of these marks associated with prehistoric sites all over Scotland. The people who processed past the massive recumbent stone were certainly very different from us in many ways, but there is also a degree of continuity, especially in matters of belief. That much is clear at Fortingall. When Christian pilgrims travel to venerated places, there are often shrines by the wayside and part of their function is to mark a journey between the secular and the unrepentant, and the sacred and the penitent. Perhaps the cup and ring marks at Croft Moraig were the last of these wayside shrines on the way to the circle.

Imagining the deep past can be difficult when the present impinges too much. Even though Croft Moraig stands in a green field in the Perthshire countryside, I found the road at the bottom of the slope, the busy A827 from Kenmore to Aberfeldy, very distracting. Modern roads cut across the landscape so emphatically that it can be impossible to visualise what the builders of the stone circle saw when they hauled the huge stones upright. And this is not a matter of aesthetics but of understanding. Creating the circles demanded great labour and the choice of the site required great thought – it had to have significance. But any gossamer trace of what that was seemed to me to have been entirely lost as the landscape changed over millennia, and especially in the last hundred years or so.

The A827 does, however, have its uses and realising I was hungry I found myself in Aberfeldy only a short time after leaving Croft Moraig. Over an excellent lunch in a tearoom attached to a baker's shop (is there any more appetising aroma than freshly baked bread?) it occurred to me I was missing a big part of the point if I allowed the twenty-first century's inevitable distraction from a sense of the third millennium BC to cloud my journeys along Scotland's hidden ways. Certainly I wanted to experience a kind of walking time capsule that would encourage some pungent understanding of the past, but if one of the main purposes of that was to understand the present better, then I had better refocus my view. And stop being so grumpy as articulated lorries rumble past our prehistory. In a direct and obvious sense, the past never leaves us, it is embedded in the present, is veined through our beliefs, our diet, our traditions, our way of moving through the landscape and much else. When I walked around the well-set little town of Aberfeldy, I found a partial illustration of a better road to enlightenment.

After leaving the Crannog Centre, much impressed, I had gone immediately to Croft Moraig because I had thought it might be possible to see a journey down the Tay as a lens through which I could see back into the darkness of the prehistoric past. The valley of the Upper Tay is densely patterned with the ancient remains of barrows, stone circles, standing stones, rock art and hillforts. By using the river as a highway, as our ancestors did until recently, I imagined I might have even stumbled across the appropriate viewpoint, perhaps even made sense of the location and arrangement of these monuments raised up by so much back-breaking labour. Stripping away the intervening millennia, I might have been able to visualise a sacred landscape, the rural equivalent of looking at a cityscape and seeing its spires reaching up to Heaven.

What cheered and enthused me in Aberfeldy was a practical, if less romantic, example of how better to see my journeys into Scotland's past. General Wade's bridge across the Tay is an unexpectedly elegant component in a road network designed ruthlessly to subdue the Highland clans. Built in 1733 and designed by William Adam, father of the more famous Robert, it has a wide central arch with four obelisks, two on each parapet marking the flat part of the bridge and two arches on either side carrying the road down to the banks of the river. But as much as its beauty (and resilience after 300 winters) struck me, I was more impressed by the fact that for a time it was the only stone-built bridge across the Tay upstream from Perth.

There were fords and ferries, and also wooden bridges, but the latter were regularly washed away by flooding. And it turns out that there is no flood like a Tay flood. At 117 miles, the river may be the longest in Scotland but it is only the fourth longest in Britain. However, the geography that gives rise to it, flowing from Loch Tay out of the heart of the mountains, across the Highland Boundary Fault and on into the Lowlands, makes the Tay the biggest river in Britain. It carries by far the greatest volume of water, more than twice as much as the Thames. In fact, the latter needs to be combined with the Trent to equal the vast flow of the Tay. What that means is simple: it was much better to think of the great river as a highway than as an obstacle – and it was navigable by shallow draughted craft for all of its 117 miles.

I crossed the Wade Bridge and made my way back into town in search of the subject of a famous song. In 1787 Robert Burns visited Aberfeldy and, allegedly, took the path up the gorge of the Moness Burn to what are now called the Birk Falls. There, it is said, he sat down on a rock and composed 'The Birks o' Aberfeldy' and set it to a tune known as the 'Birks o' Abergeldie', not another version of almost the same name but an Aberdeenshire air. Since then the gorge has adopted the name of the Birks o' Aberfeldy, an early example of tourism branding. With his remarkable facility, Burns managed something generic (there is only one verse with an explicit reference to the waterfalls in the gorge) and pleasing, but in truth it could have been a celebration of almost any Scottish beauty spot.

From the car park, there is a good path through mixed, mature woodland, by no means all of it birks or birches, clearly a place where the trees have regenerated naturally for many centuries. For all Burns' artifice, the gorge has probably been long thought of as beautiful. The falls are dramatic. There are several stretches where the burn races white over steep rocky rapids, and at the top of the path are the Moness Falls, often called the Birk Falls. There the burn tips dramatically over a near-vertical face. Having climbed up to a significant height, I enjoyed the views down to the valley of the Tay. The soil being thinner and rock strewn, the tree cover had become almost exclusively birch. The gorge has been designated a Site of Special Scientific Interest because botanists have found evidence that there has been continuous woodland cover for more than 8,000 years.

When the ice finally shrank back north about 11,000 years ago, the frozen tundra began slowly to green and centuries after the temperatures rose, trees returned to Scotland. Amongst the earliest was the birch, and now it is the most common native tree. At first it grew in secluded places, out of the wind, and where there was a good water supply. Birches grow fast, as their deep tap roots reach down for moisture. Aside from the path and its occasional handrail, here was a place unchanged for millennia, where birches grew long before the stone circle was raised at Croft Moraig. Perhaps the builders of its wooden precursor had felled them, trees that grow tall and straight, to make the horse-shoe henge.

Old woods can be more than atmospheric, more than merely picturesque; they are sometimes magical. In their shadows wisps of ancient belief can be glimpsed. In what is now called lore, but is actually the residue of belief, Gaelic culture remembers the Creideamh Sìth, frivolously translated as 'the Fairy Faith'. It was associated with birch woodland and the special properties of the tree. Its sap was drained and made into a drink, its twigs were tied into brushes that were used to purify and punish (as in 'Bring Back the Birch'), its bark made canoes, its wood could be cut and used for almost any purpose, and if it was burnt it did not need to be seasoned because of the oil it contains.

The Daoine Sìth, the Spirits of Nature, perhaps also understood as ancestors, were said to walk unseen amongst the living. In Ireland, the same phrase translates more freely as 'the People of the Mounds', the barrows where the prehistoric dead had been buried. These Shadow-Walkers, the Daoine Sìth, were said to be perfect, entirely beautiful but capable of spite and great cruelty if they were not respected. In places like the birch woods at Aberfeldy their parallel world somehow seemed closer, like a flicker of movement glimpsed out of the corner of an eye. By the time I began to walk back down the gorge, it was early evening and the sun was sinking fast in the west. It was close to gloaming, an evocative Scots word for the slow process of darkling. It is a near-synonym for a word that came echoing back across the years to me.

In modern parlance, glamour means simply charm, allure, attractiveness, beauty, but its meaning was originally much more precise and interesting. It comes from another old Scots word that was certainly in use in the Borders in the 1960s when my grandmother used 'glammer' or 'glimmer' to mean a spell, or the power to enchant. More, she used 'glamoury' (perhaps academic orthographers would spell it as 'glam-ourie', but I never saw the word written down) to mean magic in general, but neither in a good or a bad sense. Perhaps the neutrality was what allowed glamour to come to be attached to beautiful women and their charms. I now think its use was a memory of natural magic as it was understood by country people.

By the time I reached the car park at the foot of the Birks path, the sun was behind the western mountains, their silhouettes dark against the golden glow. I wasn't sure, but I fancied I could make out the highest of them. At more than 3,000 feet, Schiehallion and its rocky summit glowers over the Upper Tay Valley in more than one sense. Its name translates as the Magic Mountain of the Caledonians. The first element is cognate to 'sìth' and the second to the name given, probably by the Romans, to the kindred who inhab-ited the valley 2,000 years ago. Schiehallion may have been thought magical because it was a shape-shifter – it looks very different from several viewpoints. And perhaps its magic floated over the lives of the people of the great river, their monuments and their shadowy woodlands.

The Caledonians were reckoned to be ferocious warriors and at the root of their name is 'caled', meaning hard. It may also mean rocky and be a reference to the nature of their territory, but I prefer the notion of tough, of hard men. As I crossed the line of General Wade's road, I reflected that the warriors of the mountains had long been feared for their ferocity, and before they raised their broadswords to make their last charge into history they remembered the Creideamh

Sith. When the government army formed up on the moor near Culloden House on the morning of 16 April 1746, they faced the army of the clans, the descendants of the Caledonians. It was a family army: fathers stood next to sons, brothers were there with their cousins and uncles, and in the moments before battle was joined they did something characteristic of a Celtic host. They summoned the army of the dead. In what is known as *Sloinneadh*, the naming of the names, each man recited his genealogy, and many could go back twenty generations. Before they charged across the heather into the gunfire, the clansmen wanted to recall their ancestors and fight in their shadows. In a modern culture where many can scarcely recall the names of all four of their grandparents, a sense of the importance – and the power – of ancestors has been all but lost.

Beyond Aberfeldy, I found an abandoned railway trackbed that hugged the southern bank of the Tay. Near Grandtully (pron. Grantly), the river runs white over rocky rapids upriver from the bridge across to Strathtay. Several evil-looking black rocks sit well proud of the water. Apparently national championships are held on this stretch of the river, canoe or kayak slaloms where competitors steer between hanging gates in an attempt to record the fastest time down the course. There was no one on the river when I passed, but at home I watched the Scottish Championships online. The skills of the kayakers were simply stunning, and their strength in pulling around their small craft against the rushing current to pass under gates upstream was immensely impressive. I would have drowned, or expired from terror.

These men and women are the heirs of a tremendously long tradition of travel on the waters of the Tay. At Friarton, on the southern fringes of Perth, an ancient dugout canoe was found. It may have been 6,000 years old and was buried in anaerobic deposits of clay. The prehistoric boat has been lost: perhaps the old wood dried out when exposed to the air and crumbled to dust. Between 1829 and 1889, six other ancient wooden boats were found in the mud flats of the Tay estuary, but apart from one they too have all been lost. The fragile husk of a canoe found at Carpow, at the head of the estuary, can be seen in Perth Museum. What these fleeting finds show is that canoes have paddled the Tay for millennia, although it is likely that, rather than seeking them out, prehistoric people will have avoided the rapids at Grandtully and carried their craft around them.

While the fast flow and white water of the Tay could make adrenalin surge, it also encouraged the growth of great and beautiful treasure on the river bed. When I reached the confluence with the River Tummel at Logierait, the great river seemed not only to swell but also to surge. I noticed a branch with green leaves borne quickly along. Allied to water purity, a fast current encourages freshwater mussels to thrive in the mud and silt of the river bed. These can be very large, the size of a hand, and live to a great age, some-times for as long as a hundred years. They were gathered for food, but as our ancestors pulled them up from the river bed and prized them open they sometimes found pearls. These could be very large and very beautiful, their pale, limpid lustre a memory of all the years they took to form in the mussel's dark heart. In 1967 a professional pearl fisher, Willie Abernathy, found a pearl in the Tay that is the size of a marble. It is on display at Cairncross, a jeweller's shop in Perth.

British pearls have long been sought after. In his biography of Julius Caesar, Suetonius listed the dictator's reasons for undertaking the risky crossing of the Channel in 55 BC and one was the abundant supply of freshwater pearls. Less enthusiastic, Tacitus wrote at the end of the first century AD that he thought them dusky and brown, inferior to oriental pearls. In 1764 the Welsh traveller and historian Thomas Pennant found himself on the banks of the Tay bemoaning the lack of pearls. The fishing had been exhausted, he wrote, 'from the avarice of the undertakers'. But by the time of the *First Statistical Account*, thirty years later, they were being fished for once more. The Rev. James Robertson wrote an excellent description of the fishermen's methods:

> They are fished with a kind of spear, consisting of a long shaft, and shod at the point with two iron spoons, having their mouths inverted. Their handles are long and elastic and joined at the extremity, which is formed into a socket, to receive the shaft. With this machine in his hand, by way of staff, the fisher, being often up to the chin in water, gropes with his feet for muscles [*sic*], which are fixed in the mud and sand by one end, and presses down the iron spoons upon their point; so that by the spring in the handles, they open to receive the muscle, hold it fast, and pull it to the surface of the water. He has a pouch or bag of net-work hanging by his side, to carry the muscles till he comes ashore, where they are opened. The operation is much easier in shallow water.

For the following two centuries the population of mussels, or 'muscles', appeared to fluctuate, and by the 1990s they were certainly in crisis. Numbers were crashing, and in 1998 legislation banning pearl fishing was enacted. Cairncross of Perth is licensed to deal in pearls found before that date, but there seems to be little doubt that illegal fishing continues. Tell-tale piles of discarded shells are found on the banks of the Tay and other rivers, and in 2014 surveillance was stepped up.

Between dense forest on either flank the river turns south towards Perth and the Lowlands, and another place that remembers the ancient Caledonians. If Dunkeld, the Fort of the Caledonians, stood on the edge of a political frontier in the first century AD, its situation remained unchanged for sixteen centuries. When I walked into the cathedral precinct, I could see on the east gable enduring evidence of the scars of war between Highland and Lowland, a series of pock-marks and chips made by musket balls.

In 1688, the restored Stuart monarchy lost its nerve and fled when William of Orange landed at Torbay. James II and VII became an exile, and a long period of constitutional instability followed as his sympathisers, the Jacobites, fought to reinstate him and his dynasty in a series of rebellions. The first and arguably the best chance of success came a year later when some Highland clans rose behind the char-ismatic leadership of John Graham, Viscount Dundee. With Clan Cameron and only a few others at his back, he led his small army down the Tummel to Blair Atholl. On 27 July, they caught a slightly larger government army in the narrow pass at Killiecrankie and defeated them after a furious down-hill charge. Dundee had waited until the evening sun had moved around behind his position and the Highlanders swept General Hugh Mackay's dazzled soldiers off the field. But the prospects of the insurgents were badly dented after Dundee died of wounds received in the brief battle.

Across Lowland Scotland, many believed that the return of the Stuarts would mean a return to Catholicism and too many Protestant martyrs had died for that to be coun-tenanced. James II had encouraged the persecution of the Covenanting movement and one of its most heroic figures was Richard Cameron. He died in the period known as the Killing Times, but the memory of his piety lived on and his followers were determined that his sacrifice would not be wasted. In April 1689, more than 1,200 men came together to form a regiment of foot. The Cameronians were organised into companies of twenty and each had an elder assigned to organise prayer and worship. Recruits were given a Bible. These singular traditions endured, and when in 1968 the regiment was asked to merge with another, they chose to disband and held a field conventicle to lower their colours.

In August 1689, the new regiment was ordered to march to the defence of Dunkeld. On the banks of the Tay, the town would undoubtedly be a target for the victorious Highland army after their success at Killiecrankie, and if they could take it, the Lowlands would lie open. What followed was one of the most dramatic moments in Scotland's history, an episode so graphic – and filmic – that its parallels with the defence of Rorke's Drift in the Zulu Wars of the 1870s are not exaggerated.

The Cameronians were led by Lt. Col. William Cleland, a brave and remarkable man. A published poet, he would write a mock-epic entitled 'On the expedition of the Highland Host who came to destroy the western shires in winter 1678'. In this lengthy and ponderous piece, Cleland left no reader in any doubt as to his view of the clansmen. They were savages, and for the most part either Catholics or episcopalians. But in the same way as the defenders of Rorke's Drift saw the Zulus, he respected the physical courage and the battle prowess of the Highlanders.

When the Cameronians marched into Dunkeld on 17 August 1689, their captains saw immediately that the town would be impossible to defend against 4–5,000 rebels. There was no wall and no high point they could defend. Dunkeld was little more than a single street that led to the eastern facade of the cathedral and the gate into the graveyard. Closes ran off either side of the street in a classic herring-bone pattern, but behind them at the foot of their backlands were only fences. The most likely redoubt was the cathedral precinct since there was a dyke around it that might serve as a makeshift perimeter.

The Marquis of Atholl's house was more substantial than any of the simple dwellings on the single street and it stood close to the dyke. It was quickly fortified. To the south flowed the Tay and a little way downstream there was a ford. To the north-west was Stanley Hill. Covered with tall trees, it overlooked the town, but Cleland did not have sufficient men to occupy it. Having completed a rapid reconnaissance, the Cameronian captains posted sentries and the regiment bivou-acked amongst the tombstones in the cathedral precinct. Some may have mused on whether or not sleeping amongst the dead was an omen.

The following day dawned clear, and despite the fact that it was the Sabbath the Cameronians set aside their piety and dug defensive ditches around the dyke and repaired it where it had tumbled down. Lookouts climbed the cathedral steeple and almost immediately spotted small groups of Highlanders moving across the surrounding hills, less than a mile away. It must have been an anxious moment since the defences, such as they were, still needed a great deal of work. If this was the Jacobite army, they might overrun the town if they moved quickly. At 4 p.m. in the afternoon, the lookouts on the steeple called down to Cleland that they could see a large company of armed clansmen emerging from the woods on Stanley Hill. They were very close. The lookouts then shouted that they could see a messenger approaching the town with a white cloth tied to the end of a halberd. Cleland immediately got a galloper away, splashing across the Tay fords, sending the horseman south to Perth for reinforcements.

To the commander's great relief, the messenger with the white flag carried a letter that made it clear this was not the victorious Jacobite army but a company of clansmen from the glens to the north of Dunkeld who were sympathetic to the rebels. They wanted to see the town survive and presented Cleland with what amounted to an ultimatum: 'We, the gentlemen assembled, being informed that you intend to burn the town, desire [to know] whether you come for peace or war, and to certify that if you burn one house, we will destroy you.' No doubt hoping that his galloper had not been intercepted, Cleland was defiant and refused to withdraw.

To his great relief, five troops of cavalry clattered into Dunkeld the day after the ultimatum, having set out on the fifteen-mile journey from Perth that morning. They quickly engaged with the groups of clansmen in the hills and on Stanley Hill, and drove them back, well out of musket range. But then orders arrived from Perth recalling the cavalry, and despite Cleland's protests, their commander, Lord Cardross, was forced to comply. Only an hour or two after the troops of horsemen had crossed back over the Tay fords on their way to Perth, scouts galloped down the north road and splashed across the river to report that the vanguard of the Highland army had been seen at Dalguise and it was approaching fast.

Peering through the morning haze on 21 August, the lookouts on the cathedral steeple shouted that they could see the clans drawing up in battle order on the hillsides to the north of the town. They counted 5,000 Highlanders, and the Cameronians were only 1,200 – vastly outnumbered. And no retreat would be possible. Col. Alexander Cannon had taken over command of the Highland army after Dundee's death at Killiecrankie, and he had sent companies of clansmen to block the Tay fords and to close the ring around the west of the cathedral. The lookouts in the steeple could see that they were completely surrounded. All they could do was watch and wait for the inevitable.

At 7 a.m. the air was rent by the pipers playing the battle rants, the signal for the Highlanders to come swarming down off the hills and charge into the town. Cleland had set a ring of outposts, but they were quickly overrun and the Cameronians sprinted for the safety of the cathedral precinct. Lieutentant Stewart and his men had set up a more substantial barricade across the east end of the single street and they managed to hold it, the Highlanders driven back by raking musket fire from the cathedral over the heads of the defenders. But the clansmen charged in waves and Stewart was shot dead. At that moment, Cleland signalled for his men to retreat and they raced back along the street to scramble over the cathedral dyke.

The Cameronians behind the dyke knew that there could be no further retreat and were grimly determined to sell their lives dearly. Their sole advantage was that the narrow street and its lanes prevented an all-out Highland charge across a broad front, and if they could keep up a steady rate of musket fire, many of the rebels would die. As each rank took aim and the others reloaded, they kept the enemy at bay. But they were beginning to run out of musket balls. Lead was stripped off the cathedral roof, poured into moulds and the new balls rammed down the muzzles of the muskets as soon as they had been plunged into cold water.

So that they could gain an elevated position over the defenders in the precinct, Highland snipers broke into houses in the street and scored an immediate success. Lt. Col. Cleland was fatally wounded, and such was his faith and courage, he dragged himself out of the sight of his men to die. He feared they might lose heart if everyone knew he was dead. Major Henderson took command, but a few minutes later he was killed by a sniper's bullet. It looked as though the defence of Dunkeld was disintegrating. In a desperate effort to deal with the snipers, Captain Munro set covering fire and sent out parties of men with burning faggots on the end of their halberds. They shoved them into the thatch of the houses where the snipers had taken up position and locked their doors. In moments, the screams of the trapped men could be heard as they choked with smoke and were burned to death.

Gunpowder was beginning to run out, and when there was no more, the Cameronians' muskets would be no better than clubs. Munro and his officers held a hurried conference. When the supplies of gunpowder were exhausted and the Highlanders finally, inevitably stormed the dyke, the remaining men would make for the Marquis of Atholl's house and defend it to the death as a last redoubt.

But then, suddenly, the Highlanders drew back. Instead of pressing their advantage, they seemed to lose heart after the appalling deaths of their snipers and Col. Cannon had little option but to call for his pipers to sound the retreat. The clans moved back out of range of the Cameronian muskets, leaving 300 dead in the streets and houses of the town. After sixteen hours of fighting, the August gloaming was lit only by the burning houses along the street beyond the precinct dyke, and Dunkeld was deserted.

When the exhausted defenders on the dyke peered through the gathering gloom and realised they had won a very unlikely victory, they threw their caps in the air. And like the devout Covenanters they were, they raised their voices in a psalm of thanksgiving. And like the practical soldiers they had become, they set about repairing the dyke. The Highlanders might return.

Like the Zulu impi at Rorke's Drift, the clansmen had left the defenders to their victory even though it seemed that their vast numbers must prevail, but unlike that famous siege the action at Dunkeld was strategically significant. It stopped the first Jacobite rebellion in its tracks by containing it, just, in the Highlands.

Below Dunkeld the character of the Tay seems to change. Having rushed down through the narrow valley and its flanking forests, it becomes a Lowland river, more like the Tweed or the Clyde as it begins to meander through a landscape of fertile fields around Caputh and Murthly. Without the steep-sided glens to constrain it, the powerful flow of the Tay forces the river into seasonal channels, leaving oxbows and long, low river islands known as inches. From the Gaelic *innis* for an island, pronounced 'innish', it remembers a linguistic as well as a political and geological frontier.

Inchtuthil probably remembers a native landowner since it appears to mean Tuthil's Island. In 84 AD, ownership changed abruptly when the haughland by the river became the property of the Emperor Domitian. After defeating and scattering the Caledonian Confederacy at the Battle of the Graupian Mountain in Aberdeenshire, the legions withdrew south for the winter to set up temporary camps by the Tay. They began construction of a legionary fortress, what would become a large military town that would act as a base for the control of Caledonia. All Roman roads would lead to and from the place they called Pinnata Castra, the Winged Fortress, perhaps after the goddess Nike, the Winged Victory.

When I decided to visit this fascinating site on the banks of the river, I found that no roads led to it. Using my trusty Pathfinder map, I parked by some farm buildings on a B road and walked down a wooded track before reaching a cottage. I could see the river beyond some trees. Having walked up another track past the cottage, I arrived at a gate that bore the discouraging sign 'Beware of the Bull'. Beyond it was a wide area of rough grazing, a grass park, with a few stands of mature trees and no bull in sight. This was, said the map, the site of the great legionary fortress. I decided to climb the gate and risk it, keeping a wary eye. I could probably make it to one of the stands of trees, if not back to the gate. Quite what I would do after climbing a tree with a snorting bull at the bottom I wasn't sure. Especially since my mobile phone had no signal.

In 1961, long before the era of metal detectors and geophysical surveying equipment, a team of archaeologists was excavating at Inchtuthil. There was nothing to see above ground, not one stone left standing upon another, and all there was to hint at the presence of a Roman legionary fortress was a wide and deep ditch that may have formed the southern perimeter. I could see it as I walked across the park. Perhaps the bull was grazing at the bottom. Prior to 1961 several digging seasons had uncovered disappointingly few artefacts. But when a new trench was opened, the director of the excavation, Ian Richmond, noticed a pronounced discolouration in the soil.

There were edges and it looked as though a pit had been dug. When the archaeologist began to dig down, they found a six-foot layer of gravel rather than soil, and under it, they came across the remains of ten iron wheel tyres, the bands used to protect wooden cartwheels from splintering. Below these, the diggers found something odd, a solid crust of corroded iron. And beneath it, a remarkable find. Sealed from the damp soil by the iron crust, there was a huge cache of almost 900,000 Roman nails. They ranged from short tacks for securing roof tiles to long iron spikes for clenching load-bearing timbers. Nothing like this had ever been found before and this extraordinary output from legionary blacksmiths spoke eloquently of a building project on an epic scale.

The legionary fortress perimeter, clearly visible from the air, especially in winter, compassed an area of fifty-three acres and it could house 5,400 legionaries and more auxiliaries. They would live in sixty-four barracks buildings and their food and other kit would fill 170 storehouses and six granaries. There was a headquarters complex at the centre of the fortress, a hospital and a large drill hall. To protect all this, a perimeter wall was built above a two-metre-deep ditch which was breached by four heavily defended gateways that allowed entry to four principal streets. It was something the Caledonians can never have seen the like of. And more, it was a building project on a scale that would not be repeated in Scotland for another eighteen centuries.

Inchtuthil was never completed and never fully occupied. In 86 AD a serious rebellion flared at the north-eastern edge of the Empire, in what is now Romania. A legion was withdrawn from Britain and Inchtuthil immediately abandoned. Events moved quickly. Those buildings that had been completed were stripped of anything useful and set on fire. Pottery was systematically smashed and pack horses loaded with kit of all kinds. But at the fort's forges, one centurion had a problem, what to do with 900,000 nails. They were too heavy to carry and too useful to the Caledonians to be simply left, and so he ordered a deep pit to be dug, hoping it would not be noticed. And it turned out to be the right decision because, until 1961, it wasn't.

After the nails were counted (a process of epic proportions and unimaginable tedium), dated and analysed, some were given to interested parties but the vast bulk were stored at the Dalzell Steel Mill in Motherwell. Eventually they were recycled as scrap iron, and since they supplied steel to the motor industry I wondered if my ancient Range Rover was even more ancient. What also occurred to me, as I kept an eye out for the bull, was that if revolt had not erupted in Romania in 86 AD, a town would probably have grown up at Inchtuthil, just as Chester and York grew up beside their legionary fortresses.

Another intriguing thought is the odd distribution of Roman artefacts found in Scotland. In Europe, trade and exchange of other sorts sent Roman pottery, jewellery, coins and much else far beyond the Rhine–Danube frontier. On the southern coasts of the Baltic many objects had been found. And yet, beyond the Highland Line, immediately to the north of Inchtuthil, very few Roman finds have appeared, far fewer than in what is now Poland and northern Germany. Perhaps Highlanders consciously rejected the products of the Empire and refused to be drawn into its cultural orbit. If that is more than a hypothesis, then it speaks of an attractive, thrawn dignity.

As I walked back down the path from the site of the huge fortress, it occurred to me that grand scale seemed to be developing as a recurring motif, but a grand scale that was invisible and needed an effort of the imagination. The Tay is undoubtedly the biggest river in Britain, even though others are wider, longer and have been witness to more history. But its scale is subtle, not possible to see on the surface. The same is true of Inchtuthil, lying sleeping beneath its grass park, scarcely thought worthy of access or even some signage. But perhaps the most enigmatic example of grand scale on the banks of the Tay lay only a mile or two inland, not far from the buried Roman fortress.

I drove up the A93 towards Blairgowrie and stopped where the road sliced through mystery. To the right and left, flanked by the regimented edges of commercial forestry, ran a long, straight ridge broken by the road. It is one of a set of prehistoric monuments built towards the end of the fourth millennium BC. In Scotland there are thirty cursus sites, so-called because eighteenth and nineteenth century antiquaries thought they had been built as courses for chariot racing, a notion fed by the closeness of the fortress at Inchtuthil. In the wacky and zany 1960s, some were certain that aliens had laid out this cursus as a handy landing strip for UFOs targeting rural Perthshire. In fact, no one knows what the Cleaven Dyke was used for.

As I walked along its length on a damp and dreich November day, the mystery seemed to swirl and deepen. It is not a dyke but three banks that run straight for about one-and-a-half miles through the forest and on into a ploughed field, where it shows up as a cropmark. The central bank rises to about ten feet in places, although so many whin bushes had grown on it, it was difficult to tell. It is flanked by two parallel ditches dug at a distance of about 160 feet on either side. It is the sum of immense labour and must therefore have been a place of great moment and importance – but its function is almost impossible to decode.

Archaeologists have established that the cursus began life as an oval burial mound at its head, with a long tail running behind it. There are wisps of possible interpretation here. Was the mile-and-a-half-long series of ditches a burial ground of some sort? One of the many puzzles of prehistory is a simple one. In proportion to the number of people who lived in Britain between the retreat of the ice 11,000 years ago and the beginning of mass burial in the Christian era, only a tiny number of burials have been found. The question is – where are all the bodies? Were the dead cremated and their ashes scattered? And was the Cleaven Dyke a place where that ritual took place?

In prehistory, ditches generally mark off the sacred from the temporal and perhaps there were processions along the length of the dyke where ashes were scattered or even buried. Perhaps people sang or chanted or music of some kind was played as priests tipped out the cremated ashes between the banks. Or was it a prison for the spirits of the dead? In Irish Celtic culture, it is believed that these could be malign and needed to be contained in some way. Intensive archaeology has shown that the Cleaven Dyke was built in thirty-four short sections, growing ever longer with time, and presumably need. Perhaps it was a linear cemetery that expanded as the generations faded into the past and fresh areas for scatter were needed.

These are little more than hypotheses, one piled upon another, but the atmosphere of the place chimes with a sense of the funereal. Hemmed in by the dank and dripping November woods, the dyke seemed to me a dead place in all senses. As cars buzzed past on the road to Blairgowrie, visible for only a moment as the road crossed the monument because of the thick forest on either side, they were like a pulse from the twenty-first century but they did not disturb any sort of peace. Some prehistoric places have an atmosphere of calm, dream-like, pleasant other-worldliness, but the Cleaven Dyke does not: it is bleak, a place where the dead were washed away in the winter rain. A vast, nameless tomb.

In the middle of November each year we rent a large house perched on a high river cliff above the Tay, just outside the village of Stanley. After my last visit to the Cleaven Dyke and a drive back in the half-dark, I shrugged off its shiver when I stepped into the sitting room, made for the glow of the woodburning stove and a glass of something warming. The house is new, very modern in design and very beautiful. For several years, it acted as my base for journeys along the Tay. Its vast floor-to-ceiling windows (triple glazed) look down on the river as it runs towards Perth and there are often kayakers braving the rapids a few hundred metres downstream, even in November. Upriver the views are a little more restricted, but it is possible to see Stanley Mills, a fascinating industrial initiative oddly attached to a small, rural village in Perthshire. It turned out to be the nature of the great river that built the mills.

From the windows of our rented house, it is not possible to see the geographical reason why this formidable manufacturing complex was built. The Tay turns an extravagant corner, almost through 360 degrees, around a long tongue of land. And crucially when the powerful flow of the river begins this near-circle, it is twenty-one feet higher than when it completes it just below the site of the mills. The land belonged to John, Duke of Atholl, the older brother of Lord George Murray, the great Jacobite general. He and his factor conceived a clever notion. In 1729 they had a tunnel dug from the top of the bend to the bottom, and the water rushed down to power a corn mill. Atholl was then persuaded by the local MP, George Dempster, to invite Richard Arkwright to come to Stanley. He had not only patented a more efficient cotton spinning frame, the water frame, but also a rotary carding engine. This greatly speeded up the making of cotton lap, a thick sheet of fibres, an important stage in the spinning of cotton fibre and thread.

From 1780 onwards, the main mill buildings were constructed and at the top of Mill Brae a planned village was laid out. At first business prospered at Stanley, but the disruption to trade in the Napoleonic Wars caused difficulties and ushered in a cycle of boom and bust. Surprisingly, the most stable period was in the mid-twentieth century. In 1916, the mills began to produce what was known as an endless thin cotton belt. It was used in the production of cigarettes precisely at the point when these became more popular than other forms of tobacco consumption. But by 1989 market conditions forced the closure of the mills and their handsome buildings were soon converted into flats.

Below Stanley, the Tay flows into the heart of Scottishness, past the place where the idea of Scotland was first forged on a stone anvil. By the ninth century, the centre of the dominant kingdom of Dalriada had shifted eastwards from its heartland of Argyll. Having overrun the Northern Isles and taken control of the Outer Hebrides, Norse sea-lords were exerting pressure, forcing the Dalriadan kindreds and their kings to move from their place of power at Dunadd across the mountains to the valley of the Tay. Events conspired to make it the focus of a new kingdom. In 839 the Annals of Ulster reported disaster. Somewhere in Strathearn, to the south of Perth and the valley of the Tay's last major tributary, 'The heathens won a battle over the men of Fortriu and Eoganan, son of Oengus, and Bran, son of Oengus, and Aed, son of Boanta, and others almost innumerable fell there.' It is likely that the Norse sea-lords and their warriors sailed into the Tay estuary and perhaps some way up the River Earn. In any event, this crushing defeat appears to have decapitated the leadership of Pictland, killing their royalty and many of their nobility. This disaster cleared the stage for the entrance of Kenneth macAlpin, famously said to be the first to rule over Picts and Scots, and the king from whom all Scottish monarchs are numbered.

The chroniclers claimed that Kenneth ruled from 843 onwards, but the likelihood is that it took him some years to establish his authority. Other Gaelic-speaking kings had governed in Pictland (essentially the eastern Lowlands of Scotland north of the Firth of Forth), but Kenneth appears to have made Scone, on the east bank of the Tay, a mile or so north of Perth, a royal centre, the place where his successors consciously created the idea of Scotland.

Norse raiders had repeatedly attacked Iona, slaughtering monks and stealing Columba's treasure. The island monastery had been the focus of early Scottish Christianity, having sent missionaries as far as Northumbria, but it had become very vulnerable. Once macAlpin had asserted himself as undisputed king, he had the precious relics of St Columba (and perhaps the talismanic Brecbennoch, the Monymusk Reliquary – which was carried into battle by Scottish kings) brought from Iona over the Drumalban Mountains to Loch Tay and from there down the river for safekeeping at the monastery at Dunkeld. It was said that he also had another hefty piece of cultural luggage brought east. *Lia Fáil*, the Stone of Destiny, may have sat on the ancient citadel of Dunadd in Argyll, the place where Dalriadan kings were inaugurated. Apparently it was heaved onto an ox cart and probably trundled across the mountain passes to Loch Tay, where it was transferred to a stout boat. Once the stone had been brought down the Tay, it was set on what became known as the Moot Hill at Scone. Until the middle of the seventeenth century, Scottish kings became kings when they sat on this cold stone throne.

Kenneth macAlpin may have been the first to be acclaimed on the hill and it seems that the old Celtic rituals followed him over the mountains. The Gaelic version of the place name is more elaborate and it remembers something of the nature of the ceremonies. It is Scoine Sciath-Airde and it means 'Scone of the High Shields'. This is a reference to the widely attested moment when a king is acclaimed by his warriors and nobility. They raised him up on their shields and as this precarious rite took place another version of the place name added a soundtrack. Scoine Sciath-Bhinne is 'Scone of the Singing Shields', of the roar of the men around the new king, perhaps even some formal chants ('Long live the king/queen' is the sole relic) or songs now lost. These rituals lasted for centuries. Devout and raised at the court of King Henry I of England, David I of Scotland was horrified at what he saw as the pagan nature of all this tumult at his inauguration at Scone in 1124, but his grandson, Malcolm IV, nevertheless went through with it. The chronicler, John of Hexham, supplied the reason: 'and so all the people of the land, raising up Malcolm, son of Earl Henry, King David's son (a boy only 12 years old), established him as king at Scone (as is the custom of the Scottish nation)'. Tradition correctly followed conferred legitimacy.

When Alexander III was inaugurated on the Moot Hill in 1249, he witnessed what the reference to Scoine Sciath-Bhinne may have meant. After the king sat on the Stone of Destiny, the Royal Bard, *An Ollaimh Righ*, stood forward and recited the *Sloinneadh*, the naming of the king's ancestors, laying down the new king's right to rule by virtue of his bloodline.

Robert Bruce had a much more shaky claim. When he usurped the Scottish throne in 1306, he hurried north to the Moot Hill to have himself acclaimed and then consecrated in the impressive medieval abbey built close to it. Since a time out of mind, the Earls of Fife held the right to officiate at the ceremonies, but the current earl was being held hostage at the time by Edward I of England. Isabella,

Countess of Buchan, was the earl's sister and she volunteered but arrived two days late. But so important was inauguration at Scone that they did it all over again.

In 1651 a beleaguered Charles II, his dynasty clearly on the losing side at that time in the War of the Three Kingdoms (often miscalled the English Civil War), had himself inaugurated King of Scotland on the Moot Hill. He was the last to do so. But his advisors knew that it mattered: Scone lay at the heart of Scottish kingship, and that is why Edward I made a special point of having the Stone of Destiny lugged south to spend 700 years in a corner of Westminster Abbey.

What is there to see of all this drama? Events of great moment took place repeatedly on the banks of the Tay at Scone, but there is virtually no trace of them left. The great medieval abbey was badly damaged in 1559 by a mob of reformers led by John Knox (although he is said to have tried to calm them) and it has now completely disappeared. The abbot's palace became Scone Palace, a dour lump of a building, and only the Moot Hill remains. It has had a much later mortuary chapel plonked on it, and for some reason the Stone of Destiny was housed in Edinburgh Castle after its repatriation in 1996.

Scone represents yet more hidden history. Like Inchtuthil and the Cleaven Dyke, it is a place of real importance, fascinating and central, but not much visited. River traffic downstream to Scone has all but ceased, but substantial ships can travel in the opposite direction and reach Perth from the sea. The Tay becomes tidal at Scone, and below the Perth bridges a working harbour still loads and unloads cargoes at its quays. And so it remains a river road for the last few miles of its length. The estuary is benign. In July, the tides rise as high as five metres, but there is no surge like the Severn Bore. It can race up that estuary at a height of two metres. Buddon

Ness, below Carnoustie, protects the mouth of the Tay from the worst of the North Sea weather.

North of the Firth of Tay was long seen as another country. Encompasing the ancient kingdoms of Dalriada, Moray and the shifting patchwork of southern Pictland, this was marked on old maps as Scotia. It took centuries for the name to extend to the southern half of the country. Perhaps what reinforced that persistent sense of the river as a frontier was what people called it. River names are the oldest in the landscape, their meaning often long since lost. On the map of Britain made by the Greek geographer Ptolemy, working in the second century AD in Alexandria, the river is plotted as Tava; a century before, the historian Tacitus called it the Taus. It means the Silent One, somehow a fitting name for a river with so much history hidden along its banks.

Lauder

River Tweed

Trimontium

St Boswells

Cappuck

Pennymuir

Kale Water · Towford

Woden Law

Cheviot Hills

Chew
Green Fort

The Invasion Road ②

2

The Invasion Road

The Cheviot Hills to the Lammermuirs

Too often, histories of Scotland seem to begin in earnest with the coming of the Romans. After a few perfunctory pages on the vast scale of our prehistory, the nine millennia since the end of the last Ice Age, historians instinctively feel on safer ground with written sources in Latin than they do with the anonymous stones and bones of archaeology. And that is understandable. So much has survived of the Roman presence in Scotland over very short periods of time, only a handful of decades, that it is natural to want to document the story of the remarkable military machine that rumbled over the Cheviot Hills in the years after 80 AD.

There is another compelling reason for that sharp focus and that is Life of Agricola, *a biography of his father-in-law written by Roman nobleman and sometime soldier Publius Cornelius Tacitus. Brilliant, almost modern in its idiom, precise, and containing what feels like eyewitness testimony, my copies, the excellent translation by Tony Birley, have been so well thumbed that I have worn out two paperback editions and pages are already falling out of the third. Tacitus wrote some of the earliest descriptions of Scotland to survive and they are tremendously illuminating.*

The Romans built a wall across the waist of Scotland, from the Clyde to the Forth, and it must have been imposing. I considered walking along the length of the Antonine Wall but because it was constructed with turf and so much of urban Scotland overlies it, its survival has been patchy. Instead I decided to follow the line of Dere Street, the Roman road that ran from York to Edinburgh and probably beyond. Some stretches were familiar, those between Jedburgh and St Boswells, but I had not walked its line through the Cheviot Hills. It turned out to be spectacular, breathtaking. Long sections snake along the watershed ridge or are shelved into the sides of hills. A stunning engineering achievement that has endured the storms and snows of 2,000 winters, it seems almost Alpine in its sweep.

Rain clouds were darkening out to the west when I reached the old forts. After a long, steep walk up the northern flanks of the Cheviot Hills, I was glad to reach the watershed ridge and find a dry bank to sit on. Wearing a warm jumper and a heavy old waxed jacket, I enjoyed the cooling wind and hoped it would keep the clouds high and scudding across the autumn sky. It was a late September morning and there was plenty of time to get down off the hills if the weather shut down. Even in a heavy downpour I could get back to the single-track road where I had left my car, though a rain-mist would have made life more difficult. All the same, I patted my pockets for my phone with its compass and GPS app, my maps and my old tweed bunnet. I found an ancient bar of chocolate at the bottom of one of the deep inside pockets of my jacket. Maybe I needed the sugar. Hard as iron, I sucked bits of it as I began to walk around the banks and ditches of the Roman forts and marching camps.

Chew Green was almost certainly called Ad Fines by the men who built it. It means something like 'At the Edge' or 'At the Border', and while notions of Scotland or England lay far in the future, there is a sense of this ancient military complex being an end and a beginning. To the legionaries and auxiliaries who dug the ditches and piled the upcast on the banks, it must have seemed like the back of beyond. Awkward to reach now, and well preserved as a result, the fort, fortlets and camps were the consequence of something more difficult to see. They were dug next to a wide, well-metalled road, one that stretched 180 miles from the legionary fortress at York and eventually as far as the Antonine Wall at Carriden on the shores of the Firth of Forth near Bo'ness, and probably beyond. It is a spectacular engineering achievement and a road that leads 2,000 years back into the past. Known as Dere Street after the later Anglian kingdom of Deira that coalesced around York, it has been tramped by armies for millennia.

All was quiet and green on the high ridge, but the peace of that September morning was deceptive. War has swirled around the Cheviots since a time out of mind, and it was the modern needs of armies that forced me to climb through the hills from the north. Dere Street approaches Chew Green from the south, through the Otterburn Firing Ranges, a stretch of bleak moorland that runs from Redesdale across to the valley of the Coquet in the east and then up to the watershed ridge. Red flags flutter in the breeze to discourage access, as artillery launches shells across the heather, and guns for infantry and aircraft are tested. Sometimes they fall silent at the weekends, and I regularly checked the website, but each time no firing was scheduled, rain was forecast and rain duly fell.

Between 78 and 84 AD soldiers and their ox-teams hauled a different kind of artillery up through the Cheviots; ballistas that could throw large stone balls at fortifications, scorpios, powerful crossbow-like machines that could fire heavy javelins, and battering rams. As I walked up the ridge north of the forts to look for traces of the road, the old winds gusted and a splash of yellow sun suddenly lit the landscape. I could see for many miles in almost all directions and hear nothing but the wind soughing and the cry of birds, maybe whaups, in the updraughts. Entirely alone, the sheep no more than white dots drifting across the hillsides, I began to think about the ghosts and the echoes of the past, about the rumbling tread of the many thousands who had walked there before me, the clangour of armies, the creak of wagons, shouted commands, trumpeters and the jingle of harness.

In 78 AD the Empire was marching north. After invasion by the armies of the Emperor Claudius in 43 AD and the rebellion of Queen Boudicca in 60 AD, the Roman occupation of England and Wales proceeded very slowly until, with the succession of Emperor Vespasian, the pace of events quickened. He had commanded a legion in the Claudian invasion and knew southern Britain well. Emperors needed military glory to enhance their prestige in Rome and it seems that Vespasian had ordered his legions to conquer Caledonia, to make the whole island a Roman province. News of martial glory would play well in the Forum and the Senate House, and glory achieved in such a remote region held a particular attraction. Not only did it lie across the dangers of what they called the Ocean, the English Channel, the Romans believed that Britain was on the edge of the world. Beyond stretched the vast wastes of the Atlantic and the very ends of the Earth. Conquest of the north would show that the reach of the Empire was great.

The Governor of Britannia, Gnaeus Julius Agricola, led a huge invasion force of 10,000 men up through Northumberland into Redesdale to cross the Cheviot ranges near the line of the modern A68 and build the road that was to become Dere Street. To the west, another column crossed the Solway fords and struck through Annandale, and then on up where the A74 now runs. These forces were encircling a hostile kindred, the fierce Selgovae, a Celtic name that means the Hunters. Some of their warriors had probably fought against Rome in alliance with the Pennine kindreds in the south and Roman military planners would therefore have counted them as hostile. Agricola had chosen his line of march not because it was the easiest route – that lay to the east by the North Sea coast. There, his fleet could shadow the advance and readily supply the army. Instead he was driving a wedge between the Selgovae kings and a neighbouring kindred, the Votadini. According to a later Roman map, Scotland was patterned with the territories of these tribal groupings.

It was a version of the classic Roman strategy of divide and conquer. And the legions needed to secure supplies of the grain grown by the Votadinian farmers of the Tweed Valley. The fortlet at Chew Green was one of many strung out along the line of Dere Street, a manned frontier between friends to the east and foes to the west.

If any Selgovan scouts had ridden up to a distant ridge and were watching, as they surely must have been, what they saw was awe-inspiring, terrifying. Column after column of soldiers appeared, marching six abreast up the hill trail, all wearing similar uniforms – these warriors had never seen anything like it before that fateful day. Cavalry, light infantry and archers were the first to breast the watershed ridge. The vanguard followed, with detachments of auxiliaries, the fierce Batavians and Tungrians from the Rhine estuary, the heavily armed legionaries marching in step, more cavalry, standard bearers, a colour party and engineers with their gear. The gleaming eagle standards and the trumpeters used for signalling preceded the Command Group, where Agricola and his Tribunes rode. And they were followed by mules hauling artillery and battering rams. Then the main body of the legions came, their hob-nailed boots thudding even on the mud and grass of the trail they were following. The main baggage train came after them and they were all protected by the rearguard. The column may have been more than four miles long, a ribbon of high colour snaking through the green hills. For the warriors of the native kindreds, it was a belly-hollowing sight.

Now the frontier turns in a different direction, approximately north-east to south-west instead of the south to north line of forts and fortlets along Dere Street. The old road runs for a short distance along the line of the modern border between England and Scotland. I had crossed and recrossed it several times that morning. In the midst of the complex of Roman camps and forts, there are clear relics of a long continuity. In the middle of one of the fortlets I could see the foundations of a chapel, probably the largest building in what was a deserted medieval village. When the climate was relatively warm in the twelfth and thirteenth centuries, Kemylpethe was home to people who could survive high in the hills, probably herdsmen who traded fleeces and mutton for what they could not grow. But they were in no sense remote. Medieval society came to them, travelling on the hard surface of the old Roman road.

The chapel was probably maintained by the monks of Kelso Abbey. Although their magnificent and vast church stood on the banks of the Tweed, down in the broad valley, their lay workers ran great sheep ranches in the Cheviots on pasture that had been given to them by patrons. The chapel was a sizeable stone building, eighteen metres long and nine metres wide, larger than the footprint of a substantial modern detached house. It may have met the spiritual needs of travellers on the road. Known as the Gamelspath in the Middle Ages, it had survived for many centuries and its metalled surface was very attractive for those who drove carts for long distances. The village was also a place where cross-border truce days were held, so that disputes between English and Scots Borderers could be discussed and even resolved peacefully. The chapel may have been used for meetings between noblemen and officials when the weather was bad.

A little further along the line of Dere Street lie more remains. In the seventeenth and eighteenth centuries the old road was used by drovers who led their herds south in the late summer to feed England's growing appetite for Scottish beef. As the great drive for empire gathered pace in the middle of the eighteenth century, the demand for salted beef for the Royal Navy and the army soared. The foundations at Chew Green may be those of an inn that supplied the cattlemen and the shepherds with food, drink and perhaps shelter, as their animals stopped over for the night to rest and graze before continuing their journey south to English markets.

I was walking in the opposite direction, following Agricola and his legions as they moved north towards Caledonia. After Chew Green, the line of the Roman road is very clear as it follows the ridge and the rounded contours of the hillsides, and some of these are very steep. When I picked up a small stone no bigger than a tennis ball and rolled it down off the road, I immediately cursed my carelessness. The stone quickly picked up speed and hurtled towards the head of the Hindhope Burn at a lethal pace. Stupid.

The long-distance walking route of the Pennine Way follows Dere Street for a mile or two, and it is well signed and defined. The border fence runs alongside, and at Brownhart Law just beyond is another relic of the long military past. Amongst the heather, tussocky grass grows in a vaguely circular pattern and it follows the ditches around another fortlet that watched over the road. If a tall wooden structure like those built by the Romans along Perthshire's Gask Ridge had been raised inside the ditching, the views to the north, east, west and back to Chew Green would have been extensive. Perhaps it was part of a chain of signal stations, a system used elsewhere in the Empire to send simple messages very quickly over long distances. On a bright day, a shiny metal plate could flash in a version of Morse code, and at night a fire could be used in a similar way. There was certainly a Roman signal station on the singular hill of Ruberslaw. It rises thirteen miles to the north-west and is clearly visible from the fortlet at Brownhart Law. There was another signal station on Eildon Hill North and it can be seen from Ruberslaw. Perhaps this pattern of grass in the heather recalled a long chain of communication the length of Roman Britain. For me, these bluff, treeless, windy hills were beginning to come alive, history literally remembered in the grass.

The road then follows the line of the border fence, winding its way around the flanks of the pillowy hills, passing two cairns at Greyhen Rock. From there, the views to the north begin to open, but it is the foreground that is more striking. The Roman road is clearly visible, its sinuous path either shelved into the hillside or choosing to follow a ridge between two steep, grassy corries. An old dyke runs from the border fence between Hunthill and Hindhope Hill, and a sign on an iron gate directs walkers back the way I had come, to Chew Green and Dere Street. The route indicated seems clear at first, but it then peters out on the precipitous hillside down to Blackie Hope, a burn that runs down to the farm at Nether Hindhope and the beginnings of the Kale Water valley. It is confusing, and to my unpractised eye the more likely line of the old road is to the north of Blackhall Hill, less than 150 metres away but surely much more passable.

In the middle distance rises a hill that saw ancient but uncertain drama. Woden Law is impressive. While a gentle slope leads up from the line of the road to a singular summit, the north-western side is very steep and commanding. In 78 AD, and for a long time before, the law was a place of power and of mystery. Across south and western England, hillforts like it dominated the landscape in the first millennium BC: perhaps the most famous and complex is Maiden Castle in Dorset. At the time of the Roman invasion, this vast earthwork was the capital place of the Durotriges, a major Celtic kindred. After the south-east of England had been secured in 43 AD, Maiden Castle was attacked by the II Legion led by Vespasian, who would later order Agricola to march through the Cheviot Hills on a mission of conquest. He and his generals knew how important hillforts were.

Beyond the south and west of England, the greatest concentration of these earthworks was in south-east Scotland and Northumberland. Woden Law was an impressive example. On the shallower south-eastern slope four lines of ditches were dug and the upcast tamped down to form ramparts behind them. Into these the posts of a wooden stockade were rammed and there appears to have been a gateway near the centre of this run of defences. Behind this was a small oval enclosure on the summit of the law, which was protected by massive stone walling, some of it nine feet thick. Inside this there were several timber roundhouses. Although very much smaller than Maiden Castle and other hillforts in south-eastern Scotland and Northumberland, Woden Law is nonetheless formidable. But its principal function was almost certainly not defensive.

Roman generals set much store by military intelligence

and planning, and their experience in the south of Britannia will have taught them the symbolic importance of these earthworks that had cost the native kindreds so much back-breaking effort to build. Often not practical, rarely with a reliable ground supply of water and with a long perimeter to defend, their principal function was probably political in the broadest sense. Hillforts were places where power resided, where kings or lesser lords held court, probably receiving food rents and services, keeping their warbands close and playing some sort of unknowable spiritual role. Hillforts have been renamed sky temples, sacred enclosures clearly marked off from the temporal world, high places where the gods were closer. Emphatic statements in the landscape, often visible for miles, these citadels were focal points for kindreds such as the Selgovae and the Votadini. And, for the Roman invaders who marched to its lower slopes in 78 AD, Woden Law also had strategic importance.

Those who stood on the ramparts of the law looked down over what was probably already a hill trail through the Cheviots, and if a Roman road was to run at its foot, then continued occupation by a native kindred could not be tolerated.

The sun lit the contours of straight lines of ditching to the west and south of the hill, and I could see them clearly as I walked down the line of the road. They contrasted with the curves of the earthworks higher up the slope. Running at right angles, they are the remains of a decision made by Agricola; two runs of Roman seigeworks. Their habit was entirely to encircle an enemy fortification to deny it water and supplies, and since the northern flank of Woden Law is very steep, it was only in the south and the west that ditches needed to be dug. But, to my eye, they looked odd.

The lines are not connected properly and archaeologists

believe that the seigeworks were abandoned soon after they were begun. Perhaps the Selgovae kings surrendered their fortress in the face of such overwhelming odds, or perhaps they agreed on terms which meant giving it up, or perhaps the whole thing was a training exercise to keep idle soldiers busy. There are signs that the inner rampart of stone was demolished rather than destroyed by ballista balls, and the roundhouses on the summit seem to have been deliberately cast down.

There is no evidence of occupation on Woden Law for two centuries after Agricola led his men over the Cheviots. When the northern frontier of the province of Britannia settled on Hadrian's Wall in the third century AD, native kings climbed the hill once more and made a fortress on the law that commanded a Roman road no longer travelled by Romans.

After the provincial frontier retreated south in the third century, the northern section of Dere Street was no longer maintained by Roman engineers and their work gangs. As the Empire faded in the west in the fifth century, all of their accumulated expertise and knowledge seeped away, and although the great road remained in use, the rains and snows of a thousand winters frayed its edges, puddled its potholes and splashed out its hard-packed gravel surface. Where the road wound down towards the south-eastern slopes of Woden Law, I had to walk around several places where little sikes running off the hill had long washed away the metalled surface. Farmers had made some recent repairs with railway sleepers (how on earth did they heave them up there from the valley bottom?) and in places the road travelled along bedrock, where it had been hacked back into the hillside to make the going level. These stretches may have been as close as it was possible to be to the actual surface where carts creaked and trundled, and they were a reminder of how all roads before tarmac were bumpy and irregular. There must have been many breakdowns, as axles broke or wheels lost their iron trim and splintered. And while Roman roads were rightly revered through the ages as technologically far in advance of anything for the following 1,900 years, the Romans themselves were not always so complimentary. In a cache of notes and letters found at the Roman fort of Vindolanda on Hadrian's Wall, dating around 100 AD, one correspondent wrote that travel was not easy because '*viae malae sunt*', the roads are so bad.

On my right there was a beautifully made drystane dyke enclosing a large sheepfold, and I wondered how many of its stones had been robbed from the road and its ancient kerbs and cobbles. There were two quarries on the slopes of Woden Law that had probably been the source of the stone for the hillfort's inner rampart, and there must have been others where the bedrock was close to the surface. Roman roads are sometimes more easily spotted from the air, where observers can see a line of quarry pits. The dykers working up in the Cheviots, by contrast, did not have to dig because they had a ready source of stone already cut to a usable size by legionaries and auxiliaries.

By the time I had rounded the hump of Woden Law, I could see where Dere Street ran downhill to the valley of the Kale Water. It was steep, but the route was presumably not thought unmanageable for ox-carts. The principal purpose of Roman roads was not so much to make marching or riding easier (although they did make for a faster pace) since infantry and cavalry only need firm ground; it was more to provide a metalled surface wide enough for wheeled vehicles, usually ox-carts. They were needed to carry essential supplies – all year round – of all kinds, as well as military hardware. Going down a steep incline could be as difficult as going up. Gravity exerted pressure behind the beasts, encouraging their natural instinct to flee something they could not see, and drivers had to take it slow on downhill stretches and use their brakes whenever they felt the wheels were beginning to turn too quickly.

At the top of the run down to the river valley, I saw a strange, block-like building, four rubble-built walls without windows and only a door on the south-eastern side. Surrounded by what looked like lambing pens, it was probably a bothy, the darkness inside made bearable by the shelter the solid walls gave from the days and nights of whistling winter winds and driving rain. The line of the road was much harder to see, and I followed a winding sheepwalk along where the map placed it until I reached a stile and a well-cropped field full of fat and woolly sheep. I had to climb down the stile very carefully since the wire of an electric fence ran worryingly close. I'd had enough excitement for one day. Finally, I climbed another stile over the fence by the single-track road. Half an hour later I was glad of a seat in my car.

Sitting on the back seat was my constant companion, Tacitus' *Life of Agricola*. Although it was written 2,000 years ago, it is a masterpiece. The sense and expression are fresh, and it reeks of the febrile politics of the imperial court in Rome, as well as the excitement and dangers of campaigning in unknown territory. Unlike more modern historiography, it makes little effort to be objective. Agricola was Tacitus' father-in-law and a great part of his purpose in writing the short biography was to burnish the governor's reputation as a soldier and a provincial administrator. Tacitus means something like 'Quiet Man', and while the Emperor Domitian ruled, the faithful son-in-law was forced to keep his opinions

to himself. Domitian appears to have been a ruthless, inse-
cure tyrant whose suspicions could have savage consequences,
especially on those who wrote well of other men who might
be seen as potential rivals. And so Tacitus lived up to his
name and kept silent.

By 96 AD Domitian had too many enemies and was assas-
sinated and replaced with Nerva, an old man who was to
reign for only two years, long enough to ensure the succession of the highly capable soldier Trajan. Tacitus rejoiced at
Domitian's death:

> Just as the former age [the reigns of Vespasian and Titus]
> witnessed an extreme in freedom, so we have experi-
> enced the depths of servitude, deprived by espionage
> even of the intercourse of speaking and listening to one
> another. We should have lost our memories as well as
> our voices, were it as easy to forget as to be silent.

Tacitus had almost certainly ridden to the foot of Woden
Law, accompanying Agricola as he began his tour of duty in
Britannia in 77 AD. Relatives were often appointed as staff
officers and his account of the new governor's campaigns,
especially in the early years, sound very much like eye-witness
accounts. When the legions tramped through the Cheviots,
Tacitus probably rode as part of the command group, and
when the great column reached the shoulder of the law,
Agricola may have ridden ahead with his bodyguards. Here
is a sense of the general's approach to the campaign in the
north, reported by his son-in-law:

> But when summer came, he concentrated the army,
> and was present everywhere on the march, praising
> discipline and keeping stragglers up to the mark. He

chose the sites for pitching camp himself and recon-
noitered estuaries and forests personally [Roman
generals had a historic anxiety about being ambushed
in woodland]. And all the while he gave the enemy no
rest, by launching sudden plundering raids. When he
had done enough to inspire fear, by acting with clem-
ency he showed them, as a contrast, the attractions of
peace. As a result, many states [kindreds] which up to
that moment had operated on equal terms abandoned
violence and gave hostages [as a guarantee of good
behaviour]. They were also surrounded by garrisons
and forts, with such skill and thoroughness that no new
part of Britain ever came over with so little damage.

And then something more specific:

The third year of campaigns opened up new peoples
with the ravaging of the territories up to the Taus [Tay]
(that is the name of the estuary). This action so intimi-
dated the enemy that they did not dare challenge the
army, although it was harassed by wild storms. There
was even time to spare for establishing forts. Experts
commented that no other general selected sites more
wisely. No fort established by Agricola was ever taken by
the enemy by storm or abandoned either by capitulation
or by flight. In fact they could make frequent sallies, for
they were assured against long sieges by supplies to last
for a year. Hence winter had no terrors; the garrisons
were self-sufficient. The enemy were baffled and in
despair, because they had been used to making good the
summer's losses by successes in winter and now they
were under pressure in summer and winter alike.

When Agricola had made his way down the north-eastern slopes of Woden Law, his horse splashed over a vital resource. When he crossed it at Towford, the Kale Water had barely begun its journey out of the Cheviots, but its flow was enough to supply the needs of 10,000 thirsty men and their animals.

In an ancient landscape where bridges were all but unknown until the Romans came, the location of fords helped form the pattern of trails used by the native peoples. Rivers and broad, deep streams were real barriers to movement and where their flow was slow and shallow, that was where people, animals and carts crossed. Fords were also favoured meeting places, and not always friendly: battles were often fought near places where warriors and horses could wade across.

Most fords were only passable in summer, and next to the crossing at Towford I saw a tall, white indicator with the levels the flooding Kale can reach marked off on it. They seemed remarkably high for what is little more than a stream, and even when the flow reached the first two or three of the lowest marks, the ford would have become impassable. The relative reliability of river crossings was one compelling reason why armies tended to campaign from midsummer into autumn.

Fords were also part of the language of travel before tarmac and bridges. Many places names still carry the 'ford' suffix, and some offer clues to the run of ancient roads. When a bridge was deemed unnecessary, the Romans sometimes paved the bed of a ford so that ox carts could trundle across safely. Although I could not find its exact location, the Crhachoctrestrete crossed the Eye Water with a ford that once carried the old name of Eiforde. The equally old medieval place name of Staniford, a crossing of the Ale

Water between Selkirk and Hawick, is very suggestive of a lost Roman road that linked Agricola's two lines of advance in 78 AD. The place name means the Stone Ford, more precisely the Paved Ford. The road that crossed it ran through the Craik Forest and is thought to have joined Dere Street just to the south of St Boswells.

A long time before my walk through the Cheviots, in the summer of 2013, on a sunny July day, I had gone off in search of Staniford in my ancient four-wheel drive, a twelve-year-old Range Rover – the only inanimate object I was ever passionate about, even forgiving its fuel consumption of fifteen miles a gallon, on a good day. The weather had been dry for a few days, the water should not have been high, and I reckoned a safe crossing would be possible. I thought I knew where the ford was, but first I had to find the roads that led to and from it.

The old Pathfinder series, no longer published by the Ordnance Survey, was an adornment to life in Britain and it is more than sad that these compact, highly detailed little maps have been discontinued. Out of doors, where many people tend to consult a map, the Landranger and Explorer series (maddeningly double-sided – a serious case of a false economy) are simply too large, especially when the wind blows. On the handy Pathfinder, I could see a track that ran from the north down to what was simply marked as a ford at Syntonmill. And so, with all the thoughtless bravado of someone who has watched too many mud-spattered TV adverts, I swung into what was at first a rutted but hard road, made a little deeper by the huge tyres of modern tractors. The crest was difficult to see because the grass on it had grown so tall, but I felt no scraping or ominous bumps that might damage my exhausts or worse. The high clearance on my trusty old four by four should have been enough. Should have been.

Straight at first, the track then turned sharply and slightly uphill. The tractor ruts disappeared after a field entry on the left. That should have sounded a warning, but no, I ploughed on regardless through high willowherb, nettles and tall grass, only staying on the track surface because the dykes on either side gave me a rough idea of where it might be. And then, and then. The gradient suddenly became very steep indeed, as it descended through a dark, leafy tunnel of mature trees. There was no gap in the dykes where I could turn and not a chance the clutch would enjoy reversing back up the incline, even if I could see where – exactly – I was going. When I saw the Ale Water at the foot of the hill sparkling in the summer sunshine, it did not occur to me how pretty or picturesque it was. How deep? That was all that mattered. I just had to get across because there was nowhere else to go. In fact, the shimmer off the water gave me no sense of how deep it was. Easing off the brake, I came to a short, flatter five metres of track and then ploughed in, slowly. I was hoping against hope that the Roman engineers had done a good job. And that their paving had lasted 2,000 years. Or was there at all.

It wasn't. There was no paving of any sort to be seen. But a little way upstream, I could see a half-submerged log lying across the line of the ford and it told me to stop fretting about its depth. The bed of the Ale Water was indeed stony and, rubbed smooth by millennia of flow, the stones were oddly uniform in shape, mostly about the size of a pack of butter, and there were no boulders to be seen. It didn't need to be paved, and I bumped across with no bow wave and pulled up on the opposite bank in front of a field gate. Thank goodness. If I had found myself marooned in midstream, I didn't fancy the call to the AA, or my wife.

Beyond the ford there was a big old barn built from the

whinstone characteristic of the district. It might have been eighteenth century, at the beginnings of the agricultural revolution, or even earlier. What struck me, though, was that it stood astride the exit/entrance to the ford, forcing the road to turn left to get around it. Clearly there was very little modern traffic across the Ale at the Staniford. Just the one idiot who should have looked at his Pathfinder more closely and approached from the south, or parked up at the top of the steep slope and walked down.

The languages of early travel not only included many variations on fords and their descriptions (Woodford, Romford, Brentford), they also had something to say about the riverbank on either side. As I had discovered, the approach to a ford could be steep and this sort of incline became known in Scotland as a 'peth' or 'path'. And it may have been particularly applied to Roman roads. The term appears in Gamelspath and Kemylpethe, and also in the modern village of Pathhead. It sits on either side of the A68, the successor to Dere Street as it strikes through Midlothian towards Edinburgh and the Forth. The village is at the 'Head of the Peth' and at its foot is the hamlet of Ford and the place where Dere Street crosses the River Tyne before very clearly climbing north through Chesterhill (a name that hints at a marching camp). The old road then disappears into the suburbs of Dalkeith.

But that is to move ahead of ourselves, and by some distance. Back in the foothills of the Cheviots, and reaching back through almost twenty centuries, Agricola kicked his horse across Towford (which is definitely paved and still in use) and had his surveyors peg out the lines of the ditches and banks that would enclose a marching camp. There then followed a miraculous transformation. Especially when they were moving through hostile territory, a Roman army always dug overnight entrenchments to protect sleeping soldiers from attack. The Roman military expert Vegetius wrote that it was as though legionaries and auxilliaries carried a walled town in their packs. Each man had an entrenching tool (known as a dolabra, it was like a cross between a pick and a spade, close to the design of a traditional mattock) and a wooden stake, and all knew exactly what to do and where.

Guarded by detachments who remained in full armour with their weapons at the ready, soldiers dug ditches and piled up a rampart before ramming their stakes into it or forming them like caltrops by tying them together to make large, bristling, star-shaped spikes. Roman marching camps were all very similar in layout. Tent lines were pegged out in the same places each time and units always pitched in the same part. This was not simply a matter of habit or bureaucracy. It meant that in the panicky moments of emergency soldiers knew exactly where to run and to muster when trumpets sounded or commands were shouted. Even in the darkest, moonless night, they could fall properly into their ranks, ready for command.

Between the lines of tents and the rampart a wide space known as the intervallum was left. This ensured that missiles, slingshots, arrows or javelins launched from beyond the ramparts could not reach where the soldiers slept and kept their kit. It also served as a place where units could form up in battle order. The Roman military instinct was not to seek shelter or the high ground but to get out into open field to fight. In restricted spaces their great advantages in equipment, tactics and discipline were less determinant. Visitors to Roman camps and forts are often surprised at the number and width of the gates. Used to looking at medieval castles with only one heavily defended entrance, they wonder at such obvious points of weakness. But in fact the gates were designed to allow Roman soldiers to get out of their camps and forts in as large a number and as quickly as possible.

When Agricola and his legions pushed northwards beyond the Tay, Tacitus wrote that they were moving 'as if into another island'. What he meant can seem unclear to a modern traveller, but it was a fact of geography that dominated landward movement between southern and northern Scotland for millennia. Between the marshy head of the Forth estuary, with its tidal pools and uncertain ground, and the great expanse of Flanders Moss to the west, there was only one road that an army could take. It ran below the glowering rock of Stirling Castle and crossed the River Forth close by, where it can be forded in summer at Kildean. The sixteenth-century Scottish chronicler Hector Boece reckoned that Agricola had 'come to Strivelyng . . . and nocht lang efter he byggit ane bryg ouir Forth'. Any traces of a Roman bridge have disappeared since it was probably a wooden structure, if it existed. This narrow neck of dry land saw many flashpoints of conflict, perhaps the most famous being at Bannockburn and Stirling Bridge.

As the legions tramped north beyond the Forth and the Tay, their route can be intermittently traced by a line of huge marching camps. At one of these, somewhere in the Angus Glens, disaster almost befell the Roman invaders. In what sounds like a surprisingly poor decision (naturally not mentioned by Tacitus), Agricola had decided to commit the cardinal sin of dividing his army.

> To avoid encirclement by superior forces familiar with the country, he himself divided his army into three divisions and advanced.
>
> When the enemy discovered this, with a rapid change

of plan they massed for a night attack on the Ninth Legion, as being by far the weakest in numbers. They cut down the sentries and burst into the sleeping camp, creating panic. Fighting was already going on inside the camp itself when Agricola, who had learned of the enemy's route from his scouts and was following close on their tracks, ordered the most mobile of his cavalry and infantry to charge the combatants from the rear and then the whole army was to raise the battle-cry. At first light the standards gleamed. The Britons were terrified at being caught between two fires, while the men of the Ninth regained their spirits and now that their lives were safe began to fight for glory. They even ventured on a break out and a fierce battle followed in the narrow passage of the gates. Finally the enemy were driven back before the rival efforts of two armies.

So that I could cross the Kale dryshod, I used the footbridge at Towford and walked up the tarmacked road that now covers Dere Street. On my left, I came across a sign for Pennymuir Camps with the jaunty headline 'Camping by Numbers'. This was the site Agricola had chosen, a flattish expanse of rough moorland close enough to a source of water. Near the sign, there was a stile – and another strand of electric fence wire to negotiate. Carefully ducking under, I walked up through the tussocky field to look at what remained of the work of all the mattlock-like dolabrae. At Pennymuir, there may not have been the drama of the marching camp of the IX Legion, but it was fascinating nonetheless. The ridges and ditches nearest the fence were those of a smaller camp dug into the south-east corner of a much larger perimeter and they were very easy to see. The Romans often used part of a pre-existing camp to build another, smaller version. When I walked around the perimeter of the larger, probably original camp, I could just make out the gates (having cheated by checking them on a map), or lack of them. Facing the entrances there were short runs of ditches and banks intended to slow down and break up a charge on the men guarding them. They were clearly not effective at the camp of the IX Legion. In places, the ramparts seemed more than a metre high and the ditches roughly a metre deep in places. They will have filled over time and been originally much more impressive.

The area of the largest of the four camps at Pennymuir is eighteen hectares, easily sufficient to accommodate Agricola's army. The soldiers stayed there long enough to build the abortive siege-works on Woden Law and the subsequent smaller camps were dug by later military traffic on Dere Street. The name of Pennymuir is a memory of all that earthworking. On the Pathfinder, it refers to the crossroads at the top of the slope above the camp, where there is a village hall (and no sign of any village), and it means something like 'At the Head of the Walls'.

The hall is also the focus of an annual event that brings people and colour to this normally deserted landscape. The Pennymuir Show takes place in September, when the hill shepherds bring down the best of their flocks to compete in the Blackface, North Country Cheviot, Cheviot and Interbreed classes. Border Collies and Border Terriers also show their paces, and the keen eye of the former still astonishes me. Some look almost human, their brains assessing you as they stare fixedly. Without doubt, collies are the most intelligent dogs on the planet. I asked an old shepherd, splendid in his russet tweed suit, what his dog's name was. 'Blacker.' Why? 'Because it's blacker than the last yin.' Which sounded as though there might have been a lack of individual affection. Pride perhaps describes better what the old shepherds feel for their superbly trained dogs. When I asked the old man if Blacker was particularly clever, he turned and looked at me with a withering eye. 'Clever?' he said. 'That yin could knit you a pullover.'

In the village hall, the Pennymuir Show seems to hark back to a bygone age, long before vans decorated with a pyramid of perfect strawberries 'freshly clicked' delivered food. Here in the foothills of the Cheviots was bountiful evidence that people still made and grew things. There were cups for the winners of the 'Best Four Potatoes', 'Best String of Onions' and 'Best Exhibit in Eggs, Jam and Needlework' sections. You had to move faster than I did before the tables of the Bakery section were cleared, but I did make a superb purchase: a straight hazel rod made into a shepherd's crook with a handle carved from the horn of a Cheviot ram. With Tacitus, my Pathfinders, compass, phone and chocolate, it became another constant companion as I walked the hidden ways.

Dere Street is a single-track tarmac road up to Pennymuir Hall and its crossroads. Leaning forlorn against a wall, a wooden sign pointed me in the direction of a straight and grassy track running beside a drystane dyke. The old road was clearly discernible, but in places I found deep and what looked like recent ruts. Apparently Dere Street is a legally accessible right of way and sometimes used by well-heeled vandals for some exciting off-road driving. After the courts confirmed their so-called rights, there was nothing the local authority could do to prevent these idiots from badly damaging 2,000 years of our history. Where were Agricola and 10,000 Roman legionaries when you needed them?

Despite being vexed at the ruts, I found myself swinging into a good walking rhythm. The sun was shining, and for about a mile there was only a gentle gradient and the views over the open moorland were wide. Directly to my front I could see the low hump of Braid Knowe and the road rising over its eastern shoulder. Entirely alone in the landscape, with the walking easy, for some reason I began to sing, belting out pop songs and hymns at full volume. An odd medley whose unifying criterion for inclusion was that I could remember at least two verses. Blake and Parry's *Jerusalem* has long been a favourite, even though I was walking through Scotland's green and pleasant land and without a dark, Satanic mill in sight. I cannot hold a tune and only occasionally hit the right note by accident, or perhaps a process of elimination. But I had the impression that the sheep had heard worse.

Two thousand years before I serenaded the heather, the Romans brought chariots, spears, swords, arrows and bows as their feet marched in ancient time. And they also chanted and sang as their column threaded its way through the landscape. With 10,000 men making up a massive male voice choir, the din must have been terrifying to native ears. And given that the soldiers wore uniforms, something never seen in Celtic society, the impression of a monstrous and noisy snake sliding quickly through the landscape would have been understandable. Some texts have survived to hint at a surprising soundtrack for the Agricolan invasion. *Bacche*, by a poet called Florus, was a hymn very different from Blake's:

Bacche, vitium repertor, plenus adsis vitibus,
Effluas dulcem liquorem, comparandum nectari.

Bacchus, of the vine revealer, let thy fullness aid the vine,
Send the dulcet juice aflowing, which no nectar can outshine.

It is unlikely that many amphorae of wine would have trundled north in army baggage carts and the soldiers had to make do with cervesa, Celtic beer. In the notes and lists found at Vindolanda, there was a plaintive request from a cavalry officer to Flavius Cerialis, the commander of the garrison: 'the comrades have no beer, which I ask that you order to be sent'.

Some of the legionaries joined the army at the age of sixteen and the average age of recruits was between eighteen and twenty. Little more than boys, many of these 'tirones' will have been virgins and their comrades sometime struck up an encouraging chant as they marched:

Cras amet qui numquam amavit,
Quique amavit cras amet.

Let him love tomorrow who has never loved,
And let him who has loved love tomorrow.

This clever play on words shows a softer side, but the men who chanted it were soldiers whose job was killing and a very different chant has survived, one that promised retribution if natives resisted the march of the Empire:

Unus homo, mille, mille, mille decollavimus.

For the loss of one man, we will cut off a thousand,
a thousand, a thousand heads.

When it stepped up to what was called the military pace, a Roman army could move frighteningly fast, making twenty-two miles in five hours. By contrast, I was ambling, stopping for a look around, a drink of water, moving slowly across what seemed an empty landscape. There were sheep and black cattle grazing, but no farmsteads, no vehicles and no people to be seen. Since I'd left the camp at Pennymuir, I had not seen a soul and the only sound above the soughing of the wind was the piou-piou of buzzards gliding in its updraughts. And yet, 4,000 years ago the silence would have been broken by the whistles and shouts of shepherds, by exchanges and meetings as the farmers on these high moorlands went about their day-in, day-out business. The climate was warmer then and the remains of cultivation terraces cut into the hillsides can be clearly seen, especially above the village of Hownam, about two miles to the east of where I walked. The soil must have been better there. Higher temperatures allowed crops to ripen at higher altitudes than they do now, and the growing season was longer. Instead of tussocky, boggy moorland, grass grew and expanded into sheep lawns as flocks cropped it short. And close to the Roman road, I came across a modest monument to prehistoric agriculture.

About thirty metres to the east, I could see a small stone circle measuring about seven metres across. Five chunky stones appeared to be hunkering down. They were almost obscured by the green spikes of tall marsh grass. The ground around was wet, easily churned. Perhaps the stones had sunk over time, as the climate grew darker, colder and more damp. This was a henge, certainly nothing as grand and spectacular as Stonehenge or Callanish, but a henge nonetheless, a monument raised by the ancient farming communities of the Cheviot ranges sometime after about 3,000 BC. Its construction was a testament to success, a society that could feed itself and, in times of surplus, have the time and energy to build a religious monument. The reason why the stones were placed here is unclear and their function can only be guessed at. If, as seems the overwhelming likelihood, the circle was a temple of some kind – the stones marking off the temporal outside from the spiritual and mysterious inside, where rituals of some kind were performed – then their choice of location is hard to understand. The circle is difficult to see from any distance (unless the stones were indeed taller when first placed in firm ground) and it appears not to relate to the landscape around it, as many henges do.

If Dere Street did indeed follow the line of a pre-existing native trail, then perhaps accessibility was the prime consideration. As I walked around the circle looking for signs of a ditch (there seemed to be none), it occurred to me that the Roman road makers had acted with restraint. Instead of breaking those big stones for use as kerbs, they left them be. And instead of giving in to the sore temptation to sit on one, I managed to persuade myself to respect the beliefs of the old peoples who had made this little temple. Even if I could not have any idea of what their beliefs were, they were clearly sincerely held, having demanded an immense amount of labour to make a place where they could be celebrated. The Romans are vivid because they left records and a great deal of archaeology, but they were incomers, not the ancestors of my own people. Perhaps precisely because the native people left so few marks on the landscape, were little more than grey figures who barely emerge from the darkness of the long past, these nameless farmers seemed to me to deserve all and any respect I could give them.

Beyond the little circle, at a small plantation of sitka spruce, the green track became more defined and dykes began to run on either side. By the time I reached a much larger plantation, my trusty Pathfinder told me that I had about a mile to walk before the old road reached Whitton

Edge. There it turned abruptly left to become a modern tarmacked road that ran in a north-westerly direction towards Jedburgh. Meanwhile, I noticed that the surface I was walking on had become harder and more stony, its surface not grassed over but visible except at its crest. But it did not look like the small Roman cobbles I had seen on the Crhachoctrestrete; it was more like hard-packed gravel. Perhaps that was all there was to hand up here in the hills. Practicalities aside, it did touch me to realise that I was walking exactly where the legions had marched, where they had carried the gleaming eagle standards and hauled their ballistas and scorpios. A departed drama, part visualised, part imagined, it gave me the schoolboy thrill of following in the footsteps of history.

As I reached the shoulder of Cunzierton Hill, long views to the north began to open. I could see the Teviot and Tweed valleys spread below and, in the distance, the Eildon Hills. At the foot of Eildon Hill North, the Romans would build a huge fort and depot by the side of their great road. When I reached the junction at Whitton Edge, where Dere Street becomes tarmac, I saw that a bench had been thoughtfully provided. I sat down to enjoy the stunning views across the Tweed Basin. Far to the north, the low humps of the Lammermuirs were hazy, hard to make out, and the rolling, freshly harvested fields of Berwickshire ran down to the sea. For Agricola and his quartermasters, it was a warming sight, for those fields grew the corn the army needed.

After Whitton Edge, Dere Street becomes more like the popular perception of what a Roman road looks like, running arrow-straight to reach destinations by the fastest and most direct route. It struck me as a historical statement of intent. The Emperor Vespasian had commanded Agricola to conquer Caledonia and bring it into the Empire as part of the province of Britannia. Since the fourth century BC the Romans had been consolidating their conquests by drawing them closer, by building a vast road network first in Italy and then across Western Europe. By enabling rapid mobility, it dramatically extended the reach and control of the army, and once provinces became settled, good roads also became arteries of trade, moving goods around, growing the imperial economy, creating revenue for the government.

After sitting too long at Whitton Edge, I walked downhill on the old straight, no-nonsense road. Trees line it and off to my right ran what the Pathfinder noted as the Avenue, another much more modern straight road leading to the farm at Upper Samieston. Perhaps it was a homage to the builders of Dere Street. At that point the road begins to cross the map like geometry, as though a ruler had been laid on the landscape – running dead straight until it reaches the banks of the Jed Water and its confluence with the Teviot. Agricola will have used scouting parties to gather intelligence about the lands that lay to the north and the kindreds who inhabited them. If, as seems likely, Dere Street was as much a policed frontier between the friendly Votadini and the hostile Selgovae, then its route will have more or less followed that political fault line. In an era when power was measured not by territory but by the strength of the bonds between kings and lords, the Roman road may have divided those loyal to the kings of the Selgovae and those loyal to the kings of the Votadini. While the pattern is by no means uniform, to the west lie the hills and the headwaters of the rivers of the Tweed Basin, while to the east are the fertile fields of the widening plain. It may be fairly claimed that Dere Street was a boundary between uplanders and lowlanders, between shepherds and ploughmen, and, for Agricola and his tribunes, between those who might pose a threat and those who needed to be persuaded to be compliant so that they could supply corn.

Further north, the Romans probably knew what to expect. As I read and re-read Tacitus, it seemed that there was a clear plan of campaign in 78 AD and the years that followed, something that can only have been worked out on the basis of forward intelligence. Dere Street not only served to divide friend from foe, it also had to bring Rome's armies to the shores of the Forth, where they could be supplied by sea, certainly at the harbour at Cramond to the west of Edinburgh, probably at Inveresk to the east. From there a route could be taken through the Stirling Gap to the north and to those Caledonian kindreds who were known to be hostile.

Once the line of a road had been agreed, surveyors set to work. Almost certainly on the summit of Whitton Edge a *groma* was planted in the ground. This was a straight vertical staff about one-and-a-half to two metres long that had two horizontal cross-pieces mounted on a bracket attached to one end and a sharp metal point on the other. Set at right angles in a cross shape, each arm had a plumb line attached at its end that hung vertically. When the staff, the *ferramento*, was pushed into the ground, it was adjusted to be exactly vertical by making sure that the hanging plumb lines and another close to the staff were in perfect alignment. A great deal of care was taken over this procedure, for all else would flow from the measurements made.

Once the *groma* was properly set, the cross-pieces were rotated on their bracket in the direction the road was intended to take. By sighting along the two arms pointing in that direction, a stake was planted in the ground at about 125 paces and lined up with the three plumb lines on the arm of the cross-piece (this was the component actually called a *groma*, but the name has come to be applied to the whole instrument). This process was repeated until the surveyors ran out of stakes. Then the *groma* would be pulled out of its original hole, taken forward to the last stake and then the whole process would be repeated as the line of the road advanced. In Italy, surveyors are still known as *gromatici*.

After I had walked past the Avenue and the sign for Upper Samieston Farm, the road began to climb towards Shotheids. The distance between there and the comfortable bench at Whitton Edge was about a mile and a half, and what I was approaching was probably the next high point where the surveyors planted their *groma*. What made Roman roads so durable and efficient (except those *viae malae* leading to and from Vindolanda) was the fact that they had proper, solid foundations. Once the line had been marked out, a deep trench, at least a metre, sometime one-and-a-half metres, was dug by the soldiers and then bottomed with stones. Roman armies used what they could find near at hand and the next layer was normally sand, if it was available. Between the Cheviot Hills and Jedburgh there is little to be had, so clay and gravel may have been used for the next layer. The original Roman road, the Via Appia from Rome to Capua, and others in Italy and Western Europe, were then paved with thick polygonal blocks of stones, but for military roads such refinements were rarely possible. Cobbles, and more often gravel, were used to finish the road and rammed down to make a metalled surface.

Rain is the enemy of good roads, so, in order that it could run off to the sides, the surface was not made level but slightly cambered or mounded in the middle. This was the *agger*, the same word used for the ramparts of a marching camp. Ditches ran on either side of the *agger* to carry off heavy rainwater, of which there is plenty in the Scottish

Borders. Kerbstones were also laid to hold the road surface together as traffic beat on it, and these must have had gaps set in their alignment, otherwise water would have pooled along the margins. At the foot of the section from Whitton Edge to Shotheids there is a trickle of a burn, at least that is how it looked in summer. Winter rains could turn it into a torrent, a road destroyer, and a culvert will have been set under it. The modern equivalent is sometimes known as an Irish Bridge.

The invention of tarmacadam at the beginning of the twentieth century has spoiled modern road users. By contrast, Roman roads were very uncomfortable for anyone travelling in a wheeled vehicle that had no springs. And none of them did. The roads were also very uneven and in need of repair after each winter. Once rainwater gets into a depression on a gravel surface and stays there, it quickly becomes a pothole. As each wheel, hoof or foot goes into it, the gravel splashes out and the hole grows larger and larger, and deeper and deeper. Walking was the most tiring but the least uncomfortable means of travel, except for those sufficiently wealthy to be carried in a litter by four or six slaves. Beside Roman roads bridleways can often be seen. Metal shoes were not used by the Romans and unshod horses will always prefer natural going to a gravel road. Although the outer horn of their hooves is hard, like our finger and toenails, the central part, the frog, is sensitive, especially to sharp stones. The Romans fitted hipposandals, leather pads secured with thongs, to protect their horses' feet, but these appear not to have been widely used. Therefore, it is unlikely that Agricola rode along the road he caused to be made.

The side drains were often dug deep along the *viae militares* as a brake on enemy warriors charging from cover, attempting to ambush a column. Road builders cleared the terrain on either side to minimise this risk, but sometimes the undulations of the ground could hide a force of attackers. I was grateful that such anxieties lay long in the past and was enjoying the shade of the mature trees lining the road up to Shotheids. When I reached what the Pathfinder marked as a crossroads, only three roads leading from it were still in use by vehicles. The fourth, the continuation of Dere Street, was clear, but it disappeared into what I would have called a green lane overgrown with bushes and thorns, and sometimes I had to thrash my way through an ambush of nettles and willowherb with my Pennymuir crook. But at least it led downhill.

After bisecting a plantation of sitka spruce, Dere Street led me into more open country. Hardwood trees lined the eastern side, while the view to the west looked out over fields towards Jedburgh, the land slowly descending to the valleys of the Jed Water and the Teviot. The road was well defined, with hedges replacing dykes, and I guessed that it had been recognised and used as a thoroughfare for so long that farmers had not been tempted to enclose its course into their fields. Perhaps the gravel and stone bottoming of the *agger* were too awkward to plough out, not worth the effort. Further north, in Lauderdale, stretches of the road had been absorbed into grass parks, permanent grazing, but its course could still be seen. As I made my way downhill towards the Oxnam Water, a tributary of the Jed, the surface improved.

I wanted to pause before crossing to have a look at a site that had something to say about the origins of the soldiers who built Dere Street and travelled on it. But when I crossed a tarmac road and made my way into the field on the left marked on my Pathfinder, I had to use my imagination. There is nothing at all to see of the Roman fort at Cappuck, not even humps and bumps in the grass. And yet the site was eloquent. Built above its steep southern bank to guard the crossing of the Oxnam Water (there is a good modern ford and therefore there was probably no Roman bridge needed), the fort was small, accommodating at most two centuries, about 160 men. In 1886, it sounds as though there was something to be seen at Cappuck. On behalf of the local landowner, the Marquis of Lothian, Walter Laidlaw excavated a stone-built granary and other buildings, and found part of an elaborate stone tablet that carried this inscription: *The Twentieth Legion, Valiant and Victorious, Made This*. It is now in the National Museum of Antiquities in Edinburgh and probably remembers the reoccupation of the fort during the reign of the Emperor Antoninus Pius (138 to 161 AD) and the reincorporation of southern Scotland into the Empire. The tablet carried the legion's mascot, the wild boar, and other decorative motifs. Based at the fortress at Chester (Deva), the XX Legion remained in Britain until the third century and they formed part of Agricola's original invasion force. By the time its men marched down to Cappuck sixty years later, many of them may have been recruited in Britain.

Subsequent excavations uncovered more and earlier inscriptions. They are fascinating. The first is a dedication to Jupiter and it reads: *For Jupiter, Best and Greatest, the detachment withdrawn from the Gaesatae commanded by the tribune, Aulus Julius Severus (made this offering)*. Soldiers often had altars carved and set up, either in thanks for victory, deliverance or some other feat of arms. Divine help was always sought. The Gaesatae, literally the Spearmen, were auxiliaries in the Roman army recruited from Gaul, modern France, and they probably marched with Agricola. Gaulish pottery datable to the later first century AD has been found at Cappuck. These men certainly understood Latin, the language of the army and the Empire, but amongst themselves they probably spoke a dialect of Gaulish, a much mutated version of which has survived as Breton.

The second inscription is longer: . . . *the First Cohort of Faithful Vardulli, one-thousand strong, part-mounted, Citizens of Rome, and Gaius Quintius Severus, of the Camillian voting tribe from Ravenna, tribune of the selfsame cohort, willingly, gladly and deservedly fulfill their vow.* This was far too large a force to occupy the fort and may only have been passing through. They had made a vow to raise an altar (the name of the god is not clear) presumably in thanks for some success in the field. The name of the Vardulli appears on several inscriptions found in northern Britain and they were originally Spaniards who probably also spoke a Celtic language, perhaps Celtiberian. Their tribune was anxious for it to be noted that he was a member of one of Rome's tribes. The closest the republic came to democracy was the Tribal Assembly, where thirty-five tribes voted on legislation and the election of magistrates, including consuls. Gaius Quintius Severus must have felt himself far removed from the politicking on the banks of the Tiber as he made offerings on his cohort's altar at the little fort on the banks of the Oxnam Water. But he would have a tale to tell of the reach of the Emperor's legions when he returned.

When I crossed the footbridge handily placed next to the ford across the stream, I passed the site of much larger marching camps at Cappuck, no doubt dug there because of its closeness to a water supply. There appear to have been four camps, the largest extending to forty-seven acres. My Pathfinder showed the fields to the west of the Roman site as Ulston Moor and beyond it lay three more kindred names: Easter Ulston, Wester Ulston and Mount Ulston. This sort of clustering is usually the relic of a larger holding and the name of the man who established it appears to be preserved within it. In the documents relating to land ownership associated with Kelso Abbey, Ulston is shown to be a contraction of Ullfkeliston, with the first element a version of the Scandinavian personal name of Ulfkell. This land to the west of the great road was once Ulfkell's tun or farmstead, a place that belonged to Norse raiders who eventually settled.

At the end of the eighth century, 700 years after the legions built the road I was walking on, sea-lords sailed out of the mists of the North Sea to attack God's church on Lindisfarne and many other monasteries around the coasts of Scotland and Britain. It was as though they had come out of nowhere. As raiding developed into settlement in the generations after the monks were slaughtered or enslaved and their sacred treasures taken, men with Scandinavian names penetrated far inland to establish themselves and stamp their names on the map.

As I walked on down towards the Teviot Valley, it occurred to me that I was falling into a classic historical trap, but one that was difficult to avoid. Because the Romans left written records (inscriptions as well as documents), very much more is known about what they did and why they did it than about the largely illiterate peoples who followed them. And that means the shortest of shrifts for many centuries of experience along the line of this ancient road. Not until the monks of the great abbeys and churches began to keep records – in Latin, the language of certainty – do the dim, half-forgotten names of the period justifiably known as the Dark Ages come into any sort of focus. But who was Ulfkell? Where did he come from, whom did he and his men displace, what sort of Nordic language did they speak? I could have little sense of any of that.

Before ever I set foot on Dere Street, I had spent many

weeks assembling fragments of colour, a patchwork of images and sounds I felt would help me make a journey back into the Roman past. The soldiers' chants, the look of their kit and weapons, the thud and speed of their march; all of this helped me leap across the void between the fall of the Empire in the west in the fifth century and the founding of the Border abbeys in the twelfth. While it is not exactly 700 years of silence, there is precious little to be scarted out of what scraps of records have survived.

That, I decided, was another compelling reason to walk. If I could discover almost nothing about Ulfkell's past, his name and its origins, at least I could walk where he had walked or ridden, and I could look down into the steep-sided valley of the Jed Water as the little river flowed north to its confluence with the Teviot. But even though I understood why, it did vex me greatly to realise that this shadowy figure's descendants certainly do live in the Borders now, while the highly informative Romans were only passing through, determined to subdue, exploit and organise. I was vexed for an intensely personal reason: I know that I am the descendant of Scandinavians who came to settle in the Teviot and Tweed valleys in the centuries following the attack on Lindisfarne in 793.

I inherited my Y chromosome DNA marker of S142 from my father and it was passed on to him by his father from a line of male ancestry that reaches back at least 2,500 years into the past. My grandfather, Robert Charters (I do not carry his name because my dad was an illegitimate child born to Bina Moffat, my grannie), was from Jedburgh, the beautiful riverside town only about a mile west of where I was walking. I certainly carry his Y chromosome DNA, and I know that S142 originated in northern Denmark, southern Norway and southern Sweden. Therefore I have, I am sure, much more in common with Ulfkell than with Gaius Quintius Severus of the Camillian voting tribe of Ravenna, but I suspect I will never be able to discover anything about this Scandinavian, a man who may have been my ancestor, whose bloodline I may have passed on to my son. Nevertheless, I was walking under the same skies that he saw more than a thousand years ago.

It was early evening by the time I reached the bank of the Jed Water. Late sun dappled through the trees on either side of the old road and as I stepped onto the tarmac of a B road that cuts across its foot, I realised that in an easy walking day, with several breaks (too long on the bench at Whitton Edge), I had come a long way, in distance, in time and culturally. Coming from the windy Cheviot watershed and the open hillsides worked by shepherds and their dogs, I had made my way, more downhill than up, to the low-lying land of the Tweed Basin and its fertile fields, the province of ploughmen for millennia.

I had also arrived at a busy junction. Not only did the B road cut diagonally across the Roman road, there was also the trackbed of a long-abandoned railway, a branch line from Jedburgh to Kelso, and a few metres further north ran the modern A698 and its concrete bridge across the Jed. This tangle of routes had all but obliterated the course of Dere Street and I could not make out where it crossed the little river, or indeed if it crossed it. Tomorrow and a refreshed eye might supply some answers.

My old friend Walter Elliot worked for decades in the Border countryside as a fencing contractor and in that long time, out in all weathers, he developed a keen sense for the shape of the land. Simply by looking, he can tell immediately what features are natural and what are man-made. Allied to much experience as an archaeologist and great learning as a historian, these skills allow him to see a different sort of history, how it was written on the land as a sort of palimpsest.

He has one further advantage over desktop researchers and cloistered academics. Walter has the gift of divining. Using only two bent pieces of fence-wire of the sort he used to run over hillsides and field-ends, he can find underground features in moments. Some years ago, I had forgotten where exactly the water pipe from my well ran under the track to my farm and needed to find it urgently, before some construction work began. When Walter's rods suddenly flicked inwards, at right angles to his outstretched arms, he stopped. 'Dig here.' And we did, finding the pipe exactly where he said it would run. Walter has taught me how to use the rods. It is important to have the right L-shape and not to grip the shorter ends too tightly but allow them to sit in a loose fist. And walk slowly – with a clear head. It turned out I could find pipes, old foundations and filled-in ditches. But even though she did exactly as instructed, my wife could not make the rods work. Therein lies a little mystery: it is indeed a gift.

So-called professionals and academics discount divining as unscientific, as New Age, or even old age, quackery and it gives them leave to turn up their noses, to ignore much that Walter Elliot has discovered. But I have seen it work again and again, and archaeologically he has ultimately been proved right, again and again.

Where Dere Street meets the Jed Water and the Teviot is a confusing site, but Walter has been able to make some sense of it. Hidden in plain sight, another Roman road forms a junction close to where I had broken off my day's walking down from the Cheviots. Running west from the port at Berwick upon Tweed, a road made some time after Dere

Street now lies mostly under modern tarmac. Many long straights mark its course south of the Tweed and the decisions made by the *gromatici* still make for a rapid journey from the Central Borders to the North Sea coast. In addition to an important junction, there was also a river crossing, first of the little Jed and then the Teviot. It was an ancient hub that needed protecting and servicing.

Both by observation and divining, Walter Elliot has discovered ditching associated with at least three forts on the higher ground to the west. Their garrisons monitored military and civilian traffic and maintained the roads. Soldiers could be vulnerable at river crossings and it looks as though the safest place to bridge the Teviot was at the place now marked on the Pathfinder as Nisbetmill Cauld. There is open haughland on either bank, and perhaps it was also like that 2,000 years ago. Much more recently the cauld was built on a diagonal across the river to push water into a lade that ran to power the wheel at Nisbetmill, less than 300 metres to the west. Walter has found no trace of any Roman bridge footings in the river or on its banks and these may have been removed when the cauld was built.

Up bright and early, I walked along the southern bank of the Teviot, past the cauld, to the suspension bridge below Monteviot House. Beautifully situated, not overbearing, south-facing with sheltering woods behind, it belongs to the Kerr family. From their shady beginnings as Border reivers in the sixteenth century, they quickly and adroitly made themselves part of the British establishment after the Union of the Crowns in 1603, becoming Marquises of Lothian and Earls of Ancrum. Recent residents at Monteviot have been prominent and distinguished Conservative politicians: Philip, Peter and Michael Ancrum all held ambassadorial or ministerial posts.

Difficult to make out in the dense darkness of a closely planted pinewood, the line of Dere Street only slowly became clear. When I reached Divet Ha' Wood, the trees parted and a grassy ride led to a fence, a stile, a B road and, beyond it, open farmland. Perhaps the ancient hard standing had frustrated the tree planters. The road ran straight now, at first by a dyke and then across the flanks of Down Law, before becoming a wide avenue with hardwood trees in broken runs on either side.

While the grass and weeds were high, it was easy going and the path was mostly clear with steady gradients. The avenue of big hardwoods was more complete on the eastern side and they shaded the morning sun (of course I only went out walking on good days). The effect of increasing enclosure, even though the traffic noise of the A68 less than a mile to the west was ever present, made Dere Street feel like something of a time tunnel. I wondered if the legionaries and auxilliaries who maintained the road allowed trees to grow on either side, like the cypresses of the Via Appia in Italy. Or was the risk of ambush too great?

I began to walk more quickly, although I could never aspire to the ground-eating marching pace that could take fully equipped, pack-carrying legionaries twenty miles in a day. In fact, I heartily dislike marching. When compelled to do it for the three weeks I was in the Boys' Brigade, stamping and stumbling around a cramped church hall, I rebelled and opted for the Boy Scouts.

In the spring of 2011, I received a letter from the splendidly named General Sir Evelyn Webb-Carter. He was organising a fund-raising event for the Soldiers' Charity, a ride that would take a small party along a stretch of Dere Street. They planned to dress in historical costumes to attract attention – and money. But not as Romans. It was thought, probably correctly, that the horse-riding kit of Border reivers was more suitable. Would I meet them on the old road and talk about its history, and also about a sixteenth-century battle that took place on it? Of course I would, and a meeting was agreed at a curious monument that I found myself revisiting on my walk.

Lilliard's Stone is said to commemorate an impossibly brave woman who fought at the Battle of Ancrum Moor in 1545. When her lover was killed, the tale was spun that the Maid Lilliard set about the enemy English, and this remarkable verse offers unlikely details:

> Fair Maiden Lilliard lies under this stane,
> Little was her stature, but muckle was her fame;
> Upon the English loons she laid mony thumps
> And when her legs were cuttit off, she fought upon
>   her stumps.

Clearly the inspiration for Monty Python's Black Knight, Lilliard's story is of course apocryphal, probably arising from a tiny grain of truth, an incident in the battle.

Sir Evelyn and I had arranged to meet at the stone at twelve noon, and arriving early, I could see the riders in the distance moving off Down Law. On horseback, they were clearly visible above the high grasses, weeds and bushes. It was a stirring sight. Even though there were only seven or eight riders, about half a mile away, it looked as though they had left the present behind, a posse of horsemen from any one of the 2,000 summers of the old road's history. Once they had dismounted and found some grazing and water for their horses, Sir Evelyn and his companions sat on the low walls around Lilliard's grave to hear the story of the Battle of Ancrum Moor, the version without the Black Knight. It was a warming, eccentric, even magical episode, somehow very British.

As often in its history, Dere Street brought the combatants together. The context was the period known as the Rough Wooing. Towards the end of his reign, Henry VIII grew increasingly bloated and ill, and anxious to ensure not only the accession of his son, Edward, but also to establish English dominion over Scotland. With a mixture of force, bribery and diplomacy, he attempted to have his heir betrothed to the infant Mary, Queen of Scots. Part of the Tudor strategy was to compel compliance by pillaging the Borders and in 1545 Sir Ralph Eure led an army of 3,000 Spanish and German mercenaries, a contingent of English Borderers and a group of 700 Assured Scots. These were men who had been given pensions by the English Exchequer in return for their support.

A significantly smaller force of Scots mustered near Jedburgh and marched north up Dere Street to meet Eure's men. They were approaching from the opposite direction, having attacked Melrose, killing, burning and plundering. The Scots had a plan. To the west of where Sir Evelyn and his band were sitting is the low hill of Gersit Law and a little way beyond it is Palace Hill. When the English were setting up camp on Gersit Law, a small force of Scots attacked them. It was a feint – and it produced the desired reaction. When the Scots turned and fled over Palace Hill, the English pursued. And ran straight into the bulk of the Scottish army, which had hidden itself until that moment.

As the sun set behind them, dazzling the English, the Scots attacked. Seeing which way the battle was going, the Assured Scots tore off their St George's Cross badges and changed sides. It was decisive. With their longer pikes working in formation, the infantry drove the English backwards over

Palace Hill and scattered them. Sir Ralph Eure was killed and the Rough Wooing ended in a stalemate.

I remember watching Sir Evelyn and his fund-raising reivers (they did that differently in the sixteenth century) ride north along the old road while I made my way to the A68, where I had parked my car. Five years later, I found myself following in their hoofprints. When the road began to climb a gentle rise, the sun suddenly slid from behind thick clouds and splashed a butter-yellow light over the landscape, the transformation so abrupt that it seemed artificial, as though stage lights had flooded on at the flick of a switch. The sunlit panorama that revealed itself with each step was breathtaking. Although I had walked up what seemed little more than an undulation, and not climbed a high hill, I could see east, west and north for many miles across the broad Tweed Valley. And at the centre of what seemed like a painterly composition rather than a series of accidents of geology rise the Eildon Hills.

At little more than 400 metres, they are not high, but the Eildons are spectacular, even magical. Around their foot lies the fertile farmland of the Borders, making them singular – except they are not. There are three hills: Eildon Hill North and Eildon Mid Hill are markedly higher than the Wester Hill. Part of what makes them magical is their number. Triplicity and the ideas and symbols associated with it are embedded in many cultures. Insofar as it can be deduced, Celtic belief often saw mystery and power in threes, be they gods, events or features. This preference continued in Christianity with the Father, Son and Holy Ghost and even non-believers observe that 'things happen in threes'.

Across the centuries since Agricola first saw them, magic has swirled around the hills. Most famous is the association with True Thomas, also known as Thomas the Rhymer, and his prophesies. On the eastern flanks, under the Eildon Tree by Huntly Bank, Thomas met the Queen of Elfland. She spirited him away and showed him three marvels: the road to Heaven, the road to Hell and her own world. After seven years (another magic number), Thomas was returned to the temporal world much changed. He had been given the gift of prophesy.

True Thomas was also known as Thomas of Ercildoune, nearby Earlston, and the historical record shows that he died in 1298. Some of his prophesies, notably those that foresaw the reverses and advances of the Wars of Independence, were fulfilled and he became one of the most famous men of his day. King Arthur and other legendary figures also came to be linked to the Eildon Hills and he was believed to have ridden around and even into their hollow centre.

To the ever-practical Romans, the three hills were a handy and distinctive landmark, a target at which their *gromatici* could aim the line of their road. The name of Eildon means Old Fort in the dialect of Old Welsh that was spoken in the Borders in the centuries around the coming of the Romans. It was a place of power, both spiritual and political. Around the summit of Eildon Hill North almost 300 levelled hut platforms have been identified by archaeologists and these were occupied by a population of between 3,000 and 6,000 people from around 1,000 BC onwards. They lie inside a vast, looping rampart around the crown of the hill, banks and ditches that make up a three-mile perimeter. There are four gates. But clearly this was no fort because thousands of warriors would have been needed to defend it and its vulnerable gates. Instead it is much more likely that Eildon Hill North was a sacred enclosure, a sky temple that brought people closer to their gods. There is no well and everything else that was necessary would have to be laboriously lugged up the hill. It is likely that this was a place inhabited by a priest-king of some kind, and that he and his retinue were attended on the Celtic quarter days when food renders were made, the laws spoken and the gods honoured. There simply cannot have been a permanent population of more than 3,000: it was logistically impossible to sustain so many on that windy site. The Romans aimed for the Eildons because they needed to treat with the powerful and control them.

To the north-east of the sky temple, the legions built what became a large depot and a fort. At Newstead, close to the Tweed, the ramparts of Trimontium rose, and it probably took its name from the hillfort, in Old Welsh, Tribrynian – in English, Threehills. It seems almost certain that control of Eildon Hill North was assumed by the invaders and on the very summit they built a signal station. It could send and receive messages from Ruberslaw to the south and from the Cheviot watershed beyond.

When I reached St Boswells Burn, just to the south of the village, I came to the end of what had been a continuous journey from Chew Green. Only at the hamlet of Bonjedward did I lose the line of the road, and then for less than a mile. But at St Boswells, the A68 bends eastwards and cuts off Dere Street. From there its line is uncertain and there is no continuous path, only some fragments and part of the course of a modern road. And crucially, the old road is not marked on the Pathfinder map.

Walter Elliot has walked the ground between the last section (conveniently called The Street) and the site of Trimontium and made sense of many competing indicators. I followed his lead and what he proposes seemed highly plausible. Despite being obliterated by the trackbed of an abandoned railway, the line of the road is straight and crosses the modern A699 about a hundred metres west of the

Buccleuch Hunt Kennels. It then goes through the village of Newtown St Boswells before picking up the line of the A6091. It passes the village of Eildon, close to Huntly Bank and then makes its way down to the Tweed at Newstead. Only the last mile or so can be walked.

Only recently has Dere Street disappeared under modern development. In the medieval period, it was frequently referred to, mainly used as a boundary in landholding documents because its location was obvious and well known. It was known as the Great Road. In the charters associated with Dryburgh Abbey, a gift of land to the monks was said to lie 'west of the church of St Mary of Lessudden [St Boswells] as far as the great road that led to Eildon'. In the Melrose Abbey cartulary it is called *magnum stratum*, the great street, meaning a paved or Roman road, and elsewhere it appears as the *hie streit*. But now, from south of St Boswells to the banks of the Tweed, only gossamer traces can be found.

The late Dr Bill Lonie of the Trimontium Trust also mapped Dere Street and published his findings in 2004. His approach was clear and consistent with Walter Elliot's. After the road left the A6091, it passed through Newstead village, down Claymires Lane, to the west of the Roman fort and depot, and then crossed the Tweed before climbing up the opposite bank to Kittyfield Farm. From there it looped up the steep ridge before striking north-west to Housebyres Moss. There it became easily recognisable as a Roman road, as it made its way arrow-straight to the north.

Between Mosshouses and Bluecairn, Dere Street often runs between dykes and it is a decent walk, but only for about three miles. The countryside is upland, more moorland than the Cheviot foothills, and while the views are long, they seem to have less character. Beyond Bluecairn, a B road overlies the great road until Upper Blainslie, from where it strikes north through farmland towards the town of Lauder. A tell-tale place name marks the crossing of the Lauder Burn at Stonyford. The road then runs to the west of the town before the trackbed of a remarkable old railway covers it for about three miles.

In 1901 the Lauder Light Railway opened and its engines steamed north out of the town to the village of Oxton before looping around Collie Law to reach Fountainhall and the Waverley Line to Edinburgh. Despite formidable engineering difficulties in rough country, the line was completed on time and under budget. But it was never viable and closed to passengers in 1932. Nevertheless it was the most sophisticated transport initiative in the Leader Valley since Agricola's legions laid Dere Street.

At the point where the railway plunged into the hills at Oxton, the Roman road climbs the hills to the north, taking a line west of the steep-sided Leader Valley. Roman engineers preferred to avoid valleys; in the millennia before widespread agricultural drainage, the bottoms could be boggy or subject to seasonal flooding, and as a river or wide stream meandered, it might have been necessary to make repeated crossings. As at Mosshouses and Bluecairn, the *gromatici* kept to the higher ground and Dere Street reappears on the Pathfinder map below Dun Law. The area is now covered by a large wind farm, the giant sails turning slowly in the ever-present wind. Its builders had to lay down roads on the moorland peat to take heavy construction traffic and, again, they were the first to rival skills of the Roman road makers in two millennia. Just how sophisticated these ancient techniques were was revealed in an excavation in 2007 before the new roads were laid. The Roman builders had floated their *agger* of cobbles on a lattice-work of branches and logs on top of the peat on Dun Law. But with powerful machinery, the modern road builders could get down below the layers of peat to find bedrock. Impressive, but not as skilled.

Long after the Empire in the west had collapsed, armies still trundled up this stretch of Dere Street. On his way to defeat at Bannockburn in 1314, Edward II of England lodged at Soutra Aisle, a medieval hospital established, very deliberately, on one of the most remote parts of the old road. It was set up as the House of the Holy Trinity, both a hospital and a friary, by Malcolm IV of Scotland in 1164. Thought to be the largest hospital in medieval Scotland, it stood very close to Dere Street. In the twelfth century, it began to be noted on charters as the Via Regis, the king's road, or the Malcolmisrode.

It was a bright, graphic winter's morning when I parked by the wood opposite Soutra Aisle. There was a sugar-dusting of snow in the hills and I hoped it would show up the line of the road, its *agger* and drainage ditches, perhaps the quarry pits. But I could make out nothing, either to the south or to the north, even though I could pinpoint on the map where the road ran. From Soutra, the views to the north are sweeping, panoramic. As far as the Ochil Hills above Stirling, and even to the snow-capped mountains beyond, it is possible to make out landmarks at tremendous distances. Across the Forth, the Lomond Hills of Fife were white, and on the southern shore, the skyline of Edinburgh was overtopped by a new and strangely beautiful structure, the piers of the new Forth Road Bridge. It looked like a gigantic stringed instrument.

I realised that I could see all of the landscape through which Dere Street passed after it climbed down Soutra Hill. But it was very difficult to follow, submerged under layers of history, generations of incessant change. Modern roads occasionally pick up its line but any graspable sense of what it was like 2,000 years ago has long since fled.

The wonder is that so much has survived. As populations shifted and towns and cities began to grow, it is not surprising that the great road faded. However irrational, I felt a powerful melancholy. I know that change and loss are the stuff of history, but it saddened me that the pleasures of Pennymuir, Whitton Edge and Cappuck should be enjoyed by so few. But, equally irrationally, I was glad that I had not met another soul on any of those memorable days.

The Road to Heaven ③

3

The Road to Heaven

Earlsferry to St Andrews

It is difficult to date the beginnings of pilgrimage to St Andrews, but by the eleventh and twelfth centuries several routes found their way through the Fife countryside, and Queen Margaret had established a ferry where the Forth bridges now stand. The routes from west to east are interrupted by urbanisation and industry, and are sometimes not clear, and so I chose to follow the pilgrim road from the south, from Earlsferry to St Andrews. After a sea journey across the Forth from North Berwick, it ran north through the countryside. If only I could find it.

The Road to Heaven was only ever a track, not a road like Dere Street, and it was not obvious where it was. I was grateful for the help of Simon Taylor of Glasgow University and leaned heavily on his The Place Names of Fife to discover where the pilgrims walked. And walking was part of the experience of pilgrimage. By the later thirteenth century, this act of faith had become transactional. If the labour of pilgrimage was undertaken and the shrine of St Andrew visited (and cash contributed for its upkeep), then time off in purgatory was promised, sometimes even absolution from mortal sin. And so the track could be busy.

When I realised that access to the shrine of St Andrew in the cathedral was restricted, I understood that most pilgrimages were not sunlit strolls through the verdant summer countryside of the East Neuk of Fife. The shrine was taken out of its chapel and *processed through the streets of St Andrews (laid out for that purpose) on the feast days of major saints. That was the only opportunity that most ordinary pilgrims had to see and get close to the remains of Andrew. However, the feast of St Andrew took place on 30 November and the Feast of the Coming of the Relics in early February. If I wanted authentically to experience medieval pilgrimage, I needed to make my way north from Earlsferry in the short days of winter, rain or shine.*

It was raining hard when I reached St Andrews but my sense of this part of our past was not dampened. Edinburgh is Scotland's political capital and Glasgow its commercial heart, but St Andrews is the soul of our country, and even on a wet afternoon in February, I felt that with every step.

He was a man who knew Christ. A fisherman on the Sea of Galilee, he was the first to be called by Jesus to follow him, to become a disciple. Andrew was the older brother of Peter, and on the shores of Galilee Christ told them they would be fishers of men. And so it happened. While Peter preached in the west and was crucified in Rome, Andrew made converts in the east of the Empire and died on the cross at Patras in Greece. His was the crux decussata, the diagonal cross that became the symbol of the saltire, a symbol of Scottishness, one of our national flags.

Tangible, physical relics of the saints were venerated as vital links with the life of Christ and His church and the exemplary lives of those who came after. Through these men and women and their relics, the pious believed that they could make a real, almost tangible link with God. To visit a shrine and pray in the close proximity of these sacred bones and objects was an opportunity to be physically closer to God, to hope that He would hear prayers more clearly, perhaps even alleviate suffering, cause miracles to happen. Saintly shrines or tombs were often supported by small galleries of pillars and arches, designed to allow supplicants to kneel and put their heads into these shallow openings. There they could mutter their prayers and pleadings in what seemed like privacy and direct communion with the saint and through them with God. Relics could be magnetic; even those of local holy men and women could attract many pilgrims. But none had the power of a man who knew Christ, a man who had walked with God in the garden and who had shared His last supper.

Andrew's relics came to Scotland because of a dream. It was widely believed that St Rule, or St Regulus (a strange name, it means 'Little King'), received divine instruction in his sleep to take from Patras a tooth, a kneecap and some arm and finger bones 'to the ends of the earth'. When his ship was wrecked far in the north, on the rocky shoreline below the headland at a place called Cinnrigh Monai, or Kinrymont, the saint survived with his precious cargo and brought it safely to its resting place, to what would become St Andrews.

Much more likely was a much shorter, much less epic journey. In the early Christian centuries, there was a brisk trade in alleged saintly relics, especially in Rome and other sites of martyrdom. Acca, Bishop of Hexham in the opening decades of the eighth century, had travelled twice to Rome with his patron, St Wilfred. Part of their mission was to collect relics, and when Acca abruptly left Hexham in 732, for some unknown reason, he appears to have come to Kinrymont to found a new see. With the patronage of the Pictish king, he set up a monastery and a shrine, probably on the site of the ancient church of St Mary on the Rock. Its foundations can still be seen just beyond the walls of the later cathedral precinct. And Acca's shrine was of course built to house the relics of Andrew, the First Apostle called by Christ. He had almost certainly acquired the tooth, the kneecap and the other bones in Rome.

Churchmen collected relics because of a genuine belief in their power, but they also knew that they were very attractive to the laity. Christian pilgrimage began to develop in the fourth century (after the Roman Empire had adopted Christianity as the state religion) and its early focus was on Jerusalem, on those places associated directly with the life of Christ, his crucifixion and resurrection. But the tides of history were flooding across the east and when the Holy Land was overrun by the armies of Islam in the seventh century, the pious were forced to go elsewhere. Rome's association with St Peter and St Paul (both were martyred in the city) was attractive, and from the ninth century pilgrims walked to Compostela in Galicia, where a shrine and eventually a great church housed the relics of St James. By the time Acca, or St Rule, reached Kinrymont, it was only a matter of time before it became St Andrews.

In the centuries that followed the arrival of the relics, Scots kings fought to establish a stable kingdom, one that would eventually extend south to the Tweed and as far north and west as Norse power would allow. Fuelled by the need for an identity that was distinct from England, the relics of St Andrew were growing in fame and importance, and they needed to be housed in a church that would reflect their glory. Around the year 1070, Robert, Prior of St Andrews, had the curious tower and nave of St Regulus built. Curious because the thirty-three-metre-tall tower (not including a spire) seems out of proportion with the much smaller nave and chancel built at its foot. But the rationale for the great tower was simple: it was a sea-mark visible to pilgrims arriving by ship in the harbour below, and for those approaching from the landward side, the west, it was a landmark that could be clearly seen against the North Sea horizon. Its spire reaching up to Heaven, the shrine of a great saint shimmering on the edge of the land, what was called 'the House of the Apostle on the edge of the wave'.

The eleventh and twelfth centuries saw the agricultural economy boom during a long period when the climate was warmer and growing seasons longer. More land was brought into cultivation as the rich harvest of Fife paid spiritual and architectural dividends and great churches began to rise. And none would be greater than the cathedral built to house the bones of St Andrew. In 1160 King Malcolm IV made the town a royal burgh and at about the same time work began on the cathedral. An order of monks known as the Culdees had developed the monastic town at St Andrews, but by the twelfth century their power was waning – perhaps they were seen as old-fashioned, harking back to a Columban mission from the Celtic west and beyond that to Ireland. In the diplomatic game of one-upmanship, the great saint of Iona was definitely outranked by Andrew, the First Apostle.

The Culdees were essentially supplanted in 1144 (although they continued to exist as an order of monks for some time afterwards) when Bishop Robert had a community of Augustinian Canons installed. It would be the Prior and chapter who would decide what the new church would look like, and no doubt with royal prompting they immediately opted for grandeur. St Andrews Cathedral would be vast, the largest church ever to be built in Scotland, a fit place to house the relics of the man who knew Christ.

Following the instructions of the canons and their Prior, surveyors, or 'liners', pegged out a nave that was no less than 391 feet in length. Perhaps it was no accident that it was longer than Old St Peter's and the papal cathedral of St John Lateran in Rome. And much longer than the church that housed the rival shrine at Santiago di Compostela. A central tower with a spire would crown the crossing where two transepts were set at right angles to the nave and there would be turrets at each of the four gables. As always, the cruciform shape was laid out on an east to west axis. To the south there was to be a cloister and extensive conventual buildings. The mathematical relationship of the cloister to the nave of the cathedral showed how skilled master masons were in matters of proportion. They often used the square root of two and this could be easily derived by running a diagonal from one corner of the square cloister to the one opposite. The length of this would then be the length of the nave, or vice versa.

All that has survived the fury of the sixteenth-century reformers and the stone robbing of local housebuilders is the east gable, much of the wall of the south side of the nave and part of the west gable, and the splendid west door. But it is enough to suggest the glory of the great church built for Andrew. One of the most grievous losses, of which no trace is left whatever, is the stained glass. On sunny days the vast nave and its side chapels will have been flooded with rays of brilliant colour. For medieval theologians, light had great symbolic significance, and the great cathedrals and abbeys of the time were bathed in its rays.

It took more than 150 years to complete the cathedral, from its inception around 1160 to the splendid service of dedication in 1318 in the presence of King Robert Bruce. A violent storm in 1272 caused much delay, for it blew down the west end. Such disasters were by no means unique: in 1107 the central tower at Winchester collapsed, part of Gloucester fell in the late twelfth century, and in 1261 Norwich's spire blew down. But the dedication ceremony of this immense building was an occasion of joy and pride. Not only was St Andrews Cathedral the greatest church ever to be built in Scotland, it was the largest building until the construction of Waverley Station in 1866. Here is the account in Walter Bower's history, *The Scotichronicon*:

On 5th July the great church of the apostle St Andrew in Scotland was dedicated by Sir William de Lamberton, bishop of the same. At this dedication, in order to augment the resources for divine worship, Sir Robert the king, acting in person in the presence of seven bishops, fifteen abbots, and nearly all the nobles of the kingdom, both earls and barons, offered one hundred marks sterling to be paid annually from his treasury in commemoration of the signal victory given to the Scots at Bannockburn by the blessed Andrew, protector of the kingdom.

The cathedral dominated the skyline and the town that had been arranged around it. Some time between 1145 and 1150, Bishop Robert appointed Mainard the Fleming to supervise the layout and the building of the new burgh. His plan used the West Door as its focal point, with South Street stretching to the West Port (which still stands) and North Street striking off to welcome pilgrims who came from that direction. Wide and straight, these are not characteristic medieval streets but processional ways. On important feast days or state occasions, long processions will have made their way to and from the West Door, with canons carrying crucifixes and statuary, singing psalms and swinging censers. And the central focus will of course have been the reliquary carrying the bones of St Andrew, with a canopy protecting it from the weather. Market Street is now the principal street in secular St Andrews, but when Mainard was laying out the burgh he did not extend its length as far as the cathedral precinct. The reason for that was simple; he wanted to use North and

South Streets as a circular processional route (linked by what are now known as Greyfriars Gardens and Bell Street) and to reserve Market Street for the stalls, booths and entertainments that the crowds of pilgrims would enjoy after the ceremonial was over, and the reliquary and finery all re-entered the West Door of the cathedral.

Some of the long medieval backlands of this early town plan, especially behind houses on South Street, can still be seen. Perhaps it is also no accident that the layout of the town imitated the shape of a scallop shell, the universally recognised badge of pilgrims.

St Andrews was a magnetic focus and Fife was criss-crossed by pilgrim roads all leading in the same direction. Not only did the pious make their way to Dunfermline, especially after Queen Margaret was formally canonised in 1250, they also used her ferries in great numbers to begin what was often the last leg of a journey when they turned eastwards. In both the winter and summer months, pilgrims enriched the Fife economy as they approached by four main routes. Along these were chapels, hospitals and inns, all catering for what was for some a version of a holiday, much in the way Chaucer's Canterbury pilgrims approached the shrine of St Thomas à Becket. Most of them walked, since part of the point was to make the journey an effort; it was also an imitation of Christ's humility and poverty. Those who came to St Andrews from the west took a ferry across the Tay near Carpow, where the Earn joins it, and they continued through the Ochils towards Cupar. The Eden could be crossed near the castle at Dairsie, where it was not yet tidal. Others went to Guardbridge, where the place name describes an ancient meeting place. The first element is cognate to the French word *gare* for a station, and it was a *statio*, a place where pilgrims waited to band together before walking the last few miles, singing hymns and praying before they finally rounded the bend in the road and at last saw the spires of the holy city.

Those who crossed the Forth could make landfall in Fife at North Queensferry and the pilgrim road took them north to the healing wells at Scotlandwell. In an effort to cure what may have been leprosy, King Robert Bruce took the waters there and issued some charters that are witness to his visits. From there the road struck east to Markinch and Kennoway before crossing the pretty Bishop's Bridge over the Craigrothie Burn at Ceres. Here the pilgrim road is called the Waterless Way, perhaps a reference to the ground being dry and not crossed by burns or bogs. The route to the east aimed straight for St Andrews, and when pilgrims rounded the flank of Clatto Hill at Blebo the great church could be seen against the grey blue of the North Sea. Further along the southern shore of the Forth, the Earl's Ferry took passengers from North Berwick across the sea to the Fife village that took the ferry's name.

As at St Andrews, where the surrounding walls are extant, each monastic foundation was enclosed by a precinct around the church, a place apart from the temporal world, a place that was sacred. The earth of a precinct had been trodden by holy men, and sometimes saints, and this gave it a special quality. Burial in the holy ground, or even inside the church itself, could literally cleanse the mortal body of sin and ensure that any time in purgatory would be shorter. Wealthy men and some women were prepared to pay for this life-after-death insurance and one method of being absolutely certain of being interred in the monastic precinct was, when death was near, to take holy orders and become a novice monk or nun. This was known as entering the monastery *ad succurrendum*, literally 'at the run'.

The Earl's Ferry had been endowed some time around

1150 by Duncan, Earl of Fife and he also founded a pilgrim's hospice at North Berwick. There a house of Cistercian nuns was also endowed and they managed the crossing at both ends. Archaeologists have uncovered moulds for objects that were a key part of the pilgrimage. The nuns sold badges, usually showing images of St Andrew, for pilgrims to wear. It was thought, probably wrongly, that these would protect the wearers from thieves or ruffians, as well as act as outward signs of piety proudly worn. Other places on other routes, such as Scotlandwell, almost certainly sold similar badges. But perhaps the most prized souvenir was the badge that could be bought at St Andrews because it was only available to those who had visited the shrine itself and completed the pilgrim's road.

The effect of entering the cathedral must have been awe-inspiring, the largest interior any pilgrim had ever seen, the soaring space lit by stained glass and perhaps even the low hum of prayers being murmured. Having passed the high altar, privileged pilgrims came at last to the focus of their long journey. It is lost now, smashed to pieces by the righteous frenzy of the reformers, but the shrine of St Andrew is likely to have resembled others that have survived. A large rectangular catafalque, it was probably located in the apse at the east end of the cathedral. When the covering hood was lifted, those fortunate enough to be allowed access to the relic chapel could put their heads in these arches and pray to the saint whose bones lay inside, only inches away. The remains of Andrew, the man who walked with God, were inside the reliquary and he would hear their prayers, forgive their sins and grant their fervent wishes.

However, it seems likely that access to the relic chapel was restricted to the privileged few, perhaps those who could afford a substantial donation to the cathedral canons' funds.

For most, their experience of pilgrimage was likely limited to being in the great church itself, close to the bones of the man who knew Christ, close enough for his presence to amplify their prayers and hear their pleas. On great feast days, crowds of pilgrims could see the reliquary carried in procession around the circuit of North Street and South Street. No doubt many fell to their knees as the canons carried it past.

The builders of St Andrews Cathedral had outdone Rome and created a shrine to one of Christendom's greatest saints. The layout of the town not only mirrored the shape of a scallop shell, it also closely resembled the Vatican borgo on the western bank of the Tiber. But it was more than an imitation; it was nothing less than a Scottish Jerusalem, built on the edge of beyond, a liminal place where God was close. And the faithful flocked to pray to Andrew and ask him to intercede with the man he had first met on the shores of Galilee.

*　*　*

Many of the pilgrim roads through Fife are difficult to see now. Half a millennium of development has overlaid the landscape through which pilgrims walked. But there is one route that can take a traveller back in time and that is the path from Earlsferry to St Andrews.

At seven miles, the crossing between North Berwick and Earlsferry is the shortest before the mouth of the Firth of Forth opens up to the North Sea. Equally convenient was the fact that Earl Duncan of Fife was also a major landowner in East Lothian and was in a position to gift sites and endowments to the houses of Cistercian nuns on both shores. At North Berwick, the pilgrims' hospital (a medieval term more cognate to hospitality than anything medical) was built immediately adjacent to the natural harbour. Once furnished with their badges and probably blessed by the Prioress for a safe crossing, pilgrims boarded what was likely a ferry driven by sail and oars. Noblemen and women, and those who were infirm, are known to have made the crossing and it is likely that there was a covered area to keep them dry, warm and out of the wind. Even after the Reformation had swept away the shrine of St Andrew, the ferry still crossed the Forth and the broad passage, as it was known, could be very alarming. In 1585, James Melville, a professor at the University of St Andrews, wrote of a stormy voyage from North Berwick in a coal boat with his family and others. They were extremely glad to make landfall on the Fife coast.

Once out in the firth, and beyond the Bass Rock, the ferrymen judged the strength and wash of the tide, either ebb or flood, and used the ancient technique of aiming off to set a course. Knowing that the current could take them far from Earlsferry in either direction, depending on the time and tide, they would aim at a sea-mark to the east or to the west. And there were plenty on the Fife shore. Even when visibility was poor, Largo Law, and on the coast Kincraig Hill could usually be made out.

On a brilliant, crystal-clear February morning I decided on a whim to drive up to Earlsferry and see if I could find the old pilgrim road to St Andrews. On the Pathfinder, there is no obvious memory of it, but I could make out some promising-looking tracks, especially where the contours began to bunch as the coastal plain rose up to some low hills. Having parked as close to Chapel Ness as I could, I laid out the contents of my rucksack: Pathfinder (with the putative route marked in pencil), mobile, compass (in case the battery of the mobile ran down), notebook, two pens (in case one of them ran out), two cheese and tomato sandwiches (both would run out), a bottle of water, my lightest waterproof, a hat and a Mars Bar. I knew that the nuns' chapel stood on the headland and that should be the start of the old road to St Andrews, but I wanted to see what the pilgrims saw when they disembarked from the ferry, so I walked down to the beach and looked up at Chapel Ness. The east gable is still complete and it looked monumental against the sun. I realised that the chapel must have been a sea-mark, visible on a clear day from far out in the firth. Looking in the other direction, I could clearly see the lump of the Bass Rock and the hump of North Berwick Law.

When I returned to the road and walked up to the headland, I had forgotten how high and commanding it was, certainly higher than anywhere in Earlsferry or Elie. The nuns no doubt kept lookout for incoming boats so that they could prepare for arrivals and warn those waiting to depart. Behind the chapel is a broad green area bounded to the west by stout garden walls. Benches with discreet dedication plaques reminded me what a peaceful place this is now. In the high summer of medieval pilgrimage, it will have been very different: a ferry terminal, busy with travellers preparing for a long walk across country, probably buying what they needed, wondering about the weather, the air thick with chatter and anticipation. For many it will have been the last leg of a long journey.

My watch read 12 noon exactly, a good time to be off. I set out along the main street, the old paths having probably been obliterated by the backlands of the houses that line it. When I came to a crossroads, I turned left and north up Cadgers' Wynd. Named after itinerant traders in an age before the term had become pejorative, the road bisected Elie Golf Course. On the first day of 2017 that prompted thoughts of spring, many golfers were out on this most beautifully undulating of links courses. But much of the shape of the land is not natural: it is a memory of the grim business of digging coal. Seams rose to the surface at Earlsferry and some of the carefully manicured humps and bumps that golf balls bounce over were once spoil heaps from the old coal heughs, the diggings at the exposed seams. In their draughty chapel and dormitory on the headland, the nuns will have welcomed such a handy source of warmth.

Medieval pilgrims preferred to travel in groups, not just for company but also for safety. The pilgrim badges sold by the nuns may have pleased God, but they were no protection against brigands. Travellers on the roads to the shrine at St Andrews almost always carried cash in their scrips, the pouches that hung from their belts, because they needed to buy items on the journey and also give money to the canons of the cathedral. A boatload of pilgrims who made landfall at Earlsferry was a ready-made company of more than a dozen, perhaps as many as twenty, and robbers would hesitate to take on that many.

Cadgers' Wynd rises a little to breast a low ridge above the golf links and passes some splendid Victorian and Edwardian mansions that enjoy long views south over the Firth of Forth. I was looking in the opposite direction. The wynd was clearly an old road, gently winding its way through fertile fields already ploughed for the spring frosts to break up the clods. It was sad to see that the boundary hedges had been grubbed up. The fields are part of Grange Farm, the outlying land held by the nuns at Earlsferry. Their farm may have grown food that could be sold to pilgrims, but early records note that it was surrounded by the coal heughs.

There was a steady stream of traffic on what I had thought was little more than a lane and I had to hop onto the verge often because it was so narrow. I suspected that the wynd had once been the old road to Earlsferry. Up ahead was the farm of St Ford, and Simon Taylor's excellent third volume of *The Place Names of Fife* points out that it had nothing to do with sanctity. St Ford is a corruption of Sandy Ford, a crossing of the Cocklemill Burn, and a ford is usually a sign of a long-established road. As I walked closer to the farm, I could see a Victorian bridge that forced the road off its line to climb an embankment and turn sharp right. The Pathfinder marked an abandoned railway track that led to Elie and the fisher towns beyond. In the field below, there was absolutely no trace of the trackbed, deep ploughing having obliterated any sense of where it once ran.

I stopped at the farm and peeled off my body warmer – it was doing too good a job in the February sun – and stuffed it in my rucksack. And then I heard them before I saw them: the plaintive honking of swans in flight. Three of them appeared over the woods to the west, flying low, their long necks outshot, their webbed feet clearly visible, tucked up like an undercarriage. I guessed they were making for Kilconquhar Loch.

When I cut across the main road to Elie, I found the first stretch of pathway. Only a hundred metres or so, it ran through the dappled shade of a stand of young trees. Beyond it, I caught up with a couple taking two very young children and their dachshund out for a walk. Unlike me, they were scarved and wrapped against the cold. As I marched past, the father asked if I was on a long walk. I must have looked purposeful.

Pronounced 'Kinneuchar', Kilconquhar is strung out along a single street below its ancient kirk. Planted on a high mound, the nineteenth-century kirk is the successor to a very old dedication. The mound itself is suggestive of even greater antiquity and the first element of the place name is common in Scotland. 'Kil' is a version of the Latin *cella* and it meant a monastic cell, a chapel, a church. Whose chapel is more obscure. The balance of scholarship tilts towards an interpretation of the name as the deposit of the settlement of an old and bitter dispute.

Celtic or Columban Christianity had spread from the Atlantic west across Scotland, even reaching down into what is now England and the great foundation at Lindisfarne. So-called Roman Christianity moved north from Augustine's mission and his church at Canterbury, and included the minster at York. They met and contended for power in the glittering kingdom of Northumbria, the first flowering of Anglo-Saxon culture, whose territories were once wide, encompassing southern Scotland and northern England as far as the Humber and sometimes beyond. In 664 King Oswiu convened the Synod of Whitby to decide two fundamental issues. Columban and Roman clerics disagreed about how to fix the date of Easter, the celebration and set of rituals around which the whole Christian year revolved. Their monks and priests had also adopted different versions of the tonsure. In order to imitate Christ's crown of thorns, Roman clerics shaved the crown of their heads, while Columbans shaved from ear to ear, across the crown of their heads to create a very high forehead. They also wore their hair long at the back and it is believed that this style was a legacy of the Druidic, pagan tonsure.

After heated and intricate debate, King Oswiu asked if both sides agreed that St Peter had been given the keys of the kingdom of Heaven by Jesus Christ. When they both assented, the king then gave his judgement. The Roman practice, what was endorsed by the church of St Peter, on the dating of Easter and their style of the tonsure would have to be followed. The Columban monks and their bishops withdrew and largely ignored the decision. There was a danger of dispute escalating into schism. It is believed that the saint commemorated at

Kilconquhar was instrumental in persuading the Iona community to accept King Oswiu's ruling.

The second element of the place name is 'Duncan' or 'Conchad', the latter a version closer to the original Gaelic pronunciation. He was the 11th Abbot of Iona and died in 717, according to the annalists. Historians judge that his cult became popular in eastern Scotland because the Pictish kings who ruled in Fife and Tayside wished to signal their agreement to the Northumbrian decision at Whitby. They did not want their ambitions in the south to be constrained or complicated by ecclesiastical disputes. Duncan's church at Kilconquhar is impressive and it looks over the loch to the south, but it did not always enjoy that aspect. Kilconquhar Loch is new and the consequence of blocked drainage. It used to be a wet, boggy area and that may have made it attractive to the religious practices of the first millennium BC. Then, valuable items such as weapons were often deposited in watery places as sacrifices of propitiation to pagan gods. Perhaps there was an ancient religious structure of some sort on the mound.

By the time I passed the old kirk, it was after 1 p.m. and I decided I would stop for a rest and my cheese sandwiches when I reached Pitcorthie, a crossroads I reckoned to be a mile north of Kilconquhar. Once I had left the village, a long straight road stretched north, what had looked to me the most direct route to St Andrews. Even though this was a B road, there was a great deal of traffic, much of it accelerating hard down the straight. Far from musing how pilgrims might have negotiated this part of the journey, I was concentrating on survival.

At the junction near Pitcorthie Home Farm, I could find nowhere to sit down and so I kept on up the steep incline. As the cars zipped past, I noticed that the verges were thick with litter: plastic bottles, empty cans, cigarette packets and sandwich wrappers. I was beginning to feel that any sense of the pilgrims' journey might be hard to find. But the line of the road was clearly old, as it ran along the crest of the ridge: the deep, wooded declivity of the Den Burn on one side and the ground falling away on the other probably meant that it could not have gone anywhere else. Tramping on, I eventually came to the turn off to Belliston Farm, the road I needed to take, and found a bank where I could at last sit down.

Even though the contours on the Pathfinder told me that I had climbed only 75 metres from sea level, it felt like more. From Earlsferry, I had probably walked five to six miles in an hour and a half. But the rhythm of walking at a steady pace, arms swinging, had helped and it struck me that I shared at least that with the pilgrims. I had good boots and they would have worn relatively thin-soled ankle boots or shoes that were open at the front and more like sandals. They moved over softer, more forgiving ground, and while I had been bashing along on tarmac, at least I had kept my feet dry. Many walkers in the Middle Ages expected to get their feet wet. The tooled leather decorations on a pair of brogues are a relic of the time when real holes were bored through leather uppers so that the water could run out, the principal purpose of footwear being to protect against sharp stones that might cause debilitating cuts.

As I munched my cheese sandwiches (they were a bit dry – too much cheddar, not enough tomato), I looked out at the wide panorama across the Firth of Forth and wondered if the clouds used to part over East Lothian and East Fife in the same way in the Middle Ages. I expect they did. The eleventh, twelfth and thirteenth centuries enjoyed sustained periods of good weather, what is known as the medieval climatic optimum. After the early decades of the 1300s, however, the pattern changed as the Little Ice Age began and the journey from Earlsferry to St Andrews will often have been wet and difficult. I noticed the clouds massing and thickening in the west as I rummaged around in my rucksack, looking for my Mars Bar. Having shaken everything out on the grassy bank, I realised that I had probably left it on the back seat of my car. Oh dear. Something to look forward to, I supposed. As I heaved on my rucksack, the sun was hidden by thick cloud and it grew a little colder.

The road to Belliston was quiet – at last, a real country road with well-set hedges planted over tumbledown dykes. Some of the mossy old stones were massive and beautifully squared. But when I came to the farm, a huge truck appeared from the opposite direction, going down the gears as it climbed the hill. A sign told me that this was not a grassy track between quiet fields, as the Pathfinder had suggested, but the busy road to Belliston Quarry, and at the top of the hill I could see the swinging arm of a large digger. The trucks had converted the uphill track into a wide and muddy single-lane road. When I had climbed halfway up, another truck turned off the road behind me and began its slow ascent. I moved into a passing-place as yet another truck started down-hill from the quarry. I had to scramble over a bank and into a field to avoid the traffic jam. Would I be accompanied by the internal combustion engine all the way to the cathedral?

Near the top of the hill, the Pathfinder directed me to go right along what looked like an old track with a grassy crest. A padlocked gate barred progress, but I manage to slip around the gatepost without much difficulty. I was anxious about this attempt at exclusion, but the roar of the engines and machinery at the quarry was growing less. It was soon replaced by loud barking and I wondered if the padlocked gate was a protection as well as a prohibition. Watching anxiously for the charge of slavering hounds, I approached a strange building with a row of narrow windows high up on the south side, where there were stunning views over the sea. Odd. There was a pen built onto the gable. Then I realised that it was a boarding kennels. The padlock had been for security – for the dogs. When they were able to see me walking up the track beyond the cottages at South Baldutho, they barked all the more defiantly, having seen me off the premises.

At long, long last I felt I was walking in the footsteps of the pious, the pilgrims of more than 500 years ago. It was a green lane, rutted with tractor tyres but otherwise untouched. Beyond where a farm cart had been parked, there was a half-broken wooden gate and what looked like impenetrable thickets of prickly gorse along the line of the track, making its surface invisible. I briefly considered walking up the field beside it, but, fortified by my cheese sandwiches, I decided that if badly shod pilgrims could walk here, I should stop being such a faintheart. The prickles quickly gave way, and the track seemed open and clear up as far as North Baldutho Farm on the horizon. A light aircraft droned into view and put up two flocks of migrating birds. They flew too high for identification, but their syncronised swooping and wheeling was almost hypnotic.

Close to North Baldutho stands a monument to private enterprise. The Lochty Private Railway was used to carry freight, principally coal from the easily accessible diggings around Largoward and Cassingray. The Pathfinder is dotted with shaft (disused) areas plotted on either side of the old track. Part of the old railway was kept open by enthusiasts until 1992. What crossed the path I was walking on was something remarkable. Running from the east was a steep embankment that carried the railway to a high bridge. Both piers remain, but the crossing itself has been cast down, probably for safety. But on the west, the massive embankment has been entirely effaced, leaving no trace whatever, in what must have been a huge exercise in earth moving. Nowadays the East Neuk of Fife is a pretty tourist destination, but once a principal employer was the early coal industry.

Beyond North Baldutho, my trusty Pathfinder let me down, or so it seemed. These little maps are so detailed and accurate that I had forgotten mine was at least 30 years old. When I climbed a gate near the farm, there was a tarmac road that did not appear on the Pathfinder. Shocked, I fired up the satnav app on my phone, thinking it must be me who was in the wrong place. But it confirmed that I was where I thought I was and had not gone through a timewarp. My map was older than the road, simple as that.

When I reached the B940, yet another busy minor road, I walked along to Knights' Ward Wood, a place name that clearly remembered the pilgrims who passed this way. At the end of the twelfth century, William I of Scotland granted land here to the order of Knights Templar at Ferriby in Yorkshire. A ward simply meant an enclosed parcel of land. The Templars came into being because of the crusades and their role was to protect pilgrims on the way to Jerusalem. They almost certainly fulfilled the same role for those on their way to the Jerusalem of the north, St Andrews. Knights' Ward lies about halfway on the journey from Earlsferry and it seemed like a good place to break my journey. As I made my way to a rendezvous with a taxi, it began to rain.

The forecast for the following day was discouraging: early brightness to be chased east over the sea by a band of rain around midday, rain that would wax heavier during the afternoon. But instead of sitting comfortable and dry in my office, reading about pilgrimage, I felt I ought to experience some of its rigours first hand. Two of the great feast days took place in the winter: Andermess or St Andrew's Day fell on 30 November and the Feast of the Coming of the Relics on 6 February. On those occasions, the reliquary containing the bones of the saint would be carried around the town in procession and, very importantly, indulgences could be bought. These were documents that made for a more comfortable afterlife because they guaranteed the remission of sins. If cash was given to God's church, then he would reward that generosity in eternity with a shorter stay in Purgatory, the uncomfortable place where mortal sins were purged. And that might take a very long time for some. The prospect of purchasing indulgences and the procession with the great reliquary were powerful attractions that will have persuaded many to walk to St Andrews in wintertime. And if poorly shod pilgrims with little more than hats and woollen cloaks to keep out the weather could make the journey, surely I should be prepared to walk through the rain.

When I parked in a muddy layby near a bridge over the Lingo Burn, I pulled on a thick, quilted waterproof and stuffed a complete change of clothes into my rucksack. No room for cheese sandwiches or Mars Bars. The prospect of hot food would be an additional incentive to reach St Andrews. As I walked across the road, the sun blinked out but I could see a dense, gun-metal grey bank of cloud massing out to the west. Following the line of the burn was a well-used track with stout metal gates and the sort of robust fencing used to work cattle on the other side of them. There were recent hoofmarks, but the rain during the night meant that I couldn't tell if they were sheep or cows. I could see nothing out in the fields and none of the ring feeders had hay or silage in them. All the same, cows with calves at foot can be dangerous and I looked out for places where I could quickly get on the other side of the fence.

The way the track followed the swell and fall of the land told me it was old and almost certainly a continuation of the pilgrim road from North Baldutho. It was also hard underfoot. I reckoned I had about seven or eight miles to walk to St Andrews and that might take two hours, if the tracks marked on the Pathfinder were still open and passable. Where the Lingo Burn becomes the Dunino Burn (for some reason) is noted as Craigloun, the title of the lands granted to the Knights Templar. But as I passed I could see no sign of an old steading or any buildings.

Up ahead was a shelter belt, mostly Scots Pine. As they grow high, these majestic native evergreens usually lose their lower branches and I could see the track running fairly straight through them and almost due north. The sun warmed their rust-red bark and moved the high branches.

There is an avenue of Scots Pine leading to our farmhouse and, without exaggeration, I think they are very beautiful, almost sculptural. But the pines are old and will have to come down sometime soon, and I will weep when that happens. The greatest of them stands sentinel on a low ridge at the corner where our track turns downhill, and his roots (these are masculine trees) visibly grip the land tight. When we bought the first few acres that would grow into our farm, I asked a retired forester if he would plant an avenue of trees opposite the pine wood. Mr Lindsay said no, not this year. First he had to scrieve the holes and let the winter frosts break down the earth before he planted them the next spring. When he came with little more than sticks of birch, rowan, gean and holly, the old man told me that the pine wood had been planted in 1950 as part of a national programme of forestry regeneration after the Second World War. That meant the tall pine at the turn of the track is exactly as old as I am. I love that tree, and when he falls, part of me will fall with him.

As I approached the shelter belt, wood pigeons fluttered off the upper branches and in the distance I saw the white rump of a little roe deer bounce towards a fence, pop it, and disappear in an instant into a dense copse of woodland. The notion that the wild creatures of the landscape are merely reactive, their actions no more than a series of individual, unconnected reflexes is surely incomplete. The flap of the pigeons and the flight of the deer were all that I saw of what must have been a series of messages. They signalled the approach of potential danger, perhaps a predator, and all manner of unseen small animals will have received the messages and scurried for cover. And when I had passed they would re-emerge to scout the scene and resume the constant quest for food.

At the northern edge of the stand of Scots Pines, the track abruptly disappeared. It should have led across to a distant ruined cottage and what looked like a byre. The Pathfinder marked it as South Kinaldy and beyond it a track was emphatically plotted. There seemed to be a piece missing. Taking care with some taut barbed wire, I climbed a rusted iron gate and a fence beside it, but I could see nothing on the ground, no trace of where the pilgrims had walked. My only option was to make my way around the edges of a large ploughed field to reach the ruin in the distance. It was like walking along a narrow mantelpiece. To my right there was a shallow but steep declivity with a burn running at the bottom, and on my left perhaps only a foot or so of unploughed grass verge. I have never seen ploughing like it, so close to the margins of the field that virtually nothing was left on the edge. Such precision was almost miraculous, almost as if it had been done by computer. When I reached the corner of the field and turned north once more, there was a line of old hardwood trees on the other side of the fence, but their roots only kept the ploughshare a little further away, leaving a couple of feet where I could walk and feel less like I was on a tightrope.

Long abandoned as a cottage, the ruin at South Kinaldy still had a roof and might have been used as a byre of some sort. Next to it was a rubble-built barn that looked much older, a little like the blackhouses of the West Highlands and Islands, perhaps the relict of a farmstead. There was a grassy area in front of the cottage with what seemed like hard standing underneath, too hard to risk pulling a plough through. To the north some pregnant ewes were grazing (it was the end of February and lambing not far away) and to the side of their field stood an old dyke. Beyond that, the track re-appeared. I turned to look south, where its line might have run, but there was nothing at all to be seen in the ploughed field, no soil discolouration, no dip in level, nothing. Arrow-straight, the track ran downhill for about half a mile to the Kinaldy Burn and on one side ran a dyke built from massive boulders. Mostly unworked in any way, these had almost certainly been prised up as the surrounding fields had been cleared and manhandled to make a massive boundary. Some sat upright like milestones and I wondered if these had been cut to act as supports, like stone fence posts, for the boulder dyke.

Much of what we see in the farming landscape was made in an era before machines – diggers, tractors, huge trailers and much else. What they have created is often ugly and out of keeping: vast slurry pits, stacks of black plastic-wrapped bales, piles of discarded fencing, ploughed fields with no verges. What farm labourers, dykers and those who worked with the heavy horses created seems more appropriate to me, more natural. It was made the hard way, by muscle power and sweat, and any radical alterations to the landscape, such as creating new fields, took a long time.

Hard edges were blurred, greened, sometimes overgrown. But if our ancestors had had access to machinery that would have made their lives easier, of course they would have used it. There is nothing romantic or attractive about digging ditches in the rain. I make no judgement here in that sense. History always involves loss and change, but I sometimes think that modern farming can be brutal and make a terrible and persistent mess.

When I crossed the Kinaldy Burn, I walked off one Pathfinder map and into another, no. 363, St Andrews. It felt like real progress. Now I could see on one sheet how far I had to go and I quickened my pace. But it was too soon for thoughts of lunch, I told myself, more than once. Confident I was on the right track in all senses, the road up to Kinaldy hugged the field ends and the ridge above the burn. However, the deep ruts of big tractors meant flooded stretches and more careful tiptoeing along the verges. Beyond the farm, the track led past a large paddock grazed by sport horses, maybe eventers or showjumpers, and I could see trailers parked next to a barn that probably housed loose boxes. By the time I reached the road that led to St Andrews, the sun had fled over the North Sea, the sky had darkened and it began to spit with rain.

At a crossroads, there was a metal gate between high, dense hedges where I stopped to look at the map. The track should have continued over the field, but there was no sign. About a hundred metres to the west there was another shelter belt of Scots Pines and I walked around what looked like newly sown grass to investigate. And there it was. Between the trees an avenue followed approximately the right line and that probably meant the road out of Kinaldy had been shifted slightly to the east, taking me away from the original route. I decided to climb the fence. There was only one thorny problem. High and taut was a line of barbed wire, the new light green sort with longer and sharper barbs. This was something no medieval pilgrim ever had to negotiate, but I was determined to walk as much as I could in their footsteps. I took a plastic bag out of my rucksack and wrapped it around the jaggy wire and then, committing myself irrevocably, I hoisted the rucksack over the fence. Gripping a fencepost, I swung my leg as high as I could. And got immediately snagged. In the crotch of my jeans. A stream of un-pilgrim-like words were uttered as I tried to pull the denim off the barb, but it was caught fast. No success and a tearing sound later, I was across the other side. The spitting rain turned to drizzle as I bent double, peering between my legs to see how bad the damage was.

'Good afternoon,' said the lady walking her dog. 'Having problems?'

I hadn't seen her coming through the woods, but she had obviously seen – and heard – me harrumphing over the fence. She couldn't stop smiling. The people you meet.

Sounding like Basil Fawlty embarking on an epic tissue of lies to disguise his incompetence, I explained that I was walking the pilgrim road from Earlsferry to St Andrews. And that was why I had felt I should climb the fence – I was pretty sure she hadn't and that there was a gate into the wood I had missed, but she refrained from telling me. The trees gave some shelter, but the drizzle was becoming more insistent, and we walked north up the track as I asked her questions. No, she had never met anyone walking the pilgrim road, but she did know where the track used to run. When we reached the edge of the wood, there was a vast ploughed field, maybe 50 acres. The lady told me that many of the fields in this part of Fife had trebled or quadrupled in size in recent years because the farmers had grubbed up the hedges and demolished many of the dykes. Her advice was to walk around the edges. 'But mind you, crossing the Cameron Burn might be tricky after last night's rain.' She smiled. 'And there is a barbed wire fence on this side.'

Once again the field seemed to have been ploughed by robots, but instead of tiptoeing along the slim, occasionally non-existent margins, I walked across it without damaging the crop. There were tyre tracks, presumably from the tractors that had pulled the seed drill. I followed these and eventually made out what looked like the pilgrim road climbing up the hill to South Lambieletham Farm. It was about a mile away, I reckoned, but across very open fields, the line of tyre tracks aimed straight at it. Halfway down one field, so much clay sticking to my boots they were like snow shoes, I saw a place where a dyke had simply stopped in the middle. It looked as though it would sink into the ground as the surrounding corn grew up.

I wondered if I would soon catch a glimpse of the spires of St Andrews, what the poet Robert Crawford called 'a haar of kirks on the edge of beyond'. They couldn't be far away. But first I had to negotiate the tricky fording of the Cameron Burn. The lady with the dog had not exaggerated. It was high, roiling, brown with run-off from the vast fields, and there was no obvious place to cross. And there was barbed wire, old, rusty and lethal. Any more rips in my jeans and I would look like a geriatric version of Sid Vicious.

The problem with the barbed wire was that it was not attached to a fence but wrapped around a line of beech, willow and other scrubby little trees that grew along the south bank of the burn. And below them there was an immediate and sheer drop of about five feet to the fast-flowing burn – of uncertain depth. I noticed that one of the beeches had a long and stout branch that reached more than halfway across the burn. Below it were some big stones that peeped above the waterline and the opposite bank was flat with no fence; it looked like a place where cows came down to drink. Rather than Sid Vicious, I needed to channel Tarzan.

Further along the bank, I found a gap between two trees where there were only a couple of straggly strands of barbed wire, but the problem was my rucksack. Each time I tried to squeeze through, it got hanked. And an additional crucial problem was that between the trees and the burn there was not even the narrowest of shelves along which I could shuffle to grab the branch that extended across the water.

OK, time for resolve. I was not walking back up that claggy field and making a huge detour so close to St Andrews. I took off my rucksack and wedged it between the tress where the big branch was, hanging one strap around a handy stump. I then walked back to the gap, forced a way through and, holding tight onto the trunks of the beeches and willows, managed somehow to swing and scramble along to where my rucksack was. Mercifully, it was not heavy, having only dry clothes in it (not if I dropped it in the burn) and I was able to loop it across one arm. Clutching on tight to the overhead branch, I put my foot on the biggest of the stones in the burn and, thank goodness, it did not rock. And then, swinging a little to get some momentum, I was able to reach the next stone, which did rock, and then leaped for the bank. Bloody hell. The rucksack slipped down my arm into the mud as I bent over, clutching my knees, catching my breath. I briefly pictured the lady with the dog telling her Sunday lunch guests about the foul-mouthed pilgrim ripping his trousers on the barbed wire fence. At least I hoped she was, and not watching me through binoculars.

When I walked up to the farmhouse at South Lambieletham on a good, straight track, I was optimistic that this was the last lap, that the skyline of the Holy City would appear before me when I reached the top of the hill. As I climbed, more vast fields opened on either side; it occurred to me how the look of the land had changed radically over the millennium – and more – since pilgrims had walked up this hill with a similar sense of anticipation, hoping to catch a glimpse of what chroniclers called 'the House of the Apostle on the edge of the wave'.

In the early medieval period, the tracts of land to the south of St Andrews were known as the Cursus Apri, in Scots the Boar's Raik. It means something like 'the Boar's Run' or 'Range' and was probably wild, uncultivated land where the king and his entourage hunted. In East Fife solid evidence of the ancient passion for hunting has been found. At Scoonie, on the outskirts of Leven, and at Largo, two Pictish symbol stones have been found that show hunting scenes, where horsemen and dogs chase deer, sometime in the eighth or ninth centuries. The Boar's Raik appears early in the historical record because Alexander I of Scotland gave at least part of this territory to the canons of the cathedral. It was a grant that affirmed an earlier endowment by a Pictish king, Aonghas or Hungus. A very early name for the area around St Andrews was Muchros, and it translates from Gaelic as 'the Boar's Headland'. At an early date, perhaps in the ninth century, at least some of this wild land began to be cultivated. In the twelfth century, records show that some of the Boar's Raik was held by a man with a strange Gaelic name. Maolsneachda means 'the Follower of the Snows', a wonderful name around which mystery swirls. In 1085 Mael Sneachtai was hailed as King of Moray, a successor to Macbeth. Were they related? Was it a title rather than a name?

Now, the Boar's Raik seems a great deal less mysterious, and with the disappearance of the dykes and the hedges much of its character appears to have been effaced. Less the habitat of wild animals of any sort, more a windswept prairie.

When I reached South Lambieletham and the top of the rise, disappointment lay on every side. To the east I could see the North Sea, and to the west the Eden Estuary and the distant Angus coast. But smack in front stood the bulk of Wester Balrymonth Hill; hidden behind it, the House of the Apostle on the edge of the wave.

The Pathfinder told me that it was a mile or so to the shoulder of the hill, and on the 110-metre contour line I should be able to see St Andrews from there. Drizzle had thickened to steady rain and I pulled up the hood of my waterproof, not something I like to do. It forces me to focus only on what lies in front and narrows the sense of being out in the open air. But as I marched past North Lambieletham Farm, crossed a B road and started to climb the last hill, there was nothing much to see. For medieval pilgrims, it was different. They were approaching a longed-for destination, their pace no doubt quickened by a genuine piety, the certainty that they would soon be close to the bones of a man who knew Christ. Religious centres often erected boundary crosses on the roads that led to them, tangible signs that pilgrims and visitors were moving from the temporal world into the realm of the spiritual, a place where God spoke more clearly to believers. Around the nunnery at Coldingham on the Berwickshire coast, place names remember where they once stood: Applincross, Whitecross and Cairncross. None survives around St Andrews – they probably fell victim to the fury of the reformers in the middle of the sixteenth century – but pilgrims would have passed one somewhere on the road I was walking.

I came to a green sign that told me I was on a right of way and that it was one kilometre to St Andrews. At first this route appeared to be a ditch with a lot of water running down it beside another marginless field, but thirty metres later a broad, well-made track began. And well before I gained the summit, the steeple of St Salvator's Chapel appeared against the grey horizon. I could even make out its famous clock, with the red face. With each step, more of the skyline of St Andrews came into view. I stopped, smiled and folded away my trusty Pathfinder. This was now very familiar territory for me, the plan of its streets engraved on my heart. I was an undergraduate at St Andrews University and, with my girlfriend, spent many happy days there. Forty-five years later, I still have the same girlfriend because in 1976 Lindsay and I were married in St Salvator's Chapel.

A strip of woodland on the right of the track obscured the cathedral ruins, but when it ran out I stopped again. Even though so little survived the destruction of the Reformation and its use as a quarry of cut stone by local housebuilders, the cathedral must have looked majestic on its headland, the endless, eternal horizon of the sea behind it. Its spire soared while the turrets at each corner of its cruciform shape defined its immense scale. When pilgrims first set eyes on the House of the Apostle, they will have fallen to their knees in prayer and given thanks for their safe journey. Perhaps they sang and rejoiced with hosannahs. At other shrines, records show that it was arranged for a priest or a novice bearing a simple cross to meet groups of pilgrims so that he could lead them on the last mile to glory.

Suburban St Andrews had crept much further up Wester Balrymonth Hill in the thirty years since my Pathfinder was printed, and after the sewage filter beds the pilgrim road became a narrow path with plentiful evidence for its use by dog walkers on each side. Not exactly the entry to the Holy City I was hoping for. At a bus shelter, I found some relief from the rain and sat down to organise myself. My jacket was waterproof but also warm; having walked seven or eight miles over muddy ground, almost emasculated myself on a barbed wire fence and swung across the Cameron Burn like an arthritic primate, I needed to cool down. Swapping my hood for a hat, and wiping my face and neck with a clean hankie, I set off for the bridge over the Kinness Burn.

As my girlfriend completed her degree in 1973, I took a teaching qualification (something to fall back on, said my dad) and spent six weeks at Kilrymont School. Each day I walked in the opposite direction through the large council estate and did my best to teach history and modern studies. A large con-temporary building with extensive grounds, its gate appeared on my right, but I could remember nothing whatever about being there. Though I do recall happy times living in North Castle Street all those years ago. Like the Cameron Burn, the Kinness was rain-swollen and I reckoned there had been a bridge for a long time where I crossed it. The houses on the far side, now Greenside Place, that lead up to the walls of the cathedral precinct are old. When pilgrims reached what is now Abbey Street, they walked north for almost 200 metres. And on their right, there it was, the towering mass of the great cathedral, journey's end. It was the largest, most awe-inspiring building almost all who came had ever seen. But it was fragile.

In 1378 fire devastated the House of the Apostle and much of the west end was badly damaged, and in 1409 a gale whistled around its walls and the gable of the south transept collapsed. More than ever pilgrimage came to matter because large sums of cash were needed to repair the fabric of the great church. At the beginning of the fifteenth century, Prior James Haldenstone began to enhance the attractions of what he called '*gloriosa domus Sancti Andree*', the Glorious House of St Andrew. So that pilgrims in the nave of the church could see it, the reliquary containing the saint's bones was raised higher than the rood screen behind the high altar. The more privileged could enter and leave the relic chapel by doors in the screen on either side of the altar, implying a steady traffic. More of the treasures of the cathedral were put on display in specially made aumbries, recessed cabinets attached the chapel wall. A new organ was installed and new forms of music played. In all that Haldenstone did to make the shrine more attractive, there is more than a hint of what now might be called 'the pilgrim experience'.

When I reached the West Door, I was impressed once more with the epic scale of this devastated building. Tall and gaunt, the east gable seemed far distant. There is now no trace of the North Porch Door where pilgrims entered, but it seems likely that they first blessed themselves with water from the holy well, much as Catholics still do, and then prayed at the various altars. In exchange for cash, a pilgrim badge could be pinned to a hat or tunic, but some who came into the church were looking for something more substantial. By chance, a certificate of completion of a pilgrimage to St Andrews has survived in northern France at the town of St Omer. It remitted a grave sin committed by a cleric, William Bondolf of Dunkirk. He had been found guilty of the murder of André d'Esquerdes, but instead of being condemned to death he was ordered to pay a large sum in compensation to the family of the dead man, have thirteen masses sung for his salvation and go on a pilgrimage to St Andrews. Not only was the shrine distant and difficult to reach, it also bore the name of the victim. Bondolf may have travelled by sea to Earlsferry and then walked the twenty miles or so to the cathedral. Going directly by ship to St Andrews was probably thought to be too easy, not enough of a penance. The dates suggest a timescale that would fit this hypothesis. No doubt in return for a handsome fee, Bondolf was given his certificate on 29 May 1333, and less than a month later, on 26 June, he was back in St Omer to present it to the judicial authorities.

It is likely that most pilgrims made shorter journeys to St Andrews, from locations in Scotland and the rest of Britain and Ireland. Most came on the great feast days. There were at least six each year and they were more than opportunities to display piety; there was fun to be had at the booths and entertainments in Market Street. Records show that preparations were elaborate. The streets were cleaned and probably cleared of beggars. The town's trade guilds spruced up the tableaux that were carried in procession, and early on the morning of each feast day pilgrims lined North Street, what is now Greyfriars Gardens (where there was a house of Franciscans), and Bell Street and South Street (where there was a house of Blackfriars or Dominicans). In the long nave of the cathedral, masters and scholars of the university colleges carried leafy branches (in imitation of the biblical palms) or flowers; the Franciscan Friars and the Dominicans were gathered there, but pride of place was taken by the Prior and the Augustinian Canons. Wearing garlands of flowers, at least on the summer feast days, or jewelled fillets on their heads, they looked resplendent in their finest vestments. Still known by its Gaelic name, the Morbrac, the Great Reliquary was carried on a bier by the canons or by wealthy laymen able to pay for the privilege. And then, when all was ready, the bells of the cathedral rang out over the town, the West Door opened and the procession moved off. Hymns were sung and carillons of bell-ringing from all of the town's churches punctuated the stately procession as St Andrews rang with praise and prayer.

The coffers of the cathedral were further swelled when it became possible to buy plenary indulgences on feast days, certainly at Michaelmas, the Feast of St Michael the Archangel, and probably at others. These were expensive documents that guaranteed remission of all earthly sins and a safe passage straight to Heaven. Their sales were also what enraged the pious German priest Martin Luther, and they set in train events that would lead directly to the destruction of the universal Catholic Church and its great cathedral at St Andrews.

By the early sixteenth century, it seemed that pilgrimage was in any case waning. In 1512, the pilgrim hospice at St Leonard's and its chapel were converted into a college of the university. The foundation charter noted that the miracles that attended the constant streams of pilgrims had ceased, as had pilgrimages themselves, because 'the Christian faith, firmly rooted in the land, no longer needed such support'. This sort of thinking nourished the seeds of reform, and at St Leonard's College young priests began to spread the ideas of Luther and others.

As the established Church attempted to ride out the storms of reform, St Andrews saw several cruel martyrdoms, culminating in the death of Walter Myln, an eighty-two-year-old former priest who was burned to death not far from the West Door of the cathedral. By the late 1550s, change had become irresistible. When the aristocratic supporters of the Reformation in Scotland, the Lords of the Congregation, occupied the town of St Andrews in the summer of 1559, John Knox came to preach. For four days he railed passionately on the biblical theme of the cleansing of the Temple in Jerusalem, when Christ had cleared away the tables of the money changers. The analogy was unmistakable, and on the morning of 14 June the cathedral was attacked and gutted. Altars and sculpture (condemned as idolatry) were broken down and burned in the very place where Walter Myln had died. Vestments, liturgical books, the images of saints and paintings of other kinds and much else were dragged out of the great church and thrown on the blaze.

What happened to the relics of St Andrew is not clear, but it is likely that they and their reliquary were also destroyed on 14 June 1559. By the end of the day the interior of the cathedral had been stripped and the stained glass (more idolatry) smashed. 'Before the sun was down', wrote one observer, 'there was [nothing] standing but bare walls.' Once the lead had been stripped from the roof and the weather allowed to invade the cathedral fabric, it was doomed. The north walls of the nave, the entire north transept, the piers and the tower and its spire all fell and much of the cut stone was removed by local people. Only sixty years later Habakkuk Bisset wrote of 'the old ruinous walls of the cathedral and sometime most magnificent kirk of the archbishopric of St Andrews'.

When I left the West Door of the magnificent old kirk, I began to take the last steps of my own personal pilgrimage. I had come to St Andrews in 1968 as a raw undergraduate, and more than forty years later I came back to walk in the footsteps of those who processed behind the relics of the man who knew Christ, to walk in the footsteps of my predecessors. Lawrence of Lindores was appointed Rector of the University of St Andrews sometime after 1419, and he and his successors undoubtedly walked around North and South Streets behind the Morbrac and the tableaux. In 2011 I was elected Rector of the university and, wearing a long purple gown and a beretta, and preceded by my mace, crowned with a silver sculpture of Lawrence, I walked in procession around the streets, academic finery replacing the gorgeous vestments of the Glorious House of St Andrew. Full circle, it seemed.

When I returned to the West Door, I picked up a tiny scrap of lime mortar from the grass near the path, a piece the size of a small coin. It sits on my desk, a badge of my own pilgrimage. Having spent formative years as a student in St Andrews and then returning forty years later to the formalities of being Lord Rector of the university, I had seen this magical, memorable place in a completely new light.

Pease Bay
Cockburnspath
Old Cambus
Hand Yards
Coldingham Moor
Press Castle
Cairncross Farm
Ayton
Lamberton
New East Farm
Berwick upon Tweed

The Great North Road ④

4

The Great North Road

Berwick upon Tweed to Cockburnspath

Highways and railways can be romantic, but motorways are rarely anything but functional. The whistle of the London train is something I vividly recall from 1950s caravan holidays near Berwick upon Tweed and, when I was only a little older, I relished tales of stagecoaches, highwaymen like Dick Turpin and Christmas cards with red-coated coachmen driving four horses in-hand through the snow.

I had always assumed that the A1 had completely overlaid the old post road, the Great North Road. But when I sat down with my excellent set of Pathfinder maps of Berwickshire I began to notice some tell-tale place names. They eventually made clear a very different route for the stagecoaches and their post-horses.

This hidden way was one of the most satisfying of all because its route was so obscure, and very beautiful. Long stretches ran through spectacular scenery, even though much of it was covered by hard standing or the tarmac of a minor road. And, unusually on my walks, I met some lovely people along the line of the Great North Road and those brief hours of good company enriched the experience.

The old queen was dying, and she knew it. In early March 1603, Elizabeth I complained that she had caught a chill while out walking at Richmond Palace and she retired to her private apartments. Refusing to take to her bed and dismissing her doctors, she lay on cushions, attended only by the ladies of her bedchamber. Two of her dearest and oldest friends had died that winter and the queen was much cast down, suffering from what contemporaries called 'an irremovable melancholy', what might be known now as depression. It seemed to at least one of her ladies that the queen had lost the will to live. Philadelphia Carey, Robert Carey's younger sister and a maid of honour at the palace, was, like most of the court, alive to the politics of what was unfolding, principally the crucial and unresolved issue of the succession.

Although she had never explicitly stated her intentions, Elizabeth I's courtiers believed that James VI of Scotland would become king of a united realm of Great Britain and Ireland. He and the old queen were cousins, descended from Margaret Tudor, who had become Queen of Scotland. Robert Cecil, Elizabeth's de facto prime minister, had written to James with advice, but nothing was certain. Philadelphia Carey sent an urgent message to her brother Robert, telling him that her mistress seemed to be slipping slowly away. Robert was Warden of the English Middle March, a professional soldier and diplomat who administered part of England's border with Scotland, and the queen's first cousin. Ambitious, dashing and good-looking, he formed a plan to take some personal advantage of these epoch-changing events. He wrote to James VI. On 19 March, his sister ushered Robert Carey into the queen's presence. 'I am not well,' she whispered.

On 23 March, the old queen lost the power of speech. When Archbishop Whitgift came to comfort her, she answered his questions by squeezing his hand. Between 2 a.m. and 3 a.m. on 24 March, Elizabeth I died and Philadelphia took a blue sapphire ring from her finger and gave it to her brother. It had been a gift from James VI. Robert had decided that long before any official communication could reach him, he would be the messenger that gave the Scottish king the news he had been waiting for all his life. Having organised a relay of fresh horses, Carey would ride like the wind to Edinburgh and Holyrood Palace. If he could be first to kneel before the new king of England and Ireland, surely his reward would be great. Speed was important. The handover of power is always a time of instability and Catholic factions, perhaps with European support, might move to prevent the accession of a Protestant king.

But there was a problem. Robert Cecil knew of Carey's plan and attempted to thwart him. The gates of Richmond Palace were locked and Carey was told he could not leave. He sought out Lord Hunsdon, his brother, and he bluffed their way out. Robert Cecil again tried to prevent Carey from embarking on his epic journey, but by 9 a.m. he was in the saddle and galloping hard out of the city and up the Great North Road.

Having walked from London to Edinburgh to fulfill the terms of a wager, the messenger knew the road well. But it was late winter when he kicked his horse on up what is now the Edgware Road, and in places beyond the city the going will have been deep and river fords swollen with rain. Astonishingly, Carey reached Doncaster late in the evening of 24 March. In approximately twelve hours, he had ridden 160 miles, probably changing horses every ten to fifteen miles, depending on the going and the gradients on the old road. No horse can gallop or canter that distance and in his account of the event in 1603, Thomas Millingham wrote of Carey 'posting', by which he meant trotting. The rider's own stamina was remarkable because the following day he covered a further 130 miles to Widdrington, his house in Northumberland.

On the night of 25 March, Carey must have slept soundly,

resting his aching legs and backside, safe in the knowledge that news of the queen's death the day before will have scarcely spread beyond London. Rising early, he gave orders that James VI should be proclaimed James I of England at the market crosses of Morpeth and Alnwick, knowing that would please the new king and also that he could outrun the transmission of the news northwards. Reaching his castle at Norham soon after midday, the horseman splashed across the fords into Scotland. Carey may have been unwilling to risk riding straight to Tweedmouth – the wooden bridge across the wide estuary was prone to damage and might have been down or impassable. Five years later, in 1608, the rickety old Berwick bridge was destroyed by ice.

Then, as Thomas Millingham relates: 'On Saturday [25 March], coming to Berwick, acquainting his worthy brother, Sir John Carey, how all things stood.'

Clearly the next stage of a well-laid plan, Robert had his brother, who was Warden of the English East March, proclaim the new king in the town. Irony of all sorts abounded. Berwick's formidable Elizabethan fortifications survive almost intact, and they are massive, thick walls built to withstand a Scottish bombardment from land or sea. But now these expensive, state-of-the-art walls were redundant, and the Careys must have realised that their jobs as March wardens were also likely to be dispensed with.

Not waiting for the proclamation at 3 p.m., Robert saddled up once more, hauled himself astride his fresh mount and rode under the Scots Gate to complete the last leg of his epic journey. But when he set out on the Great North Road once more, it is likely that the March weather turned wet.

Somewhere north of Berwick, perhaps on Lamberton Moor, Carey's horse spooked sideways, slipped in the mud and threw its rider. And adding injury to insult, it kicked Carey in the head while he lay on the ground. As often, cuts to the head bleed profusely and progress through Berwickshire slowed. But Carey posted on doggedly through the gloaming as he at last turned westwards after reaching Cockburnspath. He probably changed horses at Haddington and reached Edinburgh late in the night of 26 March. Having kicked on his tired horse, he found Holyrood Palace in the darkness, dismounted in the cobbled courtyard and demanded that the king be woken. Perhaps servants hesitated, but the English stranger seemed to be alone and he was insistent. Bloodied down one side of his face, exhausted, his cloak and boots caked in mud, Carey finally knelt before James VI. When the king asked him what letters he carried from the Privy Council, the bedraggled messenger replied that he had nothing except 'a blue ring from a fair lady'. James took it and said, 'It is enough.'

Robert Carey's remarkable ride would have been impossible if the Great North Road had not been a well established route with inns and stables with fresh horses at regular intervals along it. But it was little more than a track. Only eleven days after accepting the blue ring, James VI and I mounted a horse and with his many attendants rode briskly eastwards on the road to his destiny. But within an hour, this royal progress was halted and the king was forced to stop and dismount. In Musselburgh, his party met the funeral cortège of Robert Seaton, the Earl of Winton, who had been one of the rescuers of Mary, Queen of Scots, from her imprisonment in Loch Leven Castle and also a lifelong supporter of the Stewart dynasty. Out of respect, King James ordered his retinue to move off the narrow track, took off his hat and sat on a dyke in silence as the mourners filed past. A day later, the Berwick garrison's cannonade boomed out over the Tweed estuary as the new king was welcomed into his new realm.

North of the walled town, the Great North Road taken

by King James and his courtiers has in places completely disappeared, its route lost or mistaken. Apart from the first mile out of Berwick, it does not follow the modern route of the A1 through Berwickshire, the demands of car and lorry drivers being different from those who rode or drove horses or walked. But for 2,000 years, history moved up and down this old road: Roman legions, Dark Ages warbands, the armies of Edward I and Oliver Cromwell, and, as Robert Carey showed so spectacularly, news crackled north and south along its line.

Much of it crossed Berwick Old Bridge, and it seemed to me to be a good place to begin. After the wooden bridge was badly damaged by ice floes driven by the strong currents of the flooding Tweed in 1608, it was decided to rebuild in stone. But so little money was raised locally that James VI and I was forced to instruct his exchequer to contribute £8,000, most of the cost. This was clearly a good investment: the north road needed to remain open, and it has also stood the test of time, surviving many winter spates.

It was misty when I started from the southern approach road, from Tweedmouth, but it was the sort of wispy scarf that seemed to lie on the river on a windless morning. Perhaps the morning sun would burn it off. The roadway seems narrow now, but it was wide enough for two carts to pass each other. I liked that the roads department had painted SLOW on the orange tarmac. Like many old bridges, Berwick Old Bridge is hump-backed, reaching its highest point not in the centre of its span but within two arches of the Berwick end. I guessed that the river must be deepest there and that the arches needed to be higher to cope with floods and their driven, dangerous debris.

When I reached the walls, I saw four fishermen hauling in a net that had been spread wide, paid out over the stern of a grey rowing boat across the shallow part of the estuary on the Tweedmouth side. Many salmon used to be netted at the mouth of the Tweed and a local festival still crowns a Salmon Queen. But conservation has recently insisted that the fishing be much reduced. Hand over hand, swaying rhythmically, the fishermen pulled in the net, its floats showing the semi-circle slowly shrinking. I thought this scene ancient, something done on the Tweed since a time out of mind. The names of the sandbanks uncovered in the estuary at low tide are so old that they sound like echoes of a lost language: Calot Shad, Gardo. The local dialect word for a salmon pool is a stell; Hallowstell means the Holy Man's Pool, St Cuthbert's Pool, and Sandstell is self-explanatory.

The only thing that seemed relatively modern was the windlass one of the fishermen turned to roll up the net. And as no doubt often happened, there turned out to be no fish helplessly flapping and arcing their suffocating bodies as they tried to escape. Maybe the conservationists had a point.

The old bridge stands in the shadow of the new. Immediately upstream is the Royal Tweed Bridge, an elegant reinforced concrete structure built in the 1920s supported by four wide arches. Like the old one, it is higher at the north end, with a longer last span, probably for the same reason. Dwarfing the road bridges is the Royal Border Bridge, built between 1847 and 1850 to carry the new railway that linked England with Scotland, Edinburgh with London. Opened by Queen Victoria and designed by Robert Stephenson (the son of George), it is a splendid viaduct, more than 600 metres long and high above the river and the town. When trains cross, passengers can see a long way to the south, picking out the silhouettes of Bamburgh and Lindisfarne castles on the Northumberland coastline. The construction of these two modern bridges spelled the end of the Great North

Road, as the railway and eventually the A1 took all its traffic.

I decided to walk along Bridge Street and up West Street so that I could pass Corvi's, a wonderful chip shop. Sadly, it was too early for their superb fish and chips, served with a pot of tea and two slices of buttered bread. Beyond the aroma of Corvi's, the Marygate is still the centre of Berwick, wide and well-set. It has a weekly market, but like many town centres it is fading, withering in the teeth of fierce competition from vast and soulless supermarkets built in the suburbs where plenty of parking space is available. The winds of changes in shopping may have brought closures and charities to the Marygate, but the sense of an Elizabethan walled town has not fled.

Its buildings seem to huddle close, cheek by jowl, sheltering behind the massive fortifications, and the sense of a military town is hard to miss. In the north-east corner of the walls, there was a garrison until the late twentieth century. Detachments of the King's Own Scottish Borderers regularly drilled on the cobbles, their mirror-shiny black boots cracking down as they came to attention. In the open area beyond the walls there is a solidly built gunpowder magazine and old firing ranges.

Beyond the main street, the Great North Road began at the Scots Gate. Dark and forbidding, its central arch allows two cars to pass each other and, incredible as it may seem now, the A1 used to run through this archway, a gate in an Elizabethan fortification. Two smaller arches on either side carry the pavements, and I shouldered my rucksack and passed under the Scots Gate, absolutely certain I was walking on the old road. I crossed the railway line and made my way through housing estates, past supermarkets and hamburger outlets to the roundabout where the A1 strikes north to Scotland. From all I had read, it was clear that the Great

North Road followed the roar of the new for about a mile, as far as New East Farm.

For the first time on any of my journeys along the hidden ways, I was given clear directions on the ground that turned out to be absolutely accurate. I met my helpful guide in his garden as he weeded around the first daffodils. He had taken over the main house at New East Farm, knew a good deal of its history and understood that he lived by the side of the Great North Road. As we spoke, the A1 thundered past only fifty metres away, the top of articulated lorries visible over a new sandstone wall built at the point where the old road diverged. Its course had been concreted over as it led around another new wall and continued beyond the garden gate – quite unmistakable. Cartwheel ruts led gently uphill, heading almost precisely due north. The views were panoramic, east over the A1 and the main line to the grey horizon of the North Sea, and south to Bamburgh and Lindisfarne and the distant outlines of their castles.

It was easy walking but very windy as the road led up to Lamberton village and the moorland beyond. The landscape was treeless and very exposed, but what surprised me was not the strength of the wind but its direction. It blew not off the sea but from the west and, as I gained height, I shivered to see that it might push heavy rain clouds towards the coast. My gardener–guide had told me that each day the wind freshened in the early afternoon and sometimes it shrouded the land with sea-frets. These could be very patchy and localised. I wondered if the wind up its tail and a sudden mist had spooked Robert Carey's horse and thrown him. But, for the moment, the sun shone and I tramped on towards another country.

By the early fifteenth century, the English occupation of the town of Berwick had solidified into a political fact. Scots kings were weak, and when Robert III died in 1406, he was said to have left a miserable, tear-stained epitaph: 'Here lies the worst of kings and the most wretched of men in the whole kingdom.' He was aptly nicknamed 'Auld Blearie'. Robert's realm was riven by faction and when James I finally established himself, his attention was drawn northwards to focus on the attempts of the MacDonald princes, the Lords of the Isles, to carve out a separate Atlantic principality. Berwick was the least of his worries, and about a mile and a half from New East Farm I found myself standing in front of a capitulation.

The Border Dyke looks much like any other and, like most field ends that are also boundaries, it was difficult to cross. The dyke marks the limits of the Berwick Bounds, a substantial parcel of land amputated from Scotland in 1438 that would serve the basic needs of the people of the English town. Its farms could supply grain, milk and other necessities. The line of the Bounds remembers civic officials, as it runs from the Coroner's Meadow on the north bank of the Tweed, about five miles from the centre of the town, round to the Marshall Meadows on the North Sea coast. From where I stood, I could see the farm and the Marshall Meadows Hotel down on my right. Just beyond it stand tall flagpoles on either side of the dual carriageway of the A1, one flying the Scottish Saltire and the other the Red Cross of St George. When I crossed the border as a child, there were only modest roadside signs.

I was confronted by a much harder border. Tacked on a strainer post, a black plaque told me this was the Border Wall, and below a small St George's Cross were the words 'Permissive Countryside Access'. As in, Permissive Society? Was Scotland, what lay on the other side of the dyke, seen as the Permissive Society? Odd wording – and also inaccurate, in more senses than one. It was extremely difficult to cross the Border Wall. Three high metal gates barred the way and in front of two of them ran the wire of electric fences. I shifted a loose, old rusted gate to one side, unhooked the English electric fence, climbed the second gate and reconnected it before disconnecting the Scottish one, climbing the Scottish gate and then reconnecting that electric fence. Not what I would call Permissive.

The Berwick Bounds was seen as an important enclave, and in 1550 the Chief Marshall (whose meadow formed the northern edge) rode around them with the soldiers of the English garrison. These men, the only permanent professional soldiers in sixteenth-century Britain, checked that the Scots had not encroached, and where there were no dykes or fences, they used mature trees as markers. So that they could be recognised as such, the Chief Marshall had his men beat the bark of the trees with sticks to mark them. It is the origin of the phrase 'Beating the Bounds'. Each year, around 1 May, horsemen and women still set out to ride the Berwick Bounds in what is now a ceremonial act. They have been doing it for more than 400 years.

On the other side of the dyke and its gates and electric fences lay disappointment. The line of the Great North Road seemed to submerge. I was fairly sure it ran on the western side of a fence that led north to Lamberton because on the other side there was a ruinous dyke and the ground fell away below that. It was a park of well-managed pasture and it may be that recent deep ploughing had removed all trace of the old road. On the photographs I took, I was later able to make out the faintest discolouration in the grass that might have hinted at parallel lines of cart tracks, but on the day I could see nothing. When I walked closer to the edge of the hamlet of Lamberton, I could see that I was on the right track since the line of the road resumed. I climbed a gate onto a short stretch of tarmac. Down to my right, I could see a B road that led to a place I wanted to look at.

Lamberton Kirk is old, certainly dating from the twelfth century, perhaps even earlier. The dedication suggests that it might be ancient. St Lambert was an early Bishop of Maastricht who preached to the pagan communities of the Meuse Valley and around what is now Liège. Their conversion to Christianity may have been a little shaky at first because, in 705, they murdered him. Curiously, Lambert became associated with the virtues of marital fidelity, having denounced Pepin II, the ruler of the Frankish kingdom, for having a mistress. Over the centuries, marriage became something of a historical motif for the old church. In 1503, Margaret Tudor, the daughter of Henry VII, was escorted to Lamberton to be married by proxy (by a different national church) to James IV of Scotland. It was this dynastic union that enabled James VI to ride through the hamlet on his progress down to London in 1603. I walked past the ruins of the old kirk and down to the site of the place known as the Marriage House. This was an old toll house whose ruins were demolished in 1975 to make way for a widening of the A1. Like Gretna Green, it lay just across the border and did a brisk trade in marrying runaways. It is reckoned that almost 400 hurried ceremonies were contracted at Lamberton each year in its heyday, the first half of the nineteenth century.

When I walked back uphill to rejoin the line of the Great North Road, I passed the second gardener of the morning. She was also weeding but glad to straighten her back for a cheery greeting and a brief conversation. When I explained where I was walking, she seemed surprised, unaware that about a hundred metres from her house ran the road where the first post coaches trundled from London to Edinburgh. Being a keen walker, she had been along the coastal path and elsewhere, but not on the road ridden by Robert Carey. When she promised one day to follow in my footsteps, I felt

I had made a convert. The land where the lady's house stood was part of the Lamberton Colony Scheme, and we talked for a while about this spasm of post-war idealism that shaped the countryside she lived in and that I was walking through.

The lands of Lamberton and neighbouring Mordington and Foulden had long belonged to the Renton family, owners for more than 600 years, a remarkable continuity. But after the First World War, the government compulsorily purchased large parts of their estates under the powers granted by the Congested Districts Act of 1897. It was designed to create smallholdings. These were defined as 'an area of land . . . sufficient to employ the whole labour of a man and his family and not enough to necessitate the employment of hired labour'. After the slaughter of the trenches of Flanders, there arose a demand for land from some of the survivors, and at Foulden sixty-one plots of land of between five and ten acres were offered, with thirty-four more at Mordington and Lamberton. Poultry farming, pig keeping and market gardening were popular, and the community at Foulden developed so cohesively that a village hall was quickly built and it remains well used. But these small parcels of land were difficult to make viable and several were merged. Around Lamberton the fields I walked through were almost all grass parks, probably the best option on this windswept upland.

When I rejoined the line of the old road, it led me through a small farm steading and a group of friendly hens. Through a gate, the road emerged once more from the grass and I made good time. The rain held off and I passed a herd of very furry native ponies, their winter coats so long that when they moved, the wind parted their hair wide. When I came to 9 Lamberton (the smallholdings are recognised by the Post Office in exactly the same way as the crofts of the Highlands and Islands), I saw an old man open the back door of his white bungalow. Using his stick for support, he carefully climbed down two steps and then reached back into his doorway to pull out a plastic basket of washing. When he laid it down next to the flapping washing line, he looked up, raised his stick in greeting and shouted above the wind, 'Blustery!' Not in the least taken aback to see someone walk though the fields beside his house, I wondered if he had once been an active smallholder in a much busier landscape.

My Pathfinder led me up to a B road that ran to the east of Lamberton Moor, where the views were glorious. In contrast to the flat, grey horizon of the sea in the east, to the west I could make out the Eildon Hills, about thirty miles inland, far up the Tweed Valley. I came to a sign for Mordington and its smallholdings, and another told me I had four miles to go to Ayton, where I intended to stop, before the rain set in. Or so I hoped. In an inbye field, I saw my first lambs of the year. Gawky and unsteady, they had not been out for long and the ewes were making plenty of noise to encourage them to stay close. Most were hard up against the dykes, where there was a bield from the west wind. The road was straight, the landscape open and treeless. When I reached some woodland on the flanks of Ayton Hill and a sheltered stretch of road, I saw another spring first that warmed me. Two wagtails were hopping around in a field of black calves (who thought I had come to feed them), picking up insects around their droppings. Depending on the prevailing winds, the swallows would not be far behind.

As I breasted a rise in the road, the valley of the Eye Water opened below me, and far in the distance I could see the sails of the great wind turbine farm on the Lammermuir Hills. According to the Pathfinder, it was now all downhill to Ayton. I set myself a good pace, arms swinging, an eye out to the west and the lead grey rain clouds gathering on the horizon. It had been an unusual morning. On all of the journeys along the old roads, I had met very few people: no one at all on Dere Street, or along the banks of the Tay, and only one on the pilgrim road to St Andrews. But in a single morning I had enjoyed informative conversations with two gardeners and been heartily greeted by an old man. It occurred to me that I had walked alone for many, many miles and, to my surprise, I had enjoyed the solitude. Not distracted by conversation, except occasionally with myself, I found that I had gradually become much more observant, using my phone camera often to take pictures of whatever caught my interest. Much faster and less intrusive than stopping to make notes, the camera recorded my curiosity rather than getting in the way of it. And when I came to write down my experiences on the hidden ways, the photographs were much more useful than anything I could have hurriedly scribbled on a windy hillside.

Walking alone, sometimes in remote places, also forced me to be much more self-reliant. Each time I parked at the beginning of a journey, I set out all that I needed on the back seat and put it into my rucksack: Pathfinders, compass, phone, pens and notebook (for when I sat down at the end of a walk), spare clothing, socks especially important, bottled water and food. And on walks over rough ground, I took my shepherd's crook, my sturdy hazel stick that I had bought at Pennymuir Show. Very important were my boots, well worn in and completely waterproof. But most important of all was to be sensible. At sixty-six, I am no longer young and my stamina is definitely not what it was. Sudden aches and stiffnesses appear for, it seems, no reason – except age. I walked at a steady pace and took no more risks than I needed to because if I pulled a muscle, turned an ankle or, God forbid, broke something, I would have been in real trouble out on moorland or on a hillside. The daftest thing I did, prompted by stubbornness, was to swing across the Cameron Burn south of St Andrews. Even though it made me smile and feel a wee bit triumphant, I vowed never to do anything as silly again. But it was not a vow I kept.

Perhaps the most surprising discovery was the semi-hypnotic nature of the walking itself. If I had a long stretch of road where tarmac had overlaid the old route, and there was nothing much to interest me, I could manage three or four miles in an hour and not remember much about where I had just been. It was not tiredness but the steady, arm-swinging rhythm of putting one foot in front of another. Maybe much more experienced walkers or marching soldiers experience something similar.

When I began to descend Ayton Hill, a two-mile stretch of road walking lay ahead, and it was all downhill. I could see the red sandstone façade of Ayton Castle in the distance and I knew that I had to aim directly for it. A year before I had given a talk in Berwick Guildhall and afterwards the owner of the castle had told me that he thought the Great North Road ran through his policies. He seemed very knowledgeable and I said I would like to have a good wander round to see if I could find the line of the road.

When I stopped to look at my badly folded Pathfinder, I heard behind me, 'Enjoy the downhill!' A tall, slim lady wearing pink trainers was striding down the road, taking out her earphones as she greeted me. Her pace was twice as fast as mine and as she quickly disappeared into the distance I reflected on the unarguable fact that the people you see out walking or running do not need to. I had been looking to see where the road ran under the main line to London when a train suddenly thundered into view, seeming to race out of some bushes. The road abruptly ducked under a bridge and then turned sharp left, a sure sign that its line had been altered to accommodate the builders of the railway line.

When I arrived at a road junction and the bridge across the Eye Water that led into Ayton, I could see that it was modern and another diversion. Below the parapet, the gorge of the little river was very steep-sided, not a place where the Great North Road could have crossed. To the right of the bridge stood the religious equivalent of Miss Havisham, a little-used, ghostly church surrounded by trees and the yellowed sticks of last summer's willowherb and other weeds. Gothic, probably late nineteenth century, its run-down, part-time state saddened me, not so much the withering of belief as the fading of pride and pleasure in such beautifully built architecture. Sadness swirled on the wind around the empty church and I sensed decay would soon follow.

I walked behind it into the graveyard and found that the banks of the Eye Water became much less steep towards the east. Retracing my steps, I crossed the new bridge and found the South Lodge of Ayton Castle. By contrast, this was fairy-tale architecture, an archway that was also a house. I walked though and found a back door but no one at home. A sign said that the castle was closed and I didn't want to trespass. Fringed by budding daffodils, a long driveway stretched uphill and I reckoned that if I kept to the tarmac, I would look less like an intruder than if I started thrashing through the rhododendra looking for the line of an old road, allegedly. A white car approached from the opposite direction and the driver waved. Fine.

I did not have to look hard, the owner of the castle had been right. By the side of the driveway, as it climbed to the higher ground where the castle stood, there was a stubby little milestone, clearly old. Just discernible on one side was a large '7'. Seven miles to Berwick. Hooray! I walked up to

the castle to ask permission to thrash around in the rhododendra and saw the vans of various tradesmen parked
outside one wing of what looked like a splendid example
of the Scottish Baronial style. High, turreted and with crow-
stepped gables, the castle looked mighty impressive, and
parked outside the grand front entrance was a black Bentley
Continental. I had a momentary pang of jealousy, but it was
quickly dismissed by the certain knowledge that the exhaust
would be off after about ten metres of our farm track.
Hoping that the car meant there was someone at home, I
rang the doorbell. Perhaps a butler would appear. No one
did and I walked across to talk to the tradesmen, who showed
me where the factor's office was. No one to be found.

I walked back down to the milestone and realised that if I
could use it as a guide, I might be able to see where the Great
North Road ran. Through the leafless trees, I could make out
a wooden bridge that crossed the Eye and what seemed like
an old track zigzagging up the steep bank. It was lined by
mature trees and seemed old. Beyond the northern policies
of the castle, the Pathfinder showed a track leading across
fields and the A1 to link with a B road I was sure overlaid the
old route to Edinburgh. But that would have to wait for
another day. It began to rain and I had promised myself lunch
at Mr Corvi's excellent fish restaurant in Berwick: fish and
chips, a pot of tea, a slice of the whitest bread with the thin-
nest scrape of what was probably butter. Wonderful. And
well-fortified, I climbed back into my old car.

I found the route immediately and by pure chance. Having
driven through Ayton and up the hill behind the castle policies,
I pulled in to park by the side of the road, switched off the
engine and looked through the front passenger window to see
the Great North Road. It ran through the dappled shade of
young woodland. Unmistakable. I tucked the car in a bit tighter

off the road, sorted my gear and set off. Once out of the shelter of the trees, a very strong wind almost buffeted me sideways as it blew across the open fields, but more shocking, more deafening was the roar of the A1. About a hundred metres from where I was fighting to fold my Pathfinder, artics, vans and cars hurtled past, and the old road headed straight for its modern successor. Recent litter told me that people walked here and, in the hedge that cut diagonally across the old road, I could see a wicket gate. It had a vertical bolt-catch of the sort used by riders so that they did not have to dismount to open and close it. Since the catch no longer worked properly, someone had tied the gate to the strainer post with a scrap of electric fencing. Only metres from the whoosh and racket of the road, I guessed it had been a long time since a rider had risked their horse crossing the A1.

When I closed the gate behind me, it was as though I had passed from the nineteenth century into the twenty-first with one stride. Lorries and cars came barrelling from both directions in continuous streams, their speed dizzying, and even in the clear spring air of Berwickshire, the stink of exhaust was pungent. I looked across to the other side of the road for another gate, but could see nothing, no sign at all. The Pathfinder did not mark any track or road, just a shelter belt of pines between two fields on the far side of the road. All I could make out between the blur of the lorries was a bank of thick gorse bushes. Maybe all that survived of the old road was the 200 metres I had just walked.

After waiting for what seemed like a long time, I saw a gap in the traffic and quickly crossed. Just discernible, I saw a path through the gorse and, having pushed and prickled through it, found myself in front of an identical wicket-gate with a vertical bolt-catch. So, once in a day, riders had crossed a much slower, gentler A1 and not had to dismount on the other side

– because they had somewhere to trot and canter their horses. What I found beyond the gate delighted me. Here it was, a wide road not marked on the map, running north-west through an avenue of mature trees. The surface was metalled and it had a crest with clear traces of cart ruts on either side. And it seemed to be used. This was the Great North Road, no question, and the best preserved section I had found so far.

I walked along this excellent surface for about half a mile, all the time putting the din of the twenty-first century further and further behind me. When I came to a crossroads near Aytonwood House, I saw an even better preserved section of the road stretch away into the distance, north-west towards the coast and East Lothian. This was even wider, recently laid with gravel, certainly still used (a sign warned of tractor traffic) and with deep and well maintained ditches on both sides. These were originally cut to discourage riders from avoiding standing water on the road or in big holes by riding across the fields.

The wind whistled so strongly across the open pasture that I did not dare open my Pathfinder to check exactly where I was and how far this part of the road might extend, but I could see sheltering plantations up ahead. I stopped near the first by a line of pheasant feeders, large blue drums raised up on posts, and suddenly, about thirty metres in front, three roe deer erupted from the wood in a line, jumped the ditch, crossed the road and jumped again into the trees to disappear in a moment. The Gaels call them the 'Children of the Mist', but they are more like the Children of the Woods.

Before 1772 Berwickshire's roads were maintained by what was called statute labour raised in each of the parishes. It was reluctant and intermittent, especially in remote stretches like the one I was travelling. The Turnpike Acts created a different model, where cash was raised from road users by the payment of tolls. Economically, investment in good roads was in everyone's interest and the government occasionally assisted with the building of bridges. And in the twenty-first century, this old road had clearly been well maintained.

After about two miles, the character of the surface changed abruptly, probably signalling that I had moved from one farm to another. The road greened with tufty grass on its crest and by the ditches, and hedges appeared on either side. It looked as though we had slipped back to the nineteenth century. When the road began to climb, Cairncross Farm came into view not far ahead. On the south-western edge of the steading, the old road ran past some cottages but was barred by a green metal gate. I wondered who owned the line of the road. Was it a right of way? What happened to Permissive Access?

Cairncross seems a very modern, well-laid-out farm steading with large barns to house machinery, fodder and probably beasts over the winter. But its name recalls a different sense of the landscape. It was once a boundary, one that marked off the temporal, everyday world from a sacred place, a land of saints and prayer, a place where God was closer. Ancient, founded in the early seventh century, the time when Christianity first came to the peoples of the north of Britain, Coldingham Priory was associated with Cuthbert, the saint on whose bones Durham Cathedral was built. Cairncross marked the edge of its lands.

At the height of Viking raiding, the priory was vulnerable, being so close to the coast. In 870, it saw a grisly act of self-mutilation. St Aebbe cut off her nose and her upper lip 'to the teeth, offering a dreadful spectacle of herself to all beholders'. The Abbess believed that the pagan Vikings would be so revolted that they would not violate her and she encouraged her nuns to do the same thing. It worked, up to a point. The raiders did not rape the holy sisters, but they did burn them to death. This extraordinary act of purity, as it was seen, brought pilgrims to Coldingham and, on roads leading to the priory, crosses were set up. When Applincross, Crosslaw, Whitecross and Cairncross were reached, pilgrims knew that they were entering upon the holy ground, the sacred earth trodden by saints.

After Cairncross, the Great North Road is tarmacked and designated a B road. It begins to climb the flanks of the hills above the Eye Water, aiming straight for Coldingham Moor. At Press Castle, where it crosses the trickle of the South Grange Burn, the line suddenly kinks right after crossing a narrow bridge and then another one. I wondered if this was a later diversion, but as I walked back and forth to investigate where else it might have gone, I could see an old wall, a considerable obstruction that it might have been trying to avoid. Half-crumbled, I could see over it something that surprised me: a very modern house. Raised on steel piers, a long wooden-clad structure projected dramatically into what looked like an old walled garden. Just adjacent to the stuccoed mansion of Press Castle, that would make sense. Close to the house, a woman was working in the garden. More weeding, it must have been the season. I asked her about the age of the wall and she said that it was indeed associated with the castle. More than that, she knew that the little B road running past her house had once been an arterial highway. Very sunny and welcoming, she invited me to come into the garden and have a look at the house. Having bought it from a couple 'who had fallen out of love', she and her husband had been there for a year and they were busy adding rooms, reorganising the layout and opening up the garden. Piles of logs lay everywhere. It had all been beautifully done, a rare example of a rectilinear modern house, with edges everywhere, having warmth and personality. Perhaps that came from the couple who showed it to me. The lady told me she had just baked some gingerbread, would I like some and a cup of tea? I would, but I needed to get on. I wanted to reach the coast before late afternoon and if I had sat down, that would have been the end of the walk.

Up on Coldingham Moor, the wind blew so hard that I could scarcely hold my phone camera steady, and I began to regret refusing the kindness of tea and fresh bakery. Another wind farm whooshed vigorously on Drone Hill. At its summit, the North Sea came into view and a clutch of Second World War blockhouses looked out to the far horizons. They were probably radio stations and observation posts, reminders of a time when the cliffs below were ramparts. And then, a few hundred metres further on, the vistas out over the Forth opened up: North Berwick Law, the Bass Rock and beyond them Largo Law in Fife. It was breathtaking and I took several shaky photographs. Managing to unfold the Pathfinder, I saw that this section of the Great North Road was marked as Haud Yauds. The descent off the edges of the Lammermuirs is very steep, made to feel even more vertiginous by the cliffs a mile or so off the road and the sea clearly a long way below them. A yaud is a Scots word for a draught horse, not a riding horse but one that pulled carts or carriages. Going down such a steep incline, it was vital to hold, or haud, the yauds in a tight rein because they would feel the pressure of the load behind them and their natural flight instinct would be to run away from it. If a cart or carriage had brakes, they probably needed to be pulled on often.

Haud Yauds also remembers the age of stagecoaches, and another name for where I was walking was the Old Post Road. Although it was set up in 1516 on the order of Henry VIII, the Royal Mail was not opened to other users until 1635. In

1660, Charles II had the Post Office established at Post House Yard in London. At first journeys between Edinburgh and London could take ten days in summer and twelve to sixteen in winter. The mail coaches averaged seven to eight miles an hour in better weather, and only five miles per hour in the depths of winter. Fresh horses were needed every ten to fifteen miles, depending on the state of the road, and as the coach approached post houses and toll gates or turnpikes, the guard blew the posthorn to warn them, and also to have toll keepers raise the bar to let them through. There was undoubtedly a sense of urgency, especially in the bitter frosts and snows of winter up on the moors I had walked across, probably amongst the highest points on the old road. But at Haud Yauds care needed to be taken and passengers in the coach, travelling in either direction, got off and walked. Most important in difficult places was a skilled postilion. Coaches were pulled by three pairs of horses, sometimes four, and he rode one of the two leaders in order to control their pace.

The Royal Mail travelled heavily armed, with the driver and his guard carrying a blunderbuss, swords and at least two pistols. Especially on remote sections, highwaymen were a real threat. Guards had to stay up top at all times, and there were reports that sometimes they froze to death. The mail coach took passengers and two were encouraged (it was also much cheaper) to sit up top behind the driver and his guard to discourage thieves from jumping on the roof. As they creaked and trundled through the countryside, the mail coaches could easily be seen from a distance. Brightly painted in maroon, red and black, they also carried the royal arms on the foreboot where parcels were kept locked. Letters went into the hindboot, so-called because it was kept under the guard's booted feet.

After 1750 the roads improved with the Turnpike Acts and the journey from Edinburgh to London speeded up considerably. In 1786, a daily service took only sixty hours and business boomed. By the early nineteenth century two companies operated services, the Union and the Mail. The journey time was improved by strict protocols: coaches always had right of way and the posthorn was blown to get other road users to move aside, and if a turnpike was not lifted and the coach forced to stop, a fine was imposed on the toll keeper.

Beyond Haud Yauds, the road quickly descends to Old Cambus, where it crosses a burn. But the first real challenge is above the beach at Pease Bay, where the stream runs through a deep ravine. Until the 1780s the road was forced to turn down towards the shore and cross by a ford. Further on, at Cockburnspath, another burn and its steep-sided banks had to be negotiated. The deans or steep valleys of these burns, places where the glaciers of the Ice Age had clawed out gorges in the hillsides, presented great problems, and not only for travellers. In 1650, Oliver Cromwell's invading army encamped at Dunbar and found their retreat south blocked at Cockburnspath. The line of the road varied a great deal in this small area, more resembling a river delta than a clear route.

By the time I reached the village, I was foot-sore and very tired. But at least it was journey's end. For much of its onward course through East Lothian, the Great North Road follows the course of the A1 before disappearing in the eastern suburbs of Edinburgh. I was content, pleased to have found much more of the old road than I imagined had survived. Following its line for about twenty-five miles, I felt I had arrived in Scotland by a very different route, one that remembered the rigours of travel before the later twentieth century, but also offered the compensation of seeing the sweep of the coastline: Largo Law and the Fife coast, and, very faintly beyond, the Angus hills and the blue of the North Sea to the east.

The Road to Ruin ⑤

5

The Road to Ruin

The Old Town, Edinburgh

Almost all of the hidden ways run through countryside, and when they approach cities or large towns their traces have often been obliterated. After Dere Street reaches the southern suburbs of Edinburgh, it disappears. But it seemed perverse to ignore the cities entirely, so I decided to include one urban route that has altered little since it was laid out in the Middle Ages.

In the later eighteenth century, when the Georgian New Town was built, Edinburgh's High Street was largely abandoned by those who might be seen as the Scottish establishment: lawyers, politicians, intellectuals. They wanted 'houses by themselves' across the drained Nor Loch. Throughout the nineteenth century, the High Street's tenements were conserved almost by default, lasting long enough into the twentieth century to be saved by pressure groups.

The High Street is not long, but it is very detailed, much more than two parallel lines of tall buildings. Most of all, it was a theatre, a public space where some of Scotland's history was played out. And behind the colourful clutter of tourism, it has recently re-acquired great status, as the Scottish Parliament was reconvened there in 1999.

I love the High Street. I have a very personal connection with its cobbles, closes and vertiginous tenements because I used to work there. And although its line is in no sense hidden, its heart, soul and history can sometimes be obscure. I hope that what follows casts it in a new light.

After a dazzling series of victories in the Highland winter, James Graham, the Marquis of Montrose, found himself trapped. His royalist army was in the Great Glen on 8 January 1645 when the general met Iain Lom, the MacDonald bard. He brought bad news. Two Covenanter armies, fighting on the side of the Parliamentarians in the English Civil War, had been deployed against him, one at each end of the Great Glen, blocking any advance or retreat. At Inverness the Earl of Seaforth, Chief of Clan Mackenzie, was encamped with 2,000 troops, while at Inverlochy Castle, near Fort William, 3,000 men were under the command of Sir Duncan Campbell, a battle-hardened soldier. Although Seaforth's was the smaller force, Montrose decided to march south to meet the Campbells. With a force of MacDonalds, Stewarts and MacDonnells, there was no need to incite them to fight. Their hated blood enemies were at Inverlochy.

With superior numbers, Sir Duncan Campbell wanted to fight on open ground where his strength would tell, and he sent scouts to watch the road by Loch Lochy. Montrose and his men had to come that way, there was no other choice. And he would attack on open field, ground of his choosing. Intelligence told Campbell that he would face only about 1,500 royalists and his force ought to be able quickly to outflank Montrose, roll up his smaller army and fatally encircle them. Then the killing would begin.

Meanwhile Montrose and his great ally, Alasdair MacColla, were talking to the Camerons. This was their country and they knew of a high pass to the south-east of the Great Glen. It passed between two mountains, Carn Dearg and Carn Leac, and it would bring the small army round behind the Campbell position at Inverlochy. But it was winter, the pass rose to 2,000 feet, and there was deep snow and freezing temperatures. The Cameron scouts shook their heads, it could not be crossed.

Montrose and MacColla paid no attention, knowing that success against the Campbells depended absolutely on a daring tactic. They persuaded their men to make their way into the winter mountains and a long column quickly climbed through the snow line. Using sticks to probe the drifts, they found a path and when night fell the moon lit their way. They had to keep moving, to stop to rest was to die. Towards dawn, the leading column saw that the ground was descending and that there was a track at the head of Glen Roy. Led by the Cameron scouts, Montrose's army made their way down from the snows and along the track by the banks of the River Spean. It had taken thirty-six hours, one of the most daring, dramatic manoeuvres in Scottish military history. When dawn broke on 2 February 1645, Sir Duncan Campbell was horrified to see the royalist army drawn up in battle order on his flank. When the pipers sounded the *claidheamh mór*, the order to charge, Montrose's army tore into their enemy. It was a terrible slaughter, more than 1,500 of the Campbell army died, including Sir Duncan.

But success did not sustain, and when Montrose marched south, without Alasdair MacColla and his MacDonalds, he was defeated at Philiphaugh near Selkirk. Having escaped capture, the great general fled to Europe and to the frustrations of exile. A man of action, he fretted in his enforced impotence, and in 1650 Montrose returned to the Highlands to raise an army to fight for Charles II. But there was little enthusiasm, little fire, and at Carbisdale the royalist army was scattered. After wandering the hills, starving and despondent, Montrose sought refuge in Assynt with Neil

MacLeod at his castle at Ardvreck. And he promptly betrayed the fugitive for a large reward.

Mounted on a carthorse, Montrose reached Edinburgh on a cold Saturday afternoon in May. He and his captors entered by the Water Gate, near Holyrood Palace, and the rebel general was handed over to the hangman. Tied to a seat in a cart, he was trundled up the High Street through silent crowds lining the route. This was a dashing soldier who had won astonishing victories, not a criminal or a murderer to be jeered at and pelted with rubbish and excrement. After a day in a cell in the Tolbooth, which used to stand adjacent to the High Kirk of St Giles, Montrose was taken to a session of the Scottish Parliament, where the death sentence for treason was pronounced.

The following morning, Montrose dressed in his finest clothes, a scarlet coat over a linen sark with a white lace collar, white gloves, silk stockings, ribboned shoes and a broad brimmed hat. And he carefully combed out his long, dark brown hair. One observer thought he looked more like a bridegroom than a condemned man. And when one of the Presbyterian ministers who had been pestering him to make some sort of confession carped at Montrose for paying so much attention to his appearance, the Marquis is said to have replied, 'My head is still my own. Tonight, when it will be yours, treat it as you please.'

By two o'clock in the afternoon a huge crowd of many thousands had gathered in the High Street and as Montrose was led out of the Tolbooth to walk to his death, they did not call out or jeer. Instead, there was a low murmur of anticipation for the grisly spectacle of public execution. By the Mercat Cross, only fifty metres down the cobbled street, a high gallows had been erected on a wooden platform. When soldiers forced a path through the crowd, Montrose climbed onto it with his executioner. He was not allowed to address the thousands who watched, hushed, waiting. Instead, the hangman had been instructed to place a copy of a laudatory account of Montrose's campaigns around his neck on a string. As was customary, the condemned man handed over a few coins in return for a speedy dispatch. Leaning against the stout beams of the gallows was a wide, heavy ladder. After he had pinned Montrose's arms behind his back and tied them, the hangman guided him up its steps and put the noose around his neck. 'God have mercy on this afflicted land,' shouted the condemned man before he was pushed off the ladder.

The crowd will have gasped. If his neck did not snap, Montrose will have convulsed involuntarily, his legs kicking, looking for footing in the air, urine darkening his breeches. So that all could see that a brutal justice had been done and they would pass on news of the death of an enemy of the state, the body was left to hang for three hours. And for further effect, Montrose's head was hacked off by the hangman and spitted on a spike on the Tolbooth, where it remained rotting for eleven years. After the restoration of the Stuart monarchy in 1660, the skull was removed and replaced by a freshly decapitated head, that of Archibald Campbell, Earl of Argyll, Montrose's great adversary.

Tourists who amble down Edinburgh's High Street, snapping selfies, staring vacantly at the souvenir shops, the window displays of malt whisky bottles and shortbread, and passing the kilted guides are often vaguely aware that history rumbled over its cobbles for centuries, but they have little idea just how raw and brutal that history could be. Or that the High Street itself shaped much that took place there. It was a theatre, a cockpit, a place where rioters pursued politicians, kirk ministers and judges, where the old Scottish

Parliament was dissolved and the new reconvened. It was a densely packed rookery of tottering tenements sometimes fourteen stories high, the most crowded city in Europe, a place where by the middle of the eighteenth century 30,000 people lived in a tiny area, piled on top of each other. The High Street was a seething pressure cooker which occasionally exploded, and it was a place where debates fizzed and ideas flowered, where the beginnings of the Scottish Enlightenment dazzled the world. An English visitor of 1750, Mr Amyat, remarked that it was possible to stand at the Mercat Cross and take fifty men of genius and learning by the hand in a few minutes. Edinburgh's High Street is far from a hidden way, but behind the welter of tartanry, the shop windows, the restaurants and the hotels a half-forgotten history is hidden.

What circumscribed and compressed the city was the deposit of an emergency. After the disastrous defeat at the Battle of Flodden in 1513, when James IV and many Scottish noblemen were killed, an English invasion was thought imminent. At any moment, the Earl of Surrey would lead his victorious army up the Great North Road to plunder the defenceless city. In reality, the English army had taken severe casualties in winning their victory and was in no condition to go anywhere but home. Nevertheless the panicking burgesses ordered a wall to be hurriedly thrown up. The northern flank of the Old Town was protected by the stinking Nor Loch, where Princes Street Gardens now flourish, and the west by the cliffs of the Castle Rock. From the now demolished Netherbow Port at the foot of the High Street, the new wall ran south down St Mary's Street and from there climbed up the steep incline of the Pleasance before turning right along Drummond Street and College Street and following the ridge of Lauriston Place westwards.

Then it turned north down Heriot Place to link with the West Port and the Grassmarket. The city authorities maintained the Flodden Wall less out of a concern for defence (in places it was little more than someone's back garden wall) and more as a means of defining the city. Municipal funds derived mainly from customs paid on goods coming through the gates to Edinburgh's markets and, while it would not have resisted an army, or even a regiment, the wall did deter smugglers and illegal traders.

In 1513, the fact that the Flodden Wall defined an area of only 143 acres was less of a problem than it later became. And the nature of the site, what Robert Louis Stevenson called 'his precipitous city', also made urban life difficult. When he became king of Scotland in 1124, David I set up what he called '*meum burgum*' of Edinburgh. As they surveyed the site of the king's new town, royal officers had a defining impact. The High Street runs down what is called a volcanic tail. Edinburgh Castle is built on a plug of very hard igneous rock and when the glaciers began to rumble across the land that would become Scotland at the end of the last Ice Age, some moved eastwards, the debris of rocks and other rubbish locked inside them scarting out river courses and depositing soil and loose rock. When they came up against the Castle Rock, the glaciers divided and clawed out the deep ravines of the Cowgate and Princes Street Gardens, leaving a sloping tail of rock and soil in its leeward, eastern side. The High Street is built on this tail.

To cope with this awkward site, the king's surveyors laid out a main street along the highest point, the backbone of the tail. And so that many craftsmen and shopkeepers could enjoy a frontage onto the market street, the building plots were narrow, perhaps only twenty-five feet across, but also very long, sometimes as much as 450 feet. Pegged out by men called liners, they were also steep, running down to the ravines on either side. The plots were usually divided into forelands with a street frontage and backlands behind. These were reached by narrow closes or alleyways and some still bear the names of people who lived in medieval Edinburgh. When two or more plots were owned by a single individual and they built a continuous street frontage, the backlands could be accessed through a pend or vennel, a vaulted passageway with an arch at each end. Wealthy or aristocratic town dwellers often preferred not to live directly on the street and they built houses in the backlands, away from the bustle and stink of the busy thoroughfare, and the likes of Lady Stair's Close and Tweeddale Court remember a time when the quality lived up a close.

The medieval town was laid out around the old kirk of St Giles, and the ridge to the west, towards the castle, was thought too narrow for housing. In any case, the defenders of the ramparts wanted a clear, open field of fire at what was their only vulnerable point. In 1753 the ridge was broadened with earth dug up for the foundations of City Chambers and converted into a parade ground. Below it the Lawnmarket was where farmers brought their produce in from the surrounding countryside. Its name has nothing to do with lawns; it is a reflection of old pronunciation. Out of the mouths of medieval townspeople 'land' sounded broader, like 'lawnd'. The street was laid out by the liners so that it was also broad, wide enough to allow the erection of stalls selling vegetables, grain, eggs and other essentials.

The line of the High Street narrowed dramatically at St Giles, where the ramshackle Tolbooth intruded and created a bottleneck only twelve feet wide. Demolished between 1811 and 1813, this old building was the centre of commercial and civic life, as well as acting as a prison for the likes of

Montrose, and it was where customs dues were paid by stallholders and merchants. Nothing remains of it now except a heart-shaped design picked out in cobbles near St Giles. It is also a reference to Walter Scott's famous novel, *The Heart of Midlothian*. The selfie-takers sometimes have to suddenly skip sideways in disgust when a local person spits on it, often without pausing. They do it in memory of the Tolbooth. It was said that when prisoners were taken out to face execution, they spat in a gesture of defiance.

One such was Neil MacLeod. On 3 April 1613, MacLeod shivered in his white sark as soldiers led him from the Tolbooth to the gallows. A bitter wind blew up the High Street, straight off the sea, and the huge crowd bayed as they saw the Lewisman climb up to the wooden platform. James VI and I had sanctioned what amounted to the colonisation of part of his kingdom, the Isle of Lewis, by a group of Lowlanders who called themselves the Gentlemen Adventurers of Fife, and Neil MacLeod's crime was to resist them. He believed himself betrayed: he had given the crown information, surely he would be pardoned. MacLeod looked over the heads of the jeering crowd for the rider who would come clattering over the cobbles from Holyrood waving the piece of paper in the air.

'Come on, Bhodach!' barked one of the executioners. 'We haven't got all bloody day.' Not having a word of English, all MacLeod heard was Bhodach, old man. Flying into a rage, he roared back, *'Nam bithin air deck luinge far am bu duilich do fhear seasamh, stiuireadh na mara gu tric, cha bhodach dhuit mis' a mhacain!'* – 'If I was on the deck of a ship, steering over the billows, trying to stand steady, you would not call me an old man!' And then, with his hands tied behind his back, MacLeod headbutted the executioner who had insulted him. The crowd gasped and then began screaming insults, none of which the Chief of the MacLeods of Lewis understood.

As he was pelted with rubbish, the condemned man looked once more down the High Street and realised that he was lost, and what was more, his death would not be quick. Unlike Montrose, he had not thought to give coins to the hangman and there would be no quick dispatch, no hangers-on would pull at his legs to put him out of his agony. The crowd screamed abuse and the Highlander had the noose looped over his head and the rope was thrown over a high beam. When it was taut, the executioners began to pull hard and lift the choking, retching man off his feet. He pissed himself and then lost consciousness before the hangmen suddenly let go of the rope and he crashed down onto the platform. The crowd cheered as a bucket of water was splashed over MacLeod and he was dragged over to the block. There was silence as the men held him down, their feet on his back, and the axe was raised high. More blood spattered on the cobbles of the High Street.

From their bedroom windows, people watched Scotland's history rumble up and down below them. Executions were not infrequent and there were religious processions to the High Kirk, as well as the formal occasions when the judiciary and the government began their sessions and meetings. Politics took place in the open air, often in full view of the densely packed tenements that lined the High Street. They were vast, sprawling and structurally very unstable. By the seventeenth century, the Great Tenement that stood near St Giles, where the Signet Library now is, had climbed to a dizzying and dangerous fourteen floors. Fire was a constant danger and the town council banned the use of thatch, insisting on tile or slate roofing. Tenements sometimes collapsed, but such was the pressure on space, they were quickly rebuilt.

The intensity of urban life in Edinburgh meant that all sorts of people might live in the same tenement. While the legal and mercantile classes dined in elegant rooms, people far down the social scale could live in filthy, rat-infested hovels reached from the same stair. It was an ant-heap, and a map of 1724 shows an astonishing 337 closes and pends off the High Street, the Lawnmarket and the Canongate, beyond the Netherbow Port. The stink of sewage must have been ever-present. In the elegant dining rooms of the quality, sanitary arrangements were primitive. Under the sideboard in many dining rooms sat a chamber pot – the original reason why the ladies withdrew to the withdrawing room was so that the male diners could use it. The drinking culture (claret being a preferred tipple) of the Old Town was legendary. Male guests often slid off their chairs and literally drank themselves under the table. One was appalled, waking up from his stupor believing he was being strangled. 'But I'm just the laddie that loosens the cravats,' said the imagined assailant. That such a job existed is eloquent.

The Edinburgh chronicler Robert Chambers saw something of the aftermath of marathon sessions with the bottle: 'Nothing was so common in the morning as to meet men of high rank and dignity reeling home from a close in the High Street where they had spent the night in drinking.'

Another job created by this culture has bequeathed a term only used on golf courses. In eighteenth and nineteenth century Edinburgh, caddies escorted drunks who could afford to pay them through the streets and deposited them at their own front doors. Behind which, wrath no doubt waited. Caddies could interpret the vague waving of a wealthy inebriate and also fend off any who tried to relieve the man of his valuables. Although they were described as ragged, half-blackguard-looking, these men and boys had a reputation for honesty and dependability. Many will have conducted their swaying charges down the High Street more than once. Caddies also seem to have acted as an informal police force, and in the eighteenth century an English visitor reckoned that they were the reason for less housebreaking and fewer robberies than any other city. There is the sense of native guides in an urban jungle.

As a public space where the drama of raw politics played out, the centre of the old city could be a cockpit. For about a century, the Beast stalked the High Street, the Grassmarket and their closes. The City Guard, the local police force, cowered behind bolted doors when it roared. This was the infamous Edinburgh mob. Because of the intense overcrowding in the tenements, the mob could assemble in minutes as thousands poured onto the streets. Politicians were terrified of it, and if judges handed down verdicts that the Beast did not like, they were peebled – pelted with pebbles and worse. It flexed its muscles frequently and perhaps most infamously in the Porteous Riots of 1736. When the Scottish Parliament voted itself out of existence in 1707, the mob was outraged and rioting was very destructive. But the Beast could be tamed, even led and manipulated.

In the middle of the eighteenth century, a general emerged who could not only summon the Beast but control it. A cobbler who lived in the Cowgate, General Joe Smith was better known as 'Bowed Joseph' because of a severe deformity caused by rickets, a common urban condition usually brought on by childhood malnutrition. Although he was tiny and very overbent, Smith clearly had tremendous charisma. When he heard of an injustice, the little man picked up his drum and walked up and down the High Street banging it loudly. In minutes he could raise a mob of 10,000, and with them at his back, Smith set about righting wrongs.

After a poor harvest and the consequent scarcity, merchants were selling oatmeal at a premium. This was a staple, the main ingredient of porridge, but before any hardship could follow, Smith forced the dealers to restrict their prices. When one merchant was found to be giving short measures, the drum was heard in the High Street and not only was the miscreant forced to deal out full measures, but the mob also ransacked his shop and house. Powerless to act, the City Guard watched.

Bowed Joseph became an unelected Tribune of the People. The Town Council was forced to defer to him often, and actively sought his services as a mediator and peacemaker. He always insisted that the burgesses pay for a hogshead of ale for the mob. His power appears to have derived from his probity. There is no record of him prospering because of his position and he seems always to have acted in defence of the rights of ordinary citizens. Nevertheless, the Provost and his council no doubt breathed a sigh of relief when news came that Smith had fallen off the top of a stagecoach bringing him home from Leith Races in the summer of 1780 and died of his injuries.

In the closes off the High Street, a ferment of a different sort bubbled. The cheek-by-jowl intensity of life in the Old Town was undoubtedly a factor in the cultural phenomenon known as the Scottish Enlightenment. All of the great men knew each other and met often. Before being conducted home by the caddies, they talked and argued long into the night. Clubs and societies were formed, pamphlets and periodicals written, and institutions formed. The High Street now shows little sign of that remarkable period in the second half of the eighteenth century. How could it, except for the erection of plaques at places like Anchor Close where *Encyclopaedia Britannica* was founded? Perhaps the most concrete legacy of the Enlightenment was the demise of the Old Town as the centre of the city. In 1767, James Craig won a competition to find the best layout for a New Town. The site was across the Nor Loch on what was called Bearford's Parks and building soon began.

In what was called the Great Flitting, the wealthy and aristocratic moved out of the evil-smelling rookeries of the High Street and across to 'houses to themselves'. As carts were piled high with their possessions, the poor and ordinary came out to see them off, no doubt shouting good riddance after them. The Old Town quickly became run-down, although the law courts and the city government stayed in the High Street.

Between 1976 and 1981, I worked in an office at 176 High Street, next to Old Assembly Close. At the tender, inexperienced age of 25, I found myself running the Edinburgh Festival Fringe and, in the happy years I spent in that job, I came to love the High Street. I still do. It seemed to me to pulse with life, some of it reputable, some disreputable, all of it exciting. Up the street was the Court of Session and pinstriped advocates inhabited the pubs around, while almost across the road were the offices and printing works of *The Scotsman* and the *Edinburgh Evening News*. Local government went on in City Chambers and in those days up at the headquarters of Lothian Region on the corner with George IV Bridge. Each year when the General Assembly of the Church of Scotland met in May, a detachment of soldiers marched up the High Street, heading for the castle. I was never quite sure why they did that, but we all turned out of the Fringe Office to watch anyway. It was part of working in the High Street.

What was less exciting was the condition of many of the buildings. The Old Tron Kirk was empty, weeds grew out of the guttering on some of the high tenements above the shops on the High Street and down many of the closes; it was squalid. Rubbish of all sorts lay around and few people wanted to live in the dark, old medieval backlands. Over in the New Town flats were huge and filled with light. My wife and I lived in one. But compared with the Old Town, the straight lines and grey ashlar of the Georgian terraces were a little soulless.

In 1979, I had an idea. We had built the Fringe into the largest arts festival in the world and hundreds of thousands came to our shows. I was determined to do more and expand our audience, and so I had the idea of turning the High Street back into a theatre. But rather than mounting public executions, popular though they would have been, I wanted to encourage Fringe performers to do bits from their shows for free on platforms, off the back of lorries, on the drying greens off the closes on the south side. We would close the High Street at George IV Bridge and North Bridge, and so that disruption was at a minimum we would do all this on a Sunday during the festival. Fringe Sunday. It would bring thousands, many of them having their first glimpse of the shows that played all over the city. Great idea.

No, said the police. Not a great idea: the crowds would be difficult to control, traffic would snarl up in the centre of the city, and the minister at St Giles would object to actors 'cavorting' outside while he held his Sabbath service. They actually used the word cavorting. Like the callow, accepting young man I was, I did not think to question this. But then, I thought, why not go and ask the minister at St Giles what he thought? The Rev. Gilleasbuig Macmillan thought it was a great idea, and no, the police had not talked to him. This time with the support of John Crichton, Convener of Lothian Region, and a thoroughly good man, I went back to see the police.

On Sunday 24 August 1980, Shona Munro, my lovely assistant, held one end of a rope attached to a lamppost while I ran across the High Street to close it to traffic. Jenny Brown did the same down at South Bridge. For the first time in generations, the High Street was closed to traffic, and then the fun began. The police were right about one thing, thousands came, maybe ten thousand on that first afternoon. Bowed Joseph would have been proud. Rowan Atkinson, Richard Curtis, Will Bowen and their crew had converted the Wireworks into a theatre, and on the drying green opposite Pete McCarthy and the Cliffhanger Theatre Company made crowds laugh and cheer. It felt to me that the High Street had come alive again, and since 1980 traffic has been much reduced and life has spilled outside once more, Edinburgh weather permitting.

On a sunny 1 July 1999, another sort of procession made its way up the High Street. Led by the Queen and Prince Philip and Donald Dewar, the first First Minister of Scotland, newly elected members made their way to the Church of Scotland's Assembly Hall on the Mound, the temporary home of the Scottish Parliament. Almost 300 years after the last meeting and the riots in the High Street, a new elected body reconvened to govern Scotland. In two decades, its presence in its permanent home at the foot of the Canongate has revitalised Edinburgh's Old Town and put the High Street back into the centre of the city's life.

Every August, during the Edinburgh Festival Fringe, I make a point of walking up the High Street. After some excellent coffee at the Netherbow Centre, I make my way through the crowds to the Tron Kirk, where the street becomes pedestrianised. The Fringe is what makes the Edinburgh Festival different from all of the other festivals in the world: its performers spill onto the street to advertise their shows, and jugglers, acrobats, fire-eaters and all sorts of entertainers stand at the centre of small crowds who happily put coins into a hat. I like to pass my old office and then move on to the High Kirk of St Giles, where the Tolbooth stood and the grim rituals of execution took place. Instead musicians and mimes perform, a theatre of a very different sort but just as venerable in its way. During the Fringe, the High Street comes alive – and as I walk up it, a smile never leaves my face. I am proud to have been part of its flowering and glad that it makes so many others smile.

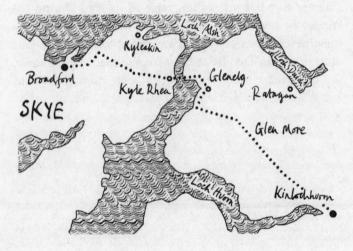

The Green Roads 6

6

The Green Roads

Glenelg into the Mountains

This is a series of snapshots. The great drove roads of Scotland that led out of the Highlands and Uplands and down to markets in the Lowlands and beyond are often very long, and I decided not to risk a walk that would have taken several days through remote and sometimes trackless terrain. One of my guiding principles was not so much endurance as enjoyment.

However, the drove roads were very important in their time and all have fallen out of use. No survey of Scotland's hidden ways could omit them. For practical reasons, I decided to begin the road that ran from Skye and follow it into the mountains – but not far, and relying on distant memory as well as recent experience.

That memory of the drove roads was what sparked my own interest in the Gaelic language. Later in my life I learned a little and thereby understood far more of the Highlands, its history and how to pronounce its geography. When I returned to Glenelg last year, I remembered how perfectly attuned the landscape and its language can be.

Anxious to make an early start, I brewed some strong coffee, poured it into a lidded mug and stuck it in the holder just below the dashboard of my ancient Range Rover. It was black-dark, moonless and still. When I fired the engine and switched on the headlights, the crows squabbled and lifted off the Top Wood. Bumping down the track to the tarmac road, I began a long journey back into my past and also a time that has long vanished into the darkness of the deeper past. Too early for much traffic up Gala Water and the usual congestion on the Edinburgh Bypass, I found myself on the empty M9 to Stirling by the time the sun was climbing into the eastern sky. It picked out the tops of the Ochil Hills and, beyond them, the mountains.

Fifty years ago, on a school hiking holiday, I had made the same journey and it has stayed with me all these years. We stayed at a youth hostel at Ratagan on the southern shore of Loch Duich, and when I reached Shiel Bridge and the turn off for Glenelg I parked the Range Rover nearby. What had been a very basic and draughty building now looked spruce, even inviting. The sun glinted across the loch and, although it was early October, the leaves were still on the trees by the roadside. My main memory of that school trip was a sense of otherness, of literally incomprehensible difference, and of the climate. The last time I had been at Ratagan it had rained. Incessantly.

Youth hostels had a strict policy of expulsion. After breakfast all those staying had to leave and were not allowed back under the hostel roof until late afternoon, whatever the weather. As the endless rain fell steadily out of leaden skies, day after day, we mooched around, sometimes sitting for hours in a large bus shelter, hands in pockets, complaining, bored. Sometimes we just plodded along the shore road, getting wet. We eked out cups of coffee at the roadside café at Shiel Bridge, trying to sit as long as possible in the dry. But it was closed on a Sunday, this being the Sabbatarian Highlands, and I decided to brave the penetrating drizzle and go for a walk along the road by the loch. Around a corner, I came to a large, nondescript green hut with a green corrugated-iron roof, but it seemed a popular destination. Cars were drawing up, parking on the verge, and out of them appeared men and women in their Sunday best. On closer inspection, the hut turned out to be a church, a Free Presbyterian Church.

Having become very wet, my militant teenage atheism seemed less important than shelter. It was packed inside and I found space on a bench at the back. From, it seemed, nowhere the minister appeared, stately in his black robes. He had a mane of white hair and a jutting jaw, much like the Scottish actor Finlay Currie, who occasionally played God in Hollywood epics. Raincoats steamed gently in the warmth. The minister bowed his head and intoned what I took to be a prayer. I had no real idea because he spoke a language that was not English, or even a Highland version, but something I had never heard before. And then the minister smiled, looked directly at me and said something like, 'Vissitors are alwayss welcome. Ass you can see, there iss a hymn book in the pocket on the back of the chair in front, if you take my meaning.' I picked it up and prepared to intone 'Onward Christian Soldiers' or 'Be Thou My Vision'.

Before I could open the hymn book, the minister reverted to Gaelic and there began the most extraordinary church service I ever witnessed, before or since. '*Air ceann na seinn*, Iain MacRae,' the minister announced, and a tall, cadaverously thin man stood forward and turned to the congregation. With no accompaniment, he started to sing. At first it seemed off-key, not conventionally melodious, more like chanting than singing – but it was hypnotic. Once Mr MacRae had sung a line, the congregation sang it back to him in a surge of harmony, hung with grace notes that swooped and soared like flocks of birds, and almost before they had finished he began a second line. The noise was immense, almost deafening, but it was dramatically counterpointed by Mr MacRae's reedy solo voice. Having no Gaelic, I had no idea what any of it meant, but it was astonishingly beautiful, the musical equivalent of the majesty of the mountains, the sweep of the high passes and the elemental power of the ocean. Even though it was to be many years before I would understand something of the words, the devotion and raw emotion behind them was palpable. I have heard sung masses in Italian cathedrals, but nothing compares to this remarkable expression of profound belief in the majesty of God and His Creation. As the rise and fall of the singing and its apparent seamlessness reverberated in the little church, I was silent, transfixed, and it felt as though a history and a culture closed to me was beginning to open.

Back in my old car, I drove up the steep road to Glenelg, hugging the flanks of Mam Ratagan. After a series of dizzying bends, there appeared a car park just at the point where the view to the north opened. East of the head of Loch Duich was Beinn Fhada, the Long Mountain, and beside it the peaks of the Five Sisters of Kintail. Even after all these years the psalms echoed in my head and their cadences seemed a perfect accompaniment to all the glory I could see from the side of Mam Ratagan.

By the time I parked at the Glenelg Inn, it was early afternoon and I quickly dumped my bag in a spare, chilly bedroom at the back. In the bar a welcome fire blazed and the food was good. But I wanted to make the most of what daylight was left and drove a short distance further north so that I could climb a hill. Glenelg is on the mainland shore of the Sound of Sleat, the slice of the Atlantic that makes Skye an island, and its waters narrow dramatically at Kyle Rhea. Despite the recent bridge at Kyle of Lochalsh, a ferry still crosses the straits near Glenelg. I did not have to climb very high to see what I had come to see.

To the north, the narrows of Kyle Rhea open out into Loch Alsh, a sea loch that also fills from the west through the straits at Kyleakin. Both create a funnelling effect that forces the falling and rising tides through very quickly, sometimes at seven or eight knots. But the paradox is that Loch Alsh was also very attractive to shipping, especially in the centuries of sail, because it was a safe anchorage, sheltered from the worst of the Atlantic storms. And it could also be effectively defended at the two straits. King Haakon of Norway and his sea-lords knew it well and that was why their great fleet mustered in Loch Alsh before sailing south to Largs and defeat at the hands of the forces of Alexander II in 1263. At least 120 warships bobbed at anchor, their colours flying, and it must have been an awesome sight. It clearly impressed those who watched from the shore, for the occasion created the place name of Kyleakin. In Gaelic, it means 'the Narrows of Haakon'.

Once I had climbed high enough above the shortest crossing at Kyle Rhea, and the ferry ramp was well below me, the swirl of the sea fascinated me. The tide seemed to be flooding from the north, filling from Loch Alsh, but inshore there were eddies running in what looked like the opposite direction. A wind was getting up when I began to make my way back down to the road. It was blowing hard up the Sound of Sleat and against the flooding tide. Whitecaps flecked the surface and the sea roiled, making shallow troughs. All of which caused me to marvel at the skill and courage of the Highland cattle drovers.

For more than 150 years, the cattle trade was a vital part of the Highland economy, in effect the sole cash crop the region produced. After the Union of the Parliaments in 1707, markets in England opened up and they expanded dramatically as Britain embarked on its great drive for Empire. From 1739 to 1815, British armies and fleets were continuously in action all over the world, and after the spectacular successes of the Seven Years' War (1756 to 1763), when vast tracts of territory were gained in North America and dominance in India established, a huge demand for supplies was created. Soldiers and sailors on active duty needed to be fed and one of their principal staples was salt beef. The small black cattle of the Highlands were driven to market in their millions in the eighteenth and nineteenth centuries to sustain Britain's long imperial wars and the conflict with France and Napoleon.

Broadford in southern Skye was a gathering place for herds from across the Hebrides. Cattle were shipped from Lewis, Harris, the Uists and Benbecula to Uig and then driven south. In the late summer of 1723 a large drove was collected on Skye and then moved eastwards to the shore at Kyle Rhea, to the narrow straits. An account of 1813 tells what happened next:

> All the cattle reared in the Isle of Skye which are sent to the southern markets pass from that island to the mainland by the ferry of Kylerhea. Their numbers are very considerable, by some supposed to be 5,000 but by others 8,000 annually, and the method of ferrying them is not in boats . . . but they are forced to swim over Kylerhea. For this purpose the drovers purchase ropes which are cut at the length of three feet having a noose at one end. This noose is put round the under-jaw of every cow, taking care to have the tongue free. The reason given for leaving the tongue loose is that the animal may be able to keep the salt water from

going down its throat in such a quantity as to fill all the cavities in the body which would prevent the action of the lungs; for every beast is found dead and said to be drowned at the landing place to which this mark of attention has not been paid. Whenever the noose is put under the jaw, all the beasts destined to be ferried together are led by the ferryman into the water until they are afloat, which puts an end to their resistance. Then every cow is tied to the tail of the cow before [in front] until a string of six or eight be joined. A man in the stern of the boat holds the rope of the foremost cow. The rowers then play their oars immediately. During the time of high water or soon before or after full tide is the most favourable passage because the current is then least violent. The ferrymen are so dextrous that very few beasts are lost.

Once the cattle had shaken off the sea water and been untied, the drovers moved them inland from Glenelg to Glen Shiel before reaching the Great Glen at Fort Augustus. From there they pushed on into the mountains and over the difficult Pass of Corrieyairack and thence to Dalwhinnie and on down the Tummel towards the Lowland markets.

Scotland is patterned by hundreds of droving routes and many preferred to strike through the hills and mountain glens and avoid the hard surfaces of roads. Raised on rough upland pasture in the summer and on the soft winter grazing down in the glens, black cattle had soft feet and it was essential to avoid the risk of lameness. A beast that slowed the herd was a liability and drovers would sometimes be forced to slaughter it and either sell the carcass wherever they could or eat the beef themselves and feed the offal to their dogs. Having managed the dangers of the Kyle Rhea crossing, some drovers took an alternative route to avoid Glen Shiel and turned up into Glen More and the mountains beyond. They left behind an indelible trace in the landscape.

Having packed my bag at the Glenelg Inn, I turned off the road back to Shiel Bridge and bumped over a weather-beaten track flanked by commercial forestry. And when the track petered out I parked on the banks of a fast-flowing burn. Once across, I could see the open uplands of Glen More, and on a rise about a mile away an old bothy. Clearly still in use, the door was bolted with a wide hasp and padlock, but there was a welcome bench outside. The path up from the plantation had been difficult and the burns all swollen by recent rain. But from the bothy I could see something remarkable – a trail that had not been travelled for 150 years but was still fresh. On the floor of the glen, as it rises towards the pass between the Saddle and Beinn nan Caorach, there are several wide areas of very lush grass. Mostly free from ferns, bracken and heather, they are luminous in the spring and lush in the autumn, oases of brilliant lime green amongst the darker colours of the mountainsides. No freaks of botany or climate, these verdant splashes are not natural but a legacy of droving. These are stances, places where the Skye drovers stopped overnight with their huge herds of black cattle. Late every summer, they were halted in the same place and they mucked the same ground until it became unusually fertile. Every ten or twelve miles, through some of the remotest mountain passes, these extraordinary green memories of the tramp of more than a million beasts can be seen.

Once over the pass, the drovers guided their herds slowly downhill to the head of Loch Huorn, to a farm place marked on the map as Kinlochhuorn. It is one of the most remote, most beautiful places in Britain.

Many years ago I decided to walk with some friends as

far as we could without using a road, not by avoiding them but by making a journey where there was none, travelling only on foot or perhaps on horseback. Even as a young man I liked maps and had begun to collect the Ordnance Survey Pathfinder series. Knoydart took my fancy, a place known to history as 'the Rough Bounds': a mountainous peninsula bounded by sea lochs, Nevis to the south and Huorn to the north. After a long train journey to Mallaig, we caught the ferry to Inverie on the northern shore of Loch Nevis. Ferry was perhaps an overstatement. It was little more than an open skiff with a good engine, a cabin at the front for the helmsman and open seats behind for passengers. Mercifully, the weather was good. Once we cleared the harbour, the aspect of Knoydart from the sea was stunning, and forbidding. We planned to reach Kinlochhuorn in two, maybe three days, and since I had at least another day or two days' walking beyond that, we sent a small parcel of food to the farmer, a Mr Macdonald, and asked him to keep it for us. I understood that the post came along a single-track road from Invergarry at least once a week and I hoped it would bring some tins of stew, beans and some biscuits, supplies that were too heavy for our rucksacks. I wouldn't care if our jammie dodgers were broken. As I stepped off the ferry at Inverie, I just hoped that the parcel had arrived.

On the first night, we slept in a bothy by a lochan below the glowering summit of Luinne Bheann. There were bales of hay at one end, probably put there by the farmer to feed his sheep in the bad winter weather. We decided not to risk a fire in the soot-blackened grate and, to my surprise, we fell fast asleep as soon as darkness came.

The following morning we found the walking easy, even though we were following sheepwalks. They are usually too narrow for human feet, but we made good progress up through the Barrisdale Pass. It must have been afternoon when we saw the farmhouse at Kinlochhuorn. I have a clear memory of it, looking down from a height at the house nestling at the foot of Buidhe Beinn, the Yellow Mountain. But it seemed to take a long time to reach it.

When at last I knocked on the door, an older lady answered, not in the least perturbed to have visitors. I told her my name and that I had been in correspondence with Mr Macdonald, but she made no reply and just smiled. My spirits sank and my companions sighed. But this had to be Kinlochhuorn, the only house for ten miles in any direction. I asked again for Mr Macdonald, more slowly. 'Ah,' she said at last and turned to look up to the slopes of the mountain. 'Macdonald iss approaching.'

When he and his dogs finally arrived, Mr Macdonald nodded to me without a word, disappeared into the house and returned with our small parcel. Glory be. I thanked him profusely and he smiled and nodded again. I am not sure when I realised that Mrs Macdonald was not deaf or very shy but that she spoke very little English, and Mr Macdonald preferred not to. He had certainly understood my letter because he wrote back in the stamped addressed letter I had enclosed. Thinking about that encounter now, it seems likely that Kinlochhuorn was a blessed oasis, with no access to a radio signal and certainly not TV or telephone. Why would Mr and Mrs Macdonald speak anything else except Gaelic to each other and their dogs? That snapshot, taken forty years ago, was of a world that was fading, fast disappearing as English advanced into the mountains and the glens.

In the eighteenth and nineteenth centuries the drovers who brought their herds down to the pasture at Kinlochhuorn spoke to each other in Gaelic and may also have had very little or no English. As late as 1891 there were 44,000 monoglot Gaelic speakers out of a speech community of 211,000 and most of them lived west of the Great Glen. It was not only their language that made the drovers seem strange, even alien to many Lowlanders. They looked different. As Highlanders, they wore 'belted plaids, girt, like women's petticoats down to the knee: their thighs and half of their leg all bare', as one observer wrote in 1723. Others thought the drovers bear-like, bearded and swathed in thick tweed that stank of heather, peat smoke and worse. Wild men, they might also be very dangerous because each was armed. All carried swords and daggers at their belts and some had pistols. The Disarming Acts that followed the Jacobite Rebellions of 1715 and 1745 specifically exempted drovers and they were legally allowed to bear arms – because they needed them.

Cattle raiding was common and the herds were much more vulnerable when they were on the move. The most famous Highland cattle thief was romanticised by Walter Scott and several modern films have also turned Rob Roy MacGregor into a hero. In reality, he was a blackmailer – the term originated amongst the Border Reivers and it literally meant 'black rent', or protection money. Scott put a good description of attitudes to MacGregor in the mouth of Bailie Nicol Jarvie:

> Troth, I wad advise only friends o' mine to gree wi' Rob; for watch as they like and do what they like, they are sair apt to be harried when the lang nights come on. Some o' the Grahame and Cohoon gentry stood out; but what then – they lost their hail stock the same winter; sae maist folk now think it best to come into Rob's terms. He's easy wi' a'body that will be easy wi' him, but if ye thraw him ye had better thraw the deevil.

The drovers who passed by Kinlochhuorn will have been watchful, particularly if they had omitted to pay blackmail. In the Rough Bounds of Knoydart, one of the most notorious protection racketeers was Colin MacDonell of Barrisdale. He levied what seems like an extortionate (which, of course, it was) £500 a year for 'cattle protection' on his neighbours and if they could not or would not pay, he stole their beasts. The Skye drovers must have known of MacDonell and made plans – either way. The green roads could be very dangerous indeed, and those who travelled through the territory of the Camerons, the Mackenzies and the MacGregors needed to be well armed and well aware, or have brought cash with them.

Beyond Kinlochhuorn, the drovers struck out east to Glen Quoich and the northern shoreline of the loch. From there, they made for Invergarry, where they crossed the Great Glen to climb up and over the Pass of Corrieyairack and on to Dalwhinnie. In the late summer of 1723, a drove was observed by a travelling clergyman, Bishop Forbes. The skills of the drovers impressed him:

They had four or five horses with provisions for themselves by the way, particularly blankets to wrap themselves in when sleeping in the open air, as they rest on the bleak mountains, the heathy moors, or the verdant glens, just as it happens, towards the evening. They tend their flocks [he means herds] by night and never move till about eight in the morning and then march the cattle at leisure that they may feed a little as they go along. They rest awhile at midday to take some dinner and so let the cattle feed and rest as they please. The proprietor does not travel with the cattle but has one [man] for his deputy to command the whole and he goes to the place appointed against the day fixed for the fair. When the flock is very large, as the present, they divide it, though belonging to one, into several droves that they may not hurt one another in narrow passes, particularly on bridges many of which they go along. Each drove has a particular number of men with some boys to look after the cattle.

At the beginning of the time of the Highland drovers, Crieff was their principal destination and in the first half of the eighteenth century it was the greatest centre for the circulation of money in Scotland; more cash and bills of exchange were handed over in this small town on the fringes of the Highlands than in either Glasgow or Edinburgh.

By 1800, Falkirk had become the preferred destination and, as this account of 1849 by Thomas Gisborne shows, the cattle markets were tremendous spectacles. It is a wonderfully vivid description worth quoting at length:

[At Falkirk people] will there witness a scene to which certainly Great Britain, perhaps even the whole world, does not afford a parallel . . . There are three trysts [markets] every year – the first in August, the second in September, and the last and largest in October. The cattle stand in a field in the parish of Larbert at a distance of nearly three miles from Falkirk, at a place called Stenhousemuir. The field on which they assemble contains above 200 acres, well-fenced and in every way adapted for the purpose. The scene, seen from horseback, from a cart, or some erection, is particularly imposing. All is animation, bustle, business and activity; servants running about shouting to the cattle, keeping them together in their particular lots and ever and anon cudgels are at work upon the horns and rumps of the restless animals that attempt to wander in search of grass or water.

The cattle dealers of all descriptions, chiefly on horseback, are scouring the field in search of the lots they require. The Scottish drovers are for the most part mounted on small, shaggy, spirited ponies that are obviously quite at home among the cattle; and they carry their riders through the throngest groups [of cattle] with astonishing alacrity. The English dealers have, in general, large, stout horses, and they pace the ground with more caution, surveying every lot carefully as they go along. When they discover the cattle they want, they enquire the price. A good deal of riggling takes place, and when the parties come to an agreement, the purchaser claps a penny of arles [a deposit] into the hand of the stockholder, observing at the same time 'It's a bargain'. Tar dishes are then got, and the purchaser's mark being put upon the cattle, they are driven from the field. Besides numbers of shows, from 60 to 70 tents are erected along the field for selling spirits and provisions . . . What an indescribable clamour prevails in most of these party-coloured abodes!

Far in the afternoon, when frequent calls have elevated the spirits and stimulated the colloquial powers of the visitors, a person hears the uncouth Cumberland jargon and the prevailing Gaelic, along with innumerable provincial dialects, in their genuine purity, mingled in one astounding roar. All seem inclined to speak: and raising their voices to command attention, the whole of the orators are obliged to bellow as loudly as they can possibly roar. When the cattle dealers are in the way of their business, their conversation is full of animation, and their technical phrases are generally appropriate and highly amusing.

The trysts were not the end of the trade. Only the beef of fat cattle can be successfully salted. When the salt reacts with the fat, it better draws out the moisture from the microbial cells that cause meat to rot, and crammed into barrels well-salted beef can keep for many months. This meant that the herds had to be slowly driven south and fattened on the lush pastures of Lincolnshire and East Anglia before going on to Smithfield in London. Those drovers who were not farmers and forced to return home for the harvest often continued the journey south and only left the beasts when they had settled on the grass of eastern England.

There exists a remarkable footnote to the droving years, a memory of journeys made not by the cattle or their masters. Most herds were guided by pastoral dogs, the ancestors of collies, sometimes six or seven of them working together around a large drove. When they reached East Anglia and Lincolnshire, many of the drovers made for the nearest port to buy a passage on a ship sailing north to Scotland. To save trouble and expense, they often left their dogs behind to find their own way home, moving up the length of England and Lowland Scotland, hundreds of miles. These unaccompanied dogs were seen passing through villages and they were fed by innkeepers and farm places where they had overnighted on the way south. The following summer the drovers paid for the food their faithful dogs had eaten the year before.

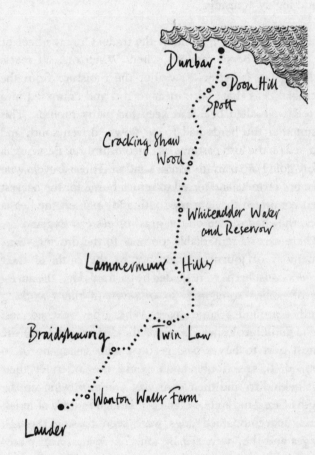

Dunbar
Doon Hill
Spott
Cracking Shaw Wood
Whiteadder Water and Reservoir
Lammermuir Hills
Braidshawrig
Twin Law
Wanton Walls Farm
Lauder

The Herring Road ⑦

7

The Herring Road

Dunbar to Lauder

I walked all but one of the hidden ways on my own, relishing the solitude and the sense of peace and singular purpose. But I realised that few people in the past walked alone. For one thing, it was risky. Not only were the roads preyed upon by robbers, there was no one to help a lone traveller if mishap befell them, an accident or the onset of extreme weather. And so it was good to walk with Nat Edwards, my partner in the Hidden Ways project, and to have his knowledge and observations at my side as we walked the Herring Road.

This was a remarkable commercial route along which fresh and salted fish travelled. Its sheer difficulty and the hardiness of the men – and the women – who walked across the tops of the Lammermuirs carrying tremendously heavy creels astounds me still. Their dogged and necessary determination puts most of our complaints about our cosseted lives to shame. None of these routes were easy in an age before engines, but of all the hidden ways the Herring Road demanded the most physical strength and stamina. Women carrying huge weights on their backs, planting one weary foot after another in soft and tussocky ground, their heads bowed into the whistling winds – I thanked providence that I did not have to do what they did.

In the late sixteeth century, as the fires of Reformation burned brightly across Scotland, ministers, readers, elders and their congregations were passionately engaged in a great enterprise, the establishment of a Godly Commonwealth. Having purged the nation of corrupt Catholicism, or so they thought, the reformers desired to make a society that lived by biblical precepts, by *God's ain law*. More, the most zealous believed that the Scots were a chosen people and they began to write and talk of Christ's Kingdom of Scotland. One of the pillars of the Godly Commonwealth was respect for the Sabbath, the Lord's Day; it was a day of rest and of worship, and most emphatically not a working day. If the Sabbath was broken, then *God's ain law* was broken.

On a bright, warm and windless Sunday morning in August 1577, the Reverend Andrew Simpson was walking to his church in Dunbar. Overlooking the old harbour, this was what is now Dunbar Parish Church, originally founded in 1342. The minister was surprised, and utterly appalled, to see many boats being made ready to go fishing, men piling nets into the sterns of large seagoing rowing boats. This was an affront to God's law; the Sabbath must be respected. It may even have been worse than a lapse, a return to the laxity of the Roman Church, an abomination so recently banished. These were the early years of a better country and the faith had to be kept.

Simpson marched over to the rocky shore to reprimand the fishermen. Most were not known to the fiery minister; they had come to Dunbar from all along the North Sea coast – it was said later that some boats had come across the sea from Holland – and they ignored his ranting. So many fishermen had gathered because out in the Forth there was treasure, in abundance: enough for all who cared to take it. The Lammas Drave had swum into the mouth of the firth. A vast shoal of herring, like nothing any fisherman had seen before, the surface boiled with the silver swirl of hundreds of thousands of fish.

The Reverend's rants made little impact: the men were

hurrying. The herring were practically jumping out of the water. But at last Simpson saw someone he recognised, one of his parishioners. And he saw that he had an ally. John Crawford was making ready his boat, but beside him stood his wife Agnes and their bairns. She was pleading with him not to go fishing, not to break the Sabbath. Simpson is said to have said, 'Know ye not that ye are now braving the wrath o' Him for whom the mighty ocean is just a drop?' The fisherman ignored the minister. 'John Crawford, harken unto ma voice, tae the voice o' yer wife and that o' yer bairns! And be not guilty o' this gross sin.'

John kissed his wife and weeping children, pushed his boat out into the deeper water and joined the huge flotilla as they rowed out into the Forth and into the midst of the Lammas Drave and its silver darlings. Meanwhile, the Reverend Simpson climbed his pulpit to deliver a thunderous rebuke. God's laws were being flouted, Christ's Kingdom of Scotland polluted. Sitting below in the congregation, Agnes Crawford wept, ashamed at her husband's impiety and, as the daughter of an elder of the kirk, ashamed for her family.

At this point in the story, its authorship becomes clearer. As the sermon reached its crescendo, the congregation heard the wind whip up off the firth and then they saw the skies darken. The roof of the kirk began to shake as the wind blew up into a storm. It was as if God was displeased. Then part of the steeple crashed to the ground. Women and children ran from the kirk to the shore, where the sight of carnage greeted them. A flat August calm had become a roiling, foam-flecked monster. Huge waves had swamped most of the open rowing boats and those on the shore gasped as they saw many had capsized and fishermen's bodies were being tossed on the crests of towering breakers. Their eyes stung by spindrift whipping off the firth, the women on the shore were helpless, transfixed by the scale of the unfolding tragedy. Perhaps 200 boats had gone out on that fateful Sunday morning and all seemed to have been inundated.

Suddenly someone in the crowd called, 'Look! Look! One still lives!' Close to the shore, a fisherman was being thrown around like a rag doll in the foaming sea, but he was moving, calling out across the howling wind for help. When he was lifted up by a billowing wave, some of the women recognised him. It was John Crawford. Agnes ran through the crowd and dived into the boiling sea to rescue her beloved husband. But her long skirts immediately wrapped around her legs and she began to founder. Others tried to reach her and were beaten back. Somehow, Agnes reached her drowning husband but the power of the undertow pulled them both back out to sea. Then a giant wave picked them up and threw them on to the rocks by the harbour. Before the sea could race back to pull them under, rescuers reached them quickly and dragged both back to dry land.

Agnes was half-drowned, retching, coughing up seawater, but beside her, John was not moving, not breathing. Onlookers cried out that he was dead, but Agnes pounded his chest. Suddenly he shuddered, then he breathed.

The Crawfords survived what became known as the Sabbath Wrecks, but more than 300 fishermen did not. The late sixteenth century reformers were not renowned for their empathy, and no doubt the Reverend Simpson played on themes of divine retribution and the paramount need to heed *God's ain law*. However, the storm and its calamitous consequences had another name attached, probably by fishermen rather than ministers. They called it the Lost Drave. It remembers how important the shoals of autumn herring were to Dunbar and many other fishing communities. Lives had been lost, but so had livelihoods.

The shoals used to appear off Scotland in a predictable cycle. The dense swirling draves, moving like vast flocks of glinting silver birds, darting and swooping in perfect unison just below the surface of the sea, were first seen off the shores of the Hebrides in May or June. Two week later, they had moved east to Shetland and by early August the Lammas Draves entered the Moray Firth and the Firth of Forth before they moved on south. The herring were no respecters of the Sabbath and that was why John Crawford and hundreds of other fishermen had to go to sea immediately. By the following day, the great shoals might have gone, moving down the North Sea coast.

Women also followed the shoals. Many came from the Hebrides. In Gaelic, they were called *Clann nighean an Sgadain*, the Herring Lasses. When the catch came ashore, their job was to gut the fish and pack them into barrels of salt and brine to preserve them. Some could work at dizzying speed, gutting a herring in three or four seconds. They worked in groups of three, and on the shore at Dunbar the tallest would pack the barrels (because she could reach the bottom), another would gut as the fish were tipped into a long trough, while a third sorted the fish by size. Because they were paid by the barrel, the herring lasses worked fast, but they never worked on a Sunday.

Not all of the fish landed were cured in barrels of brine, but if some were to be sold fresh, then they had to be sold quickly. All down the North Sea coastline fishwives gathered up herring into creels, wicker baskets, and carried them into towns where they could sell their husband's catch at markets or on street corners, often calling out their wares. 'Caller Herrin' was the traditional cry of Newhaven fishwives and it meant 'Fresh Herring'.

The Forth fishery reached its peak between 1850 and 1900.

After that stocks began to dwindle because of over-fishing and in some years the draves did not come at all. Untreated sewage from the growing city of Edinburgh and the industrial towns on the Fife shore, such as Kirkcaldy, Leven and Methil, fouled the sea badly. The great oyster beds off Leith and Portobello disappeared entirely and after the end of the First World War the great draves were never seen again.

A few boats still work out of Dunbar, many going after shellfish, but there is little left to remember the bustle of the herring industry and all its many hardships. A hidden way, however, sheds a bright light on what life was like when the shoals came into the Forth. Travelled in the eighteenth and nineteenth centuries, the Herring Road runs for twenty-nine miles from Dunbar across the Lammermuir Hills to the inland market town of Lauder. Pack horses carried creels, carts full of barrels creaked along and, astonishing as it may seem to us now, fishwives walked with creels on their backs. Some weighed a hundredweight, about fifty kilos. And they did it in a day.

I wanted to walk the Herring Road, but the Pathfinders marked several routes and in places the route seemed to peter out. And this was a journey across moorland hills with few roads and probably poor mobile signal. I needed a guide, someone who had done it before. Nat Edwards reckoned that the best, most appropriate start was McArthur's at Dunbar harbour. It is Britain's oldest fisherman's store still in use. Lobster pots and other clutter were piled next to the building, and to the east it looked over the old harbour where John and Agnes Crawford had been rescued centuries before.

I persuaded Nat that we should make a slight diversion so that we could walk past Dunbar Parish Church. A solid, foursquare, red sandstone building, its tower and nave seemed as though they had looked out over the sea for generations. In fact, apocalyptic events appear to have dogged its long history. On 3 January 1987, the church was gutted by fire, leaving only a blackened shell. But Dunbar responded magnificently and raised funds for restoration. Some of the unwavering piety of the old reformers persuaded parishioners to shiver through an Easter service in the roof-less ruins only three months after the blaze.

Most who plan to walk the Herring Road park their cars at the foot of the Lammermuirs, but Nat wanted to begin in Dunbar and then walk on a B road down to the village of Spott. Not only would it be a gentle preamble to the climb through the hills, it also allowed us to walk in the footsteps of history. And it turned out that resonances echoed at almost every turn in the quiet and green landscape.

Once we had ducked under the main line to London, just as a train thundered southwards, and cleared the southern suburbs of Dunbar, we came close to the site of a famous battle. It was a bloody contest between competing versions of the gospel truth. Led by their ruthless, charismatic general, the soldiers of another Godly Commonwealth had marched up the Great North Road to attack Scotland in the summer of 1650. The spark that ignited Oliver Cromwell's invasion flickered on a cold winter's morning in London. On 30 January 1649 'Charles Stuart, that Man of Blood' stepped through the middle window of the Banqueting House in Whitehall and onto a scaffold. Wearing a plain white shirt, he conducted himself with great dignity. When his head rolled over the boards and was picked up by the hair by the masked executioner, Charles I immediately became a martyr.

In Scotland, a group known as the Whiggamores (the ancestors of the Whig party), a fundamentalist Protestant sect, had taken over the government in what amounted to a *coup d'état* and they reacted with horror to the regicide. Known also as the 'Government of the Saints', they had supported a constitutional monarchy and quickly moved to contact the heir apparent, the man who would become Charles II. He was offered not only the crown of Scotland but also those of England and Ireland. There were conditions. The Government of the Saints insisted that Charles sign the National Covenant (this was no less than a covenant between the people of Scotland and God that had first been promulgated in 1638 and it formed one of the foundation stones of Scottish religious autonomy) and support the imposition of Presbyterianism in England and Ireland.

Now that they at last had their Covenanted King, the Government of the Saints had to look to the south and contend with Oliver Cromwell and the crack troops of his New Model Army. Scotland had proclaimed Charles II not only King of Scotland but also of England and Ireland, while less than a month after the execution of his father, the English parliament had abolished the monarchy. A collision was inevitable. In the summer of 1650 the New Model Army crossed the new stone bridge over the Tweed at Berwick, but the reaction of the Scottish government swung the balance significantly in Cromwell's favour. The Purging Committee of the Scottish army reduced its fighting effectiveness dramatically by weeding out all those suspected of having low morals or of being royalists rather than loyal to the Kirk. In all, eighty officers and around 3,000 experienced soldiers, some of them no doubt given to swearing and cursing, were dismissed. There existed a profound, fundamental belief that righteousness rather than military might was what mattered.

Like the pragmatic soldier he was, the commander of the Scottish army, Sir David Leslie, adapted his tactics. He sensibly avoided a direct confrontation in open field and instead adopted a scorched earth policy while barricading his weakened army behind strong fortifications around Edinburgh. In the absence of foraging or sourcing food locally, Cromwell was forced to supply his army through the harbour at Dunbar and when they withdrew to be closer to the port, Leslie mistook this for a general retreat. He deployed the Covenanter army on Doon Hill, which lay to the south of Dunbar, overlooking the Great North Road, Cromwell's only feasible line of march. And Nat and I were walking around its lower slopes. We could see that it was a strong position, dominating the narrow plain between the hills and the sea. The commander of the New Model Army despaired, feeling himself trapped:

> We are upon an engagement very difficult. The enemy has blocked up our way at the pass of Copperspath [Cockburnspath], through which we cannot get without almost a miracle. He [Leslie] lies upon the hills that we know not how to come that way without great difficulty; and our lying here daily consumes our men, who fall sick beyond imagination.

But righteousness once again prevailed over sound military sense when the radical ministers pressured Leslie to bring his men down off Doon Hill to attack Cromwell. Perhaps they could not wait for what seemed a certain victory for the invincible Army of the Covenant. Seeing that his enemy had inexplicably surrendered their great advantage, Cromwell ordered a general advance and his cavalry charged the Scots flank. The armies clashed on the flattish ground where the A1 and the main line now run side by side for about half a mile, not far from where Nat and I crossed them. Cromwell is said to have exclaimed, 'The Lord has delivered them into our hands!' It was more true than he knew. The Scots were utterly defeated.

The crash and clangour of war, of international politics and of the consequences of a ferocious piety seemed far distant when Nat and I walked into the pretty, picturesque village of Spott. By the side of the road stood a red sandstone doocot. With its crowstep gables and a slate roof, it is a lectern-style structure with no fewer than 1,422 nesting spaces. These look like a slightly larger stone version of the racks behind hotel receptions where they keep the keys. Nat pointed out some wild wood pigeons flapping in and out. But it seemed unlikely that anyone would go into the dovecot to wring their necks, as happened in the past. These buildings or their ruins are to be found all over rural Britain, and while they look like a quaint harking back to a pastoral past, in reality doocots were a handy source of pigeon meat.

Spott lies at the foot of Doon Hill, where Leslie's men camped in the summer of 1650, and plenty of water runs off its steep slopes. It feeds a spring known as St John's Well. On the other side of the road from the dovecot, it is an atmospheric place. Covered by a well squared sandstone structure, its water flowed in sufficient volume to supply Dunbar in the eighteenth and early nineteenth centuries. Long before then, it was the focus of an annual pilgrimage and dedicated to St John. Each summer, the Benedictine monks of Coldingham Priory walked to Spott to pray at what they believed was a holy well. Many of these had been revered in pre-Christian times and St John's Well certainly retains an elusive otherworldliness. Very much in what he saw as the demands of the here and now, Oliver Cromwell destroyed Coldingham Priory on his way north to victory at Dunbar.

Beyond the village, the landscape continues to be littered with the relics of piety, only this time one that needed to be remembered rather than celebrated. The Godly Commonwealth's greatest threat was not the flouting of the Sabbath, sinful though that was, it was the foul power of Satan. His evil agents on earth were believed to be witches and between 1560 and 1700 thousands of women and some men suffered horrific deaths after days of dreadful torture. Across Scotland, and in East Lothian in particular, witch-hunting developed into a hysterical frenzy. In 1590, a North Berwick woman, Agnes Sampson, was accused of being a member of a coven that met in the Auld Kirkyard. A sensational trial began and King James VI took an active part. Agnes Sampson was interrogated by him at Holyrood Palace as she suffered horrific torture. Deprived of sleep, she was pinned to the wall of her cell by a witch's bridle, a metal device forced into her mouth that pressed sharp prongs on her tongue and cheeks. After two days of agony, she of course confessed and was burned at the stake. The phrase 'the quick and the dead' comes from these appalling sentences, which were sometimes specific; some were fortunate to be strangled by the executioner as he tied them to the stake, but others were burned quick, while they were still alive.

On the road out of Spott, Nat and I stopped at the Witches' Stone. The Presbytery of Dunbar was responsible for the burning of more than a hundred women and men accused of witchcraft, and in the tiny parish of Spott six women and two men were killed in this barbaric fashion. And this madness was persistent. As late as 1698 Marion Lillie was condemned to suffer death at the stake in the village. It is to be hoped that she was strangled before the flames crackled at her feet.

When we looked more closely at the memorial stone

behind its iron railings, we could see withered flowers and a scatter of coins, perhaps offerings of atonement from a more enlightened age. This incident and the appalling fate of seven others changed the way I saw Spott, its tidy cottages and the avenue of trees leading to the big house. Now it is tranquil, but once an evil fanaticism lived here. Only 300 years ago, Spott's inhabitants piled wood and tar around the feet of a terrified old woman and stood back to watch as the fire consumed her, silencing her screams.

A mile or so further down the road, the flanks of the hills began to crowd around us and we walked past a dense strip of hardwood trees to reach Spott Ford. It crosses the Brock Burn, the Badger's Burn, before climbing up to a junction with another B road. Five miles or so out of Dunbar, this was the first real test for those carrying heavy creels of herring. When we puffed up the steep hill past Ice Cleugh, Nat and I turned to look north over the Firth of Forth, a panorama that was punctuated by the Bass Rock and North Berwick Law, and on our right a circular Iron Age hillfort at Chesters, now mostly ploughed flat. Having walked through the farm at Halls, we made for Hartside, climbing gently, and across the cattle grid there was a path and the first of the signs for the Herring Road.

It was hard, hard going. And soft. The line of the old road is very clear as it climbs up Hartside Edge, but centuries of feet, hooves and cartwheels have worn a cleft into the hillside and rainwater naturally drains into it. But as we ploughed on up through the tussocky grass, not often finding good places to put our feet, the ground gradually dried out. Walking over uneven, rough ground is much more tiring than ambling along a tarmac road or a good path. When your foot is not flat or slips even a little as you plant it, walking can look more like drunken skating. By the time we made it up to what seemed, thank God, like a plateau, I was tired. Hartside was not labelled as an Edge for no reason. But when I remembered that women carried a hundredweight of herring up this steep road, I stopped moaning and started marvelling at their hardihood. And in my head I heard the low rumble of my dad's voice: 'Be a man!' OK. OK.

Beyond stood the giant grey turbines of Crystal Rig Wind Farm. It is vast, the second largest in Britain, with ninety-one turbines across the Lammermuir Plateau. They seemed to me to be beautiful, almost sculptural as their sails turned gently in the ever-present breeze, much better looking than the steel pylons that everywhere disfigure the countryside. Up here, few people see them and they make use of a resource that in Scotland was previously seen as an irritant, and they are planted on land useful only for summer grazing for sheep. When construction work began in 2002, the Lammermuirs saw something unprecedented: an invasion of fleets of heavy machinery, earth movers, trucks and other vehicles. Beneath where Nat and I walked, cables connect an invisible latticework and carry off the electricity made by the wind to the national grid. But all of the seismic ground disturbance had made the Herring Road hard to find. The last time he was on these hills, on his fold-up mountain bike, Nat had found it difficult to find where the path led. That was precisely why I had persuaded him to come with me. But when we arrived in front of an information board he knew to head for Turbine 26 to pick up the line of the Herring Road.

Ignoring the metalled roads made by the turbine builders (and with a planned extension to create a farm of more than a hundred turbines, these would once again be busy), we walked on to Cracking Shaw Wood. The trees felt like a transition, taking us out of the breeze, away from the twenty-first-century technology on the wide, open plateau and into a much more intimate place. With few gradients, the path was good and we began to make much better progress (or rather I lagged behind a bit less), partly because I was feeling less tired. Nat encouraged me, saying that it was mostly downhill for the last stretch before we reached the rendezvous, where we would be picked up.

Beyond the wood, and with the turbines far behind us, the air seemed clean, even if it was beginning to move very quickly, and at last I felt we had left behind the clutter of history, of battles and witch burnings. For millennia, all that had ever mattered up here in this elemental landscape was survival. My great-great-grandfather, William Moffat, was a ploughman and, like many, he moved his family around different farms during his working life. In the nineteenth century, agricultural workers were employed at hiring fairs for terms, usually a year at a fixed fee. It was a near-feudal relationship, but good ploughmen could bargain up their fees, the quality of the tied cottage that went with them and their 'gains', or payments in kind, if their reputation was good. William Moffat worked the heavy horses in a clutch of Berwickshire farms that lay within a radius of about five miles. That suggests to me that his work was good and that he was in demand. In my sentimental opinion, it also seemed to lend him some dignity in a desperately unequal world.

The only story I have from him is about the Lammermuir Hills, his northern horizon for all of his life. My grandmother, Bina, heard it from him and she told it to me when I was a little boy and it has never left me. Nat and I were walking down to the shallow valley of the Whiteadder Water and William's story took place on the hills beyond it, Bleak Law and Moss Law. Two shepherds and their collies were moving a large flock of sheep down from the higher ground. It was late October and there was little grass left for them out on the hills. It was later said that the shepherds could smell the snow coming. The wind got up and as the sky darkened they sent their dogs arcing out over the flanks of the laws to begin the gather. They needed to get them down to the Whiteadder as soon as they possibly could. And then it came, whistling out of the west, the dense, blinding vortex of a blizzard. In less than half an hour there was whiteout. In the half-dark, visibility shrank to a metre or two and the roar of the wind meant that the shepherds could not hear each other. They were lost in all senses. The blizzard blazed on and as night fell temperatures plummeted.

The following morning the two men were found frozen to death in the snowdrifts. Crouching to preserve a core of warmth, their backs to the west wind, it seemed that each man was sleeping. And beside them were the rigid bodies of their dogs. The collies could have found their way off the hill, but they stayed. They stayed.

When we crossed the Whiteadder by a ford, we gratefully walked on the flat surface of a B road. It felt like luxury. Perhaps we (I mean I) picked up our pace a little. Beyond lay the Whiteadder Reservoir. Its dam was built in the late 1960s to supply pure Lammermuir water to East Lothian and Berwickshire. Nat wanted to point out a strange roadside memorial, something easily missed. The Packman's Grave is an arrangement of five smallish boulders, two are set up on their ends and three lie flat. It is said they mark the grave of an itinerant trader, a man who carried his wares around country roads on his back. The stones looked old, but not prehistoric, and perhaps they mark a place where a man who spent his life on the roads might be buried.

It was late afternoon, time to climb into a welcome car

seat and take the weight off my leaden legs. The forecast was good for the following day, the second half of the journey. I felt no shame that we would take two days to complete a journey done in one by women carrying a heavy creel. They were clearly made of sterner stuff.

Warmed by early sun, we set off the next morning from the same place (I resisted commenting that my legs still felt like lead), heading southwards into a deserted landscape that once buzzed with history. Penshiel Grange has been partly inundated by the creation of Whiteadder Reservoir, but once it was at the centre of a busy upland farm owned by the monks of Melrose Abbey. The ten-foot-high walls of a vaulted building still stand; they might have been part of a large farmhouse. There are traces of a courtyard beside it and the founds of other buildings round about. The wool crop from places like this was a lucrative source of income for the Abbot and his great church on the banks of the Tweed. In the twelfth century four abbeys were established in the Borders by the modernising king, David I, and each owned vast tracts of land, much of it in the Lammermuirs and the Cheviots. European and English buyers came to the markets at Roxburgh, a medieval town near Kelso that has entirely disappeared, for the raw wool was much prized for its quality by the weavers of the south, Flanders and Tuscany. Melrose, Kelso, Jedburgh and Dryburgh all sent woolpacks to the fairs at Roxburgh. The trade was so important that in the handbook of a thirteenth-century merchant, Francesco Pegalotti, the abbeys were all given Italian names: Mirososso was Melrose, Ghelzo was Kelso, and Gridegorda was Jedburgh.

Around the ruins of the abbey grange lay more, much older stories. Nat pointed out a small stone circle and beyond it an alignment of other stones. Most of these mysterious monuments were erected by communities of prehistoric farmers in the centuries on either side of 3,000 BC. The climate was likely warmer then and the bleak moorland maybe more productive than it is now.

We followed the Herring Road up the flanks of Southern Law and made our way down to Faseny Water. By now we were walking through the empty heart of the Lammermuirs, miles from habitation of any sort, and the only sign that others came here was a concrete ford over the burn. The track was also good and clearly occasionally used by vehicles, but we saw no one. After a couple of miles, my legs were feeling a little less leaden and we began to make good time. From my Pathfinder, I could see that we had crossed from East Lothian into the Scottish Borders.

From the slopes of Scar Law, we could see another reservoir, one filled by the Watch Water. Nat reckoned we should stop and have a look at John Dippie's Well. Someone had paid for a mason to carve an inscription on what looked like a tombstone: 'There is no water on the Lammermuir sweeter than at John Dippie's Well'. There followed by a version of a signature, 'Keeper Rawburn, 1865 to 1897'. It seems to have been a monument to a cheering tale.

John Dippie was a gamekeeper on these hills, where the Pathfinder still marks many grouse butts, turf banks where shooters stood, and tradition holds that the water was made even sweeter because he hid a bottle of whisky in the well. Apparently Dippie was in the happy habit of adding a dram to a draught of water for the shooting parties he led out across the Lammermuirs. Nat and I could find nothing but water, but it did taste good, clean and clear.

The track remained very good, but the Pathfinder told me we had another long climb as the contours bunched on the flanks of Twin Law. At this point the path formed part of the great coast-to-coast walking route, the Southern

Upland Way, and it was well signposted. But when we flogged uphill to the twin cairns on the summit of the hill, we met no one. Impressive, these cylindrical drystane cairns looked like miniature brochs and at their foot there was a set of steps down to what seemed like a sheltered area, what my gran would have called a bield. Lest we think these structures ancient, my online guide to the Southern Upland Way told me that these five- to six-foot-high cairns were flattened during the Second World War by Polish tank commanders out on manoeuvres. They were carefully restored and inside each is a narrow set of stairs to allow access so that beacons might be set. The reasons for lighting a beacon on Twin Law escaped me, but it would certainly have been visible for many miles to the south. The views were tremendous.

Nat assured me that while the end might not exactly be in sight, Lauder was only about five miles away. Piece of cake. Possibly. We scrambled across the burn at Braidshawrig, still on the Southern Upland Way, and by the time we reached the Snawden Burn we caught a glimpse of the Eildon Hills. It was a warming sight, one that must have given great cheer to the fishwives and carters who had brought their loads of herring twenty-five miles from Dunbar. The moorland gave way to rough grazing and then to managed grazing, all signs that we were coming down off the hills, moving from the world of shepherds to the land of ploughmen.

Walking through Wanton Walls Farm, we crossed the A6089 and made our way through some woodland into the policies of Thirlestane Castle. Beyond it lay journey's end, the town of Lauder. Never had it looked more beautiful. Despite the A68, a busy arterial road, running through its heart, this ancient royal burgh remains largely unchanged. In order to accommodate market stalls or booths, its main street widens and is dominated at the southern end by the

Tolbooth, a town hall, customs house, court room and jail. The small barred windows of its cells can still be seen on the ground floor. Closes, or alleyways, rather than streets spur off on either side of the High Street and a few very old houses present their gable ends in the streetline, clearly survivors from the medieval town. It is as though Lauder has been frozen in time. Nat and I walked into a place very little changed from the days when fishwives arrived off the Herring Road and gratefully laid down their creels at last. One sad difference is that it is no longer possible to buy fresh fish in Lauder.

How the women and men must have felt as they at last heaved their creels off their backs or pulled the barrels of salted fish off their carts can only be imagined. For us, only a little footsore and creaky, there was a sense of achievement and also of deep appreciation. The Lammermuir tops are not the mountains of the Highlands, but they can be just as bleak and elemental, and Nat and I marvelled at the sheer dogged toughness of those forgotten people who made the annual journeys on the Herring Road.

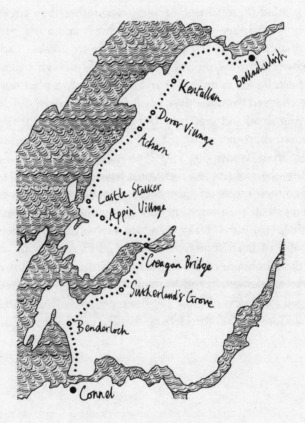

Ballachulish

Kentallen

Duror Village

Achara

Castle Stalker
Appin Village

Creagan Bridge

Sutherland's Grove

Benderloch

Connel

The Rail Road ⑧

8

The Rail Road

Ballachulish to Connel

Not all of the hidden ways need to be opened up and reclaimed from the overgrowth of history. The railway line from Ballachulish to Connel in Appin closed in 1966 and the trackbed was left in a reasonable state of preservation. This allowed long sections to be cleared and tarmacked to make a cycleway and a walkway. Although at about thirty miles it is a longish walk (I decided to do it over two days – after all, Roman legionaries were expected to march only ten to twelve miles in one day), it was easier going than almost all of the others.

An unlooked-for companion was Duncan Kennedy. Although he died some time ago, he left an excellent memoir of the building of the railway. The Birth and Death of a Railway: Ballachulish Line *was published in 1971 and it documents Duncan's involvement in the engineering work when he was a very young man. He was also a native of Appin.*

His book brought the walk alive for me because it unpacked the practical difficulties of working in such a wild landscape. Instead of thoughtlessly crossing bridges and walking through cuttings, I knew from Duncan the details of how the engineers and navvies had negotiated the difficulties of creating the line. And the views of the Firth of Lorn were breath-catching.

On 4 June 1746, a strange, highly theatrical ceremony took place at Edinburgh's Mercat Cross. Less than seven weeks before, all but two of the clan banners that fluttered over the Highland army at Culloden had been captured and brought to Edinburgh Castle. On that June Saturday morning large crowds had gathered to witness not an execution but the ritual death of a cause. Cheering and jeering on the Castlehill, the Lawnmarket and the High Street, they saw the city hangman, John Dalgleish, march at the head of a procession. He carried the personal standard of Prince Charles Edward Stuart and behind him there followed a farce. With blackened faces and sooty hands, the chimney sweeps of Edinburgh carried the clan standards, those of the MacDonald regiments, the Atholl Brigade, Clan Chattan, Clan Cameron and many others. Rather than holding them high, the sweeps trailed them through the dust and rubbish of the streets, encouraging the crowds to stamp on the silk colours, to spit on them and worse. This was a pantomime made even more bizarre because the captured flags of vanquished enemies were always treasured as trophies. But at the Mercat Cross, a fire was blazing.

From the narrow parapet around the cross, a herald proclaimed to the crowds below that these symbols of rebellion and treason were to be burned by the city hangman. These were the flags, the foul rags carried by screaming savages, people who were scarcely human. They had no value and deserved no respect. To the baying crowd, the herald read out the name of each clan as its colours were held out over the flames: MacDonald, Cameron, Mackintosh, Maclean, Chisholm, MacGillivray, Fraser, Farquharson. And each time a flag was turned to ashes, there was a thunderous cheer. But the colours of one clan were missing.

About 300 yards from the Mercat Cross, in a corner of the National Museum of Scotland, a glass case contains a much-faded silk flag, a gold Saltire on a blue ground. This was the banner of the Appin Stewarts, a clan whose chiefs had sworn everlasting loyalty to the Jacobite cause, and a clan that would be made to suffer great loss and indignity.

In the dark aftermath of the disaster at Culloden, Appin became the landscape of vengeance. A fertile coastal region warmed by the waters of the Gulf Stream, it is bounded by Loch Leven and Glencoe in the north and by the crooked line of Loch Creran in the south. On a damp April morning in 1746 Charles Stewart of Ardsheal stood at the head of the regiment of the Appin Stewarts, waiting in vain for the order to charge from his commander, Prince Charles Edward Stuart. Men were being blown to pieces by an accurate barrage from government artillery as round shot bounced over the heather and ploughed into the ranks of clansmen. Incompetence and indecision was frittering away the lives of hundreds of men until Clan Chattan could stand it no more. Roaring their war cries, they broke into the charge, racing across the heather towards the scarlet ranks of the Duke of Cumberland's army. When they saw that the Mackintoshes were away, Clan Cameron, the Atholl Brigade and the Appin Stewarts followed, their broadswords raised, Charles Stewart of Ardsheal running far ahead of his men.

They fought like furies, breaking through the front ranks on the left flank of the government army and for a moment anything seemed possible. A rider on a prancing, spooking horse watched the Camerons and the Stewarts tear into the government ranks and, to him, it seemed as though the invincible Highland charge would once again scatter their enemies. He turned his skittish horse and rode hard for Edinburgh, changing horses where he could. Clattering into the city by the West Port, the young man reported a Jacobite victory and for a few hours the city was dazed, amazed and fearful. If the young man had waited another hour, he would have seen something entirely different.

The Highlanders charged over boggy ground, collided with each other, impeded those behind them, and many failed to engage properly, especially the MacDonald regiments on the left flank. Roared at by their sergeant majors, the redcoats for once stood fast, kept their discipline, did not turn and flee, reformed their lines when they were broken, and their musketry and bayonet thrusts devastated the Highlanders. A rout began, and with the ragged remnants of his regiment, Charles Stewart of Ardsheal fled. The Appin men had taken terrible casualties: out of 300 who had charged, ninety-two were dead and sixty badly injured. Eight of Ardsheal's close family died and a further fourteen officers were killed, men who were minor lairds, tacksmen at Fasnacloich and Achnacone, Invernahyle and Ballachulish, those whose families had lived on, farmed and made the blessed and beautiful land of Appin.

The wives and children of the dead and those who had turned and fled lost everything as a rash of forfeitures deprived clan chiefs and Jacobite gentry of their estates and handed them to those who had remained loyal. The Campbells had fought in the government army at Culloden and they reaped a rich reward. But worse was to follow. More blood was spilt in the summer after the battle as rebels were hunted down and killed by government soldiers, or hanged in mass executions or transported. Their cattle were taken, their cottages burned and their women raped in what amounted to a concerted campaign of genocidal savagery directed by George II's brother, the victor of Culloden, William, Duke of Cumberland.

One of his most sadistic officers was the oddly named Captain Caroline Scott. After Clan Campbell had confiscated and sold cattle in Appin, this vicious individual led another punitive expedition. When he arrived at Ardsheal House, he evicted Mrs Stewart and then had his men dismantle her home so that he could sell its blue-grey Ballachulish slates, its timbers and even the nails that held them in place. The walls were taken down and the cut stone loaded onto carts, and the tall ash trees that protected the house and the orchards around it were all cut down. Watching all of this, hiding in a waterfall cave high on the slopes of Beinn a' Bheithir, was Charles Stewart of Ardsheal, a fugitive since the defeat. He must have wept at the destruction and the rape of Appin. A few weeks later, he and his wife escaped into exile in France.

Having driven through the brooding, sad splendours of Glencoe, I reached Ballachulish in the late morning to see spring beginning in the Highlands. Green was poking through the tussocky winter wrack in the straths and near houses occasional avenues of daffodils lit the road. It was my intention to walk the line of a remarkable railway that was built to bring Appin into the national network and carry the output of the great slate quarries at Ballachulish. Begun in 1903 and closed in 1966 it was twenty-eight miles long and ran through some of the most heartbreakingly beautiful country in the Scottish Highlands, the green heart of Jacobitism.

Before I found where the railway began, I wanted to look at the quarries. In the midst of so much history and romance, and the grandeur and drama of their setting, there was industry in the Highlands. At its peak in the 1880s, the vast East Quarry at Ballachulish was the largest in Scotland. Six hundred men produced a million slates each year and, once cut and dressed, they were loaded onto ships waiting at the quays on Loch Leven. Ballachulish slates cover many thousands of roofs in Glasgow and Edinburgh, and the great architect Charles Rennie Mackintosh delayed the completion of the Hill House in Helensburgh until he was sure to be supplied with just the right shade of blue-grey. My own house is roofed with Ballachulish slate.

Generations of quarriers have hacked a huge hole in the hillside behind the village and the effect is like an immense amphitheatre. Slate was cut in shelved levels that resemble tiered seating for giants. On the eastern side there are several vast buttresses that flank deeper inroads and one of these is veined with russet streaks of iron pyrites. It could create holes in the dressed slates and the buttress was probably not worth the trouble. But these massive outcrops seemed noble to me, sculptural, somehow defiant. By the beginning of the twentieth century, the market for slate in Britain was badly affected by cheaper imports, but the company continued in business at Ballachulish until 1955.

Armed with three maps and the satnav on my phone, I was having trouble finding where the old railway into Appin began. I knew that much of its line had been converted into a tarmac track for cyclists and walkers and had picked up a handy map of its route. The only problem was that it was difficult to work out where to join it. The lady in reception at the Ballachulish Hotel told me I should begin by climbing up a long flight of steps to the bridge over the narrows and then turn right. Really? That did not sound right, but I did it anyway. Steep slate steps, they certainly warmed me up for the day's exertions, and they also brought me face to face once more with history: a grey memorial to a grisly execution. On the rocky knoll above the loch an innocent man was hanged for a famous crime.

Known as the Appin Murder, it intrigued Robert Louis Stevenson and inspired him to write *Kidnapped*, the adventures of David Balfour and his unlikely Jacobite friend, Alan Breck

Stewart. A wonderful, utterly absorbing novel, it offers a pungent sense of the years after Culloden for the Highlanders who remained loyal to the exiled Stuart kings or were forced to live as fugitives in the mountains. And it skilfully uses the actual events that gave rise to this famously unsolved crime.

Known as the Red Fox, Colin Campbell of Glenure had been appointed factor of the forfeited estates of the Appin Stewarts. On the morning of 14 May, he had crossed the narrows at Ballachulish by ferry and was walking precisely where I had been. With Campbell were a manservant, a sheriff officer and an Edinburgh lawyer. When they reached the woods at Lettermore, a shot rang out. Hit in the back, perhaps through the heart, Campbell fell to the ground, fatally wounded. Muskets were notoriously inaccurate and it seems very likely that the marksman had been concealed close to the road when he fired. Tradition holds that he hid behind a bush, where the shoulder piece of his musket was later found. Shocked and perhaps fearful of more volleys to bring them down, Campbell's companions did not attempt to pursue the assassin and he melted back into the woods.

The surprising irony was that Glenure had not been disliked, not at all resented even by Jacobites who were losing their possessions. He appears not to have been heavy-handed, unlike Captain Caroline Scott, in his dealings with the Appin Stewarts. Nevertheless, suspicion fell immediately on Alan Breck Stewart, the foster-son of James Stewart. Known as Seumas a' Ghlinne, or James of the Glens, he was the brother of Charles Stewart of Ardsheal and in the dislocated times after Culloden the de facto chief of the clan. He had been pardoned after the rebellion and acted as a mediator between Glenure and the Stewart tenants. After the murder, Alan Breck fled and James was arrested and charged. What followed was a clear miscarriage of justice.

From the outset, it was inevitable that Stewart would be found guilty and sentenced to hang. Out of fifteen men on the jury, eleven were Campbell clansmen and the presiding judge was Archibald Campbell, Duke of Argyll and chief of the clan. And the trial was held at Inverary, the Campbell capital. When James Stewart was able to show convincingly that he had been nowhere near the wood at Lettermore on 14 May 1752, his alibi was dismissed. The charges were summarily changed. Instead of being convicted for the murder itself, he was found guilty on the Scots law charge of airts and pairts, as an accessory to murder. It was a travesty. James of the Glens had been convicted because of his political sympathies and family connections. An example would be made.

At Cnap Chaolais Mhic Phadraig, a knoll above the southern shore of the narrows at Ballachulish where the ferry used to cross, and a place where many travellers would see it, even from the other side of Loch Leven, carpenters were instructed to build a scaffold. As I discovered it was steep-sided, and before the modern bridge and some woodland hid it, the knoll would have been easy to see. On the stormy, wild morning of 8 November 1752, James Stewart climbed onto the platform, protested his undying innocence to the crowd below, saying, 'I found it was not only Glenure's murder I had to answer for but [also] the sins and follies of my forefathers such as the rebellions of 1715, 1719 and 1745.' James of the Glens then recited the 35th psalm before the noose was pulled tight around his neck. Secured by chains, his corpse was left to swing in the bitter winds for eighteen months, a blunt warning against sedition and armed rebellion that no traveller across the narrows at Ballachulish would miss.

This was by no means an isolated incident in the years

after Culloden, but Robert Louis Stevenson's interest (and that of Walter Scott, who wrote of the Appin Murder in the introduction to *Rob Roy*) and the immense and sustained success of *Kidnapped* has cast the fate of James of the Glens into a continuing limelight. Several books have set out to solve the mystery and somehow right an ancient wrong. None of them convict Alan Breck Stewart and one of the most plausible claims that James Stewart was indeed guilty of conspiracy to murder. A recent study turns the case on its head by accusing a fellow clansman, Mungo Campbell, of having Glenure shot for personal gain. He inherited his lucrative position as factor of the forfeited Stewart estates, including those of James of the Glens.

Whatever the truth lurking behind the Appin Murder, it was the spark that created *Kidnapped*, an important novel. Not only is it a tremendous adventure that starts off at a sprint and gets faster as Alan Breck and David Balfour suffer shipwreck and are chased across the heather by redcoated soldiers, it is also an accurately observed examination of many of the awkwardnesses, contradictions and romantic misconceptions in the long relationship between Highland and Lowland. Balfour's Presbyterian upbringing contrasts with Alan Breck's guile and instincts for survival, and the Highlander forgives the Lowlander for his stiff-necked attitudes because he admires the boy's physical courage. But throughout Stevenson resists judgement, even though it is clear that Balfour is on the right side of history and in the end prospers. Alan Breck Stewart lived in stirring times and escaped the consequences of his politics and his culture, but he is the more memorable, attractive – and tragic – figure.

My plan to walk through Appin arose in part from the complexities of that old cultural division. By any measure, I am a Lowland Scot in all regards. I was born in the Scottish

Borders and have come back to live and work there. I was raised by my Scots-speaking grandmother and my ancestral DNA, reaching 2,000 or so years back into the past, is Scandinavian in origin. I am emphatically not a Celt. And yet here I was in the glorious heart of the Highlands, anxious to understand something of its history, to walk through Appin and perhaps somehow understand a little better the passions that drove the Stewarts and others into the charge at Culloden. I have learned a little Gaelic and am told that I have a good *blas*, or accent. I am fascinated by the turns our history might have taken, especially if the later Stuart kings had not been so feckless. It is only our history that makes us who we are. But even though I love the Highlands, and particularly the body warmth of Highland culture and society, I would have stood in the ranks of the government army at Culloden – and yet admired the astonishing bravery of the men charging over the heather to kill me with nothing more than bladed weapons: a medieval host rather than an eighteenth-century army. A significant number of the officers who left records of the battle marvelled at the courage of their enemies and were both saddened and repelled at the slaughter. As I left the knoll where James of the Glens met his end, I reflected that even the glorious lochside landscape embodies a clear sense of its past and the vicissitudes of history. It seems to be in the air. What had once been a working landscape, alive with people and their animals, had withered into mere scenery. Once, it had been loved with a fatal passion, worth dying for. When the Highlanders charged at Culloden, their war cries were often the names of their places.

Unlike all of the forgotten roads I had walked, the line of the Ballachulish to Connel railway should have been obvious, not part of the faded map of an older Scotland but a route that had been remembered and adapted. But I still could not find it. My Landranger was too vague (again, no Pathfinder could be found for this area – and in any case it would probably have been out of date) and my phone had no signal. And then I realised that my feet had found it: I must be walking along the line of the railway. When that lightbulb flickered, I made my way back towards Ballachulish. And found it in a few minutes.

Labelled Route 78, the start of the cycle and pedestrian path is marked by two elegant iron gates offset to allow walkers and bikers to pass through with a wiggle and to exclude four-wheeled traffic. The surface was excellent, and the weather, for the West Highlands, was also excellent – only a light drizzle. And best of all, the builders of this excellent path had erected handy blue signs that gave the exact mileage, down to the quarter miles, for each stage of the journey I had planned. Excellent. On all of my previous walks along hidden ways I'd had to estimate distance and travel time, and sometimes got it badly wrong. But here was clear information. A blessing. Three miles to the old station at Kentallan. Piece of cake on this surface. Maybe I could walk the entire twenty-eight miles in a day. Or maybe not.

After a short time, I came to the remains of a station platform, a long, curving concrete sill covered in moss. This was the stop for the Ballachulish Ferry, where passengers bound for Fort William and points north were collected in a charabanc (or motor coach) and taken down to the slip for the ferry across the narrows of Loch Leven, past the rocky knoll where James of the Glens had been hanged. Ballachulish is from Baile a' Chaolais, 'the Village at the Narrows'. I am old enough to remember the car ferry: the service had only ceased in 1975, when the bridge was completed. By that time the railway had been closed for almost ten years and the age of the car was well under way.

When I started reading about the line through Appin and North Lorn, I was lucky to come across Duncan Kennedy's superb account of its construction. *The Birth and Death of a Highland Railway* is Kennedy's very personal story – the new line was to pass through a few fields of his father's farm near the village of Duror, six miles from where I started my walk. As a late teenager, Duncan's ambition was to become an engineer and here was an opportunity on his doorstep to observe that profession in action. But the young boy had some initiative and, anxious to do more than watch the line being built, he approached one of the engineers to ask him for a job. Paid ten shillings a week (knocked down from fifteen), Duncan helped the surveyors set out the centre line of the new trackbed and he began to learn his trade on the ground.

As a frontispiece for his book, Duncan encouraged the publisher to print an advertisement. It is a pungent memory of Edwardian Britain, the evening of Empire and yet a time when excursions carried a palpable sense of adventure. The advertisement was for a circular tour that involved three modes of transport. Passengers could board a train at Oban at 9.30 a.m., alight at Ballachulish at 11.05 a.m. and then take a charabanc along the bumpy road through Glencoe before turning south at the King's House Hotel. There, what is now only a track leads to the pier at the head of Loch Etive. At 1.45 p.m. precisely, passengers boarded a yacht, the *Darthula II*, and they sailed first to Taynuilt before disembarking at Achnacloish on the southern shore of the loch. The train then took them back to Oban in time for a late afternoon tea at 4.37 p.m. Wonderful. And no longer possible.

After Ballachulish Ferry Station, the track opened for a

few hundred yards to allow a sweeping view of the Appin mountains before a cutting closed in. Slicing through rock, these sections of the line are very impressive. Duncan Kennedy wrote a great deal about the gangs of navvies (from navigators, the men who dug the canals, or navigations, in the eighteenth and nineteenth centuries) who did the pick and shovel work. There were no mechanical diggers of any sort: it was sweat that moved parts of mountains, not the clanking buckets of diggers or bulldozers. When the centre line went over an outcrop, there being no way around it, the rock was sometimes shifted with explosives, but more often it was broken with steel chisels and drills hammered into the surface. To keep these sharp, there was a black-smith's forge up the line at Kentallan (now only two miles away, according to the excellent blue signs) and tools were barrowed back and forth by Allan Dubh. Even though he was eighty years old, he had a full head of jet-black (*dubh*) hair and very little English.

Occasionally the builders of the new path avoided going under the neat little bridges that carried farm roads over the line, probably because the cost of making them safe was too high, but the masonwork was very attractively done. Duncan Kennedy wrote of a quarry close to where I was walking, a place where stone for bridges, culverts and station buildings was cut, but I could not find any trace of where it had been. Further along the path, the vistas to my right began to open and I could see the northern shore of Loch Linnhe, the houses at Onich and traffic snaking along the road to Fort William. To my left, the mountainside was sometimes steep and occasional waterfalls rushed down and under the old railway. When it came to the modern road to Oban, a bridge carried the cars over the railway as it passed through to run along the shoreline. The views were breath-catching.

Across a widening Loch Linnhe, I could see the Morven mountains far to the west and over my shoulder the narrowing neck of the sea-loch as it reached north-east to Fort William and the mighty flanks of Ben Nevis. The line ran so close to the shore that there were few trees to interrupt the view as the sun splashed yellow on the top of Sgurr Dhòmhnaill on the farther shore of the loch. A breeze blowing off the sea had driven the drizzle inland and the day freshened. This must surely have been one of the most beautiful stretches of railway line anywhere. What a tragedy that Dr Beeching, the man charged by the government to shrink the rail network, was given such sweeping powers that he could insist that it be closed down in 1966.

Further along the line, I barked my shins on history once more. A sign for Leitir Mhor, Lettermore, told me that this was where Colin Campbell of Glenure was killed by a musket ball. An information board directed me to the older cairn that marks the spot and advertised the path as the Red Fox Trail. (This appears to be a nickname no one knew in 1752; it was given to Campbell by Robert Louis Stevenson. He was known as Cailean Ruadh, Red Colin, probably because he had red hair. By making him a fox, Stevenson created a handy narrative link with a predator.) Looking around, it struck me that the assassin must have been confident. He had only one escape route – back along the road to Ballachulish – because at Lettermore the mountainside is very steep and he could hardly have run past Campbell's companions on the road down to Appin. On my walk, I saw more boards about the murder of Colin Campbell and the death of James of the Glens, and I wondered if visitors might form the impression that nothing else of any note had ever happened in Appin.

Before I reached Kentallan the path climbed a little. This was disappointing. My ambition to walk the whole line in a day was in part predicated on the assumption that railway line builders, with all their cuttings and embankments, try to avoid steep gradients. Worse was to come. At Kentallan the station buildings had been converted into the Holly Tree Hotel and Restaurant and two modern houses were being built on the trackbed nearby. The blue signs directed me off it, through the little village and past the old water tower, something essential for steam trains. According to Duncan Kennedy, there was a siding at Kentallan, but it looked as though houses had been built over its line. Past the tower, a new section of the path began to climb alarmingly. After only three miles, my aspirations to complete twenty-eight miles by the end of the day were fading fast. But at the summit of this new stretch the path opened to tremendously rewarding views over the great sea-loch. And because I was much higher up, I could see further. The islands at the mouth of Loch Linnhe are where it becomes the Firth of Lorn and leads out to the mighty Atlantic. Mountains rising up out of the sea, islands breaking its surface, the fingers of head-lands reaching out – all these are elemental, dramatic, humbling. I decided to linger more, worry less about how many miles lay ahead and stop counting off those that were behind me.

As the path left the shoreline and led me inland to Glen Duror, I came to the first in a series of livestock gates. They needed to be firmly closed. I realised that I was in farming country, mostly pasture with the spring grass beginning to flush. I saw some spindly lambs and as the ewes nibbled at the sweet new grass, their rich milk would mean that the newborns would fatten quickly and be better able to survive the wind-driven rain all stocksmen fear in March and April.

Duncan Kennedy's father farmed nearby (although he nowhere gives the name of the farm and I had no luck finding out), but he seems mainly to have reared the traditional Highland staple of small and hardy cattle. So that he could rest his summer fields, Kennedy let Balnagowan Island, an islet about a mile and a half offshore in Loch Linnhe. In the spring he and his boys ferried over about a dozen yearling stirks and a score of old ewes so that they could fatten. After they had been left on the island for a year, the Kennedys returned and, like the drovers at Kyleakin, they swam the cattle back to the mainland. Which could be difficult because, not handled for a year, they had become wild on the island. No one does that now.

Near Duror village, six miles out, exactly, from Ballachulish, I met another user of this excellent track, the first I had encountered. A cyclist in full high-vis gear grunted 'Good morning' as he whooshed past. A bike would certainly have covered the whole journey in a day, but would I have stopped so often or looked around so much? The path was forced to the side of the trackbed, where it ran parallel for a few hundred yards. This may have been because the landowner did not wish to sell and what might have remained of Duror Station hid behind a paling fence and a tangle of ash trees. The air was so pure that grey clusters of lichen embroidered almost every branch and twig, leaving only the lower trunk clear.

In the village I found myself walking in what I thought was the wrong direction and I pulled out my OS Explorer map (better than the Landranger but still too big) to see where I had strayed offline.

'Would you like some 'elp?' A cyclist had silently stopped behind me and I must have jumped because she smiled. 'Are you losing yourself?' She took off her helmet and shook out her hair. She had the gamine look of Leslie Caron in *An American in Paris*. I guess I was gawping. She smiled again and I heard myself say, '*Vous êtes française?*' She nodded and

I started stammering out a stream of schoolboy French. No, she had no idea where the next section of track was. Did I care?

Leslie Caron replaced her cycle hat (why do they remind me of toasters?) and whizzed off at high speed, wishing me *bonnes vacances*. I walked down a village road, round a corner and there it was. And there she was, about half a mile in the distance, flying along. What on earth had I said to this very pretty woman? In front stretched a very long straight – after all, it was once a railway – but it was somehow discouraging. For half an hour the view would not change, but at least it was flat. Near another bridge, an information board announced that I was close to James of the Glen's farmhouse at Acharn. The information was well presented. Gaelic subtitles and translations reminded readers Stewart and Campbell did not speak to each other in English. There was a translated passage that described what happened after Culloden to the farms around where I was standing:

> Neither cow nor horse, sheep nor goat, was left to them. The blankets were taken off their beds; any part of their bodyclothes that was worth money was taken from them, and their houses put on fire.

After the bridge, the path took me off the line of the railway, and up ahead I could see the reason why. Achara House was rebuilt in 1907 in some style and the original farmhouse demolished. The property had come back into the family after the forfeitures of 1745 were eventually rescinded and successive generations of the Stewarts of Ardsheal had developed the estate. Recently it was on the market for only £1 million, and that included 200 acres and three cottages. And not a right of way for walkers and cyclists. The path swung towards the busy Oban road and a sign warned that for the next two miles I would have to walk on it. With very slim or non-existent verges, this proved difficult, even dangerous. Half a mile later I passed Duror Burial Ground, hoping not to be returning. Having survived the hurtling log lorries whose slipstreams rocked me back on my heels, I came to a stretch of the road with a pavement. Next to it the trackbed ran through a cutting. It looked wet and was very overgrown. Making up that gap in the path would be difficult.

When the blue signs reappeared and the cycle track resumed, it took me along a lovely section close to a shingle beach. Beside it grew copses of old, windbent birch trees and I noticed that someone had tied a pink ribbon to one, and further along there were another two. Was this a memory of someone who had died, a little like these sad bunches of flowers tied on roadside fences at the scene of an accident? As I made my way on through Appin, I saw more ribbons of different colours and wondered what stories they told. The builders of the excellent path had thoughtfully set wooden benches next to it at attractive viewpoints and I decided it was time for cheese sandwiches.

Having tried to keep up a good pace and climbed more gradients than anticipated, I was warm under my old Barbour jacket. Its many and large pockets had persuaded me to swap it for my usual light Gore-tex coat with its handy hood. To find my way through Appin, I needed to carry three maps, and I wanted to take my copy of Duncan Kennedy's book and a small bottle of water so that I could avoid wrestling off my rucksack if I needed either. I took off the heavier coat and draped it over my shoulders to help me cool down. The weather also decided to lend a hand and a drizzle began to smirr off the loch. Deep in one of the game pockets I had found an old tweed bunnet, and there is no better protection against the rain than a tweed bunnet. I buttoned the Barbour at the neck, pulled up the collar, put my rucksack over my lap and kept everything else dry inside this small wigwam. For twenty minutes I sat contentedly in the rain, munching my sandwiches, before standing up, sorting myself out and moving on. It was important never to sit too long when there were roads and miles up ahead.

The old railway ran alongside the modern road for a mile or so, hugging the shoreline of the loch. The builders of both had no choice in their route because there was little more than a fifty- or sixty-metre shelf between the foot of Beinn Sgluich and the sea. And then, disappointingly, the road and the path changed places and I found myself walking inside the line of the traffic and only able to see the Morvern mountains through gaps in the trees. There was occasional compensation, with some dramatic white waterfalls tumbling off the steep flanks of Beinn Sgluich. At one point I saw sheep behaving like mountain goats. One ewe had deliberately wedged herself on the high side of a birch tree so that she could get at the clumps of new grass on the rocky scree. Another looked directly at me as she teetered on an outcrop as if to say, 'So?'

A road sign told me that I had crossed from Highland Region into Argyll and Bute, the boundary a wider than usual mountainside burn. There seemed little logic in its placing halfway through Appin, a historically and culturally homogenous district. Perhaps this division of their ancient province was a late instance of more Campbell revenge on the Stewarts.

The path eventually moved away from the road into Argyll and Bute and into some woodland – and, it seemed, into a different world. Some trees had been felled, but stacks of logs lay uncollected, gathering moss and sinking into wet patches. Others had been burned, and blackened stumps poked up out of the ground. By the side of the path, a dyke was being devoured by birch trees that had rooted amongst its stones. At the risk of melodrama or daftness, it looked as though there had been a war between the trees and men, and that the trees were winning. The wood seemed alive, even malevolent. I shivered and walked on.

Shuna Island came into view, shortening the near horizon. It is a sheep farm able to support a flock of about 360 ewes and it occurred to me that lambing would probably have started, a thought that warmed me. I was glad for any newborns that it had stopped raining. Close to the lochside once more, for the first time I caught that distinctive iodine tang of the sea, a sign that the vastness of the Atlantic was around only a few headlands. The old railway track moved through a shallow cutting with rock on the sea-side only the height of a dyke. But it was enough to shelter small clumps of primroses in its lee.

A tall sign announced Linnhe Marine Moorings and I expected to see splendid yachts bobbing at anchor in the bay at Dallens. Instead they were almost all beached, held up on wooden frames, and very close there was a scrapyard dominated by a huge crane next to a boat that was either being repaired or broken up. It was difficult to tell. All sorts of metal bits and pieces lay in heaps around a wide area, most of it gently rusting in the salt air. No one seemed to be about. The path carried on under another bridge and in minutes I seemed to have travelled a long way back in time from the decaying detritus of the twenty-first century. Out in the bay, perched on a small outcrop, stood a splendid medieval castle. Tall and with a few small windows, it looked as though it had been restored. The earliest version of Castle

Stalker (from an old Gaelic word, *stalcaire*, for a hunter or perhaps a falconer) was built in 1320, as the great Atlantic principality of the Lords of the Isles was establishing itself. It was part of a network of sea-castles accessible not by road but by the fleets of birlinns, the galleys of the MacDonald princes. Down the Atlantic shore, the most prominent and powerful were built at Ardtornish in Morvern, Castle Duart on Mull, and further south at Dunollie and Dunstaffnage. They are a memory of strongpoints and staging posts on hidden sea-roads, half-forgotten voyages no longer made. No road leads to the hump of the ruined citadel at Ardtornish, but in the bay below scores of birlinns were once beached and thousands of warriors were in the service of this line of sea-kings.

The Lordship fell after the discovery of a deal done with the kings of England. In the Treaty of Westminster–Ardtornish of 1462, the terms negotiated were more than audacious: if the boy-king, James III of Scotland, could be deposed, then his realm would be divided between John of Islay, the Lord of the Isles, and Edward IV of England. When the details became known, it was Islay who was deposed, his estates made forfeit and, in 1493, he became a captive pensioner at the royal household. A dismal end for the great sea-kingdom of Atlantic Scotland.

Not far beyond the bay dominated by Castle Stalker ran the platforms of Appin Station, where up and down trains could stop at the same time. On one side stood the waiting room and the signal box, and on the other was the substantial station house. No trace remains of any of these smart buildings, but on the long straight beyond there was at least somewhere to sit. Inside a high, horseshoe-shaped drystane dyke topped with grass, slate seats had been built in a pleasing semi-circle, a welcome break from the freshening wind. The straight ran on for almost a mile to the village of Appin and in the distance I could see a tall shape moving slowly towards me, swaying slightly, and immediately recognisable as someone on horseback. It turned out to be a young girl, far too heavy for her small, black pony, and we exchanged good afternoons. I hoped she was not riding far.

It occurred to me that I might be walking too far. I judged, with the help of the excellent blue signs, that I had come fourteen miles from Ballachulish, about halfway down the old railway line. I had made good time on the excellent path and it was only 2 p.m. I decided to stop in two hours' time, wherever I was, and call a taxi to take me back to my car. My only concern was my right foot. Since I injuring my back a few years ago banging in too many fence posts, my right foot has not been hitting the ground properly. Instead of the correct heel and toe action, the ball of my right foot tends to make contact first, especially if I am tired. How this looks has never bothered me, and I harbour no ambitions as a ballroom dancer, but if I walk too far on hard surfaces, the muscles in my right leg begin to complain. So, if they started to object too loudly, I would stop before 4 p.m.

When I crossed the road at Appin village to rejoin the path, it stretched a long way, far into some woodland as it crossed the flat strath. The OS Explorer told me I was walking on the Druim na Moina, the spine of the moor. And it was dull. The drone of the nearby modern road never faded and there were only a few bridges and culverts to remember the trains that had once trundled that way. But it was vital to walk the entire length of the track! And so on I yomped, my foot not flapping too badly, and soon Loch Creran came into view.

The vistas opened once more and soon I found myself approaching the first of the great engineering achievements of the line: the Creagan Bridge. Duncan Kennedy's account of the construction of the bridge across the narrows of Loch Creran is fascinating. Unlike Loch Etive or Loch Leven, Crearan does not penetrate far inland, only two miles beyond the narrows. This meant that a smaller volume of water was forced through the bottleneck by the tides and it was therefore possible to build a central pier to carry the two spans of the bridge. Such was the expertise – and confidence – of the line builders that their engineers took on the work of putting down the foundations and completing the mason work. The steel superstructure would be prefabricated in Glasgow by Arrol's Bridge and Roofing Company. This approach stands in high contrast with major engineering projects in twenty-first-century Scotland; no Scottish company was involved in the building of the new road bridge across the Firth of Forth, so in only a century our native expertise seems to have evaporated.

Duncan Kennedy worked on the construction of the three piers for the Creagan railway bridge: on the north side a pier could be relatively easily founded on solid rock that stood above sea level, but the central and southern piers involved working in the waters of the loch. Huge steel cylinders were slowly lowered until they grabbed a solid bearing. Weighted by kentledge (I had to look this up – pig-iron used as ballast), it was clearly vital that they sit absolutely straight. When Duncan arrived on the site, he found consternation; there was a big problem. After weeks of being carefully lowered down to the bed of the loch, one cylinder had stopped before it should have (engineers had measured the depth of the water) and no matter how much more kentledge went it, it would not move. A diver discovered that the bottom rim of the cylinder was caught on a steep face of underwater rock.

Compressed air was thought to be the solution and an expert arrived from Edinburgh with the necessary kit. An air-lock was fitted and then, amazing against the modern background of health and safety, the expert asked Duncan, little more than a raw teenager, if he would like to climb down into the cylinder. And he did. Even though he was scared. There was still water at the bottom but masons came down with their chisels and mallets to cut away the rock. The debris was pulled up in buckets and soon the steep slope had been levelled. Duncan remembered that the decompression gave him nose-bleeds.

Once the middle and south cylinders were straight and level, concrete was poured in and work began on the masonry facing. There was very little space on top of the middle cylinder and the granite facing blocks had to be winched to the platform and then lowered down to where the men were building up the courses. In windy and wet weather, this must have been a dangerous place to work, but Duncan makes very few references to these factors in his brisk account. When a riveter fell off the structure, plummeting fifty feet into the loch below, he remembered that his colleagues were reassured by the fact that the boy was yelling so much. It meant he was not dead or badly hurt. The foreman made him vomit out the seawater he had swallowed, and his face and shoulder, where he had hit the water, were badly bruised. But he was fine.

Before I had the chance look over the edge, I came across another information board with more about the Appin Murder. It pointed out that I was standing in the historic borderlands between the territories of the Campbells and the Stewarts of Appin. It quoted two remarks than ran interestingly counter to the accepted version of events. 'I will yet see that a clod of Appin shall not be possessed by

a Stewart' was something allegedly said by the well-liked
Colin Campbell of Glenure. And in a letter written by Alan
Breck Stewart in 1751 this appeared: '*Bidh an glean seo gu math
cosgail dhaibh mun bi e aca*' – 'It shall be a dear glen to them
ere they shall have it.' All of which seemed to imply that
the murder was waiting to happen.

Before I stepped into Campbell country, I needed to stop
stepping for the day and sit down, have some supper and
get some rest.

The bridge at Creagan has been converted for vehicle
traffic and it has lost all of its impressive Scottish Baronial
crenellations. This has been replaced by grey steel. The
embankment on the south side has also disappeared and the
road took me downhill to where the excellent path began.
It was about 7.30 a.m. and the grey skies overhead seemed
to promise rain. 'Good morning!' I was startled out of my
reverie by an early morning jogger, the luminous colours
of her kit almost as much of an eye-opener as her sudden
appearance. The old line sliced through a cutting south of
the bridge and I remembered one of Duncan's lightbulb
points in his book. The gangs of navvies used the loose rock
and soil from a cutting to build up an embankment on either
side so that they didn't have to dig too deep.

It began to drizzle a little, but I still believed I could
complete the walk by lunchtime, having done eighteen of
the twenty-eight miles the previous day. My old Barbour
would have no trouble keeping me dry and the tweed bunnet
was firmly scrugged down. I noticed that moss had crept
right across the tarmac path in places, a testimony to too
little use and the damp, West Highland climate. I had left
my hotel early, long before breakfast was to be served, and
all I had was a bottle of water and a few squares of fruit
and nut chocolate. It would have to do. After a series of

deep cuttings where the line had bitten through outcrops of glistening rock I came to a wood where the trees reached very high. An information board welcomed me to Sutherland's Grove, a wood of Douglas firs first planted in 1870. Some of them stand fifty metres tall. John Donald Sutherland was an Oban solicitor who liked trees and helped set up the Forestry Commission in 1919.

The path had departed from the line of the railway to meander through the policies of Barcaldine House. At one point it turned three right angles around an old walled garden that had been converted into a caravan park. In the dripping birch woods I came across patches of strange flowers. Like giant tulips, they were yellow and looked like something from *The Day of the Triffids*. The mossy path was weaving its way through a landscape of great fecundity. Along its margins were rows of thousands of tiny Norway spruce seedlings, miniature trees no more than two or three inches high growing close to the giant Douglas firs.

When at last I rejoined the line of the railway, the path ran beside it for a while. Although the trackbed was easy to make out, it had become very overgrown. I passed a tree-felling operation on the slopes east of the Oban road. The harvester looked like a dinosaur grazing in the primeval forest as its saw gripped a tree trunk, zipped through in seconds and lifted it up onto a stack. Even though I know that felling is necessary, the process scars the land badly and leaves animals and other woods suddenly exposed to the weather. And a clear-felled forest takes many years to heal. One of our own woods is due to be felled this year and I will miss it badly, sad to see the mighty trees toppled, living things of such majesty killed.

Despite my prayers, the Scottish Sea Life Sanctuary was not yet open, so no breakfast for me. Its staff were arriving, but a notice said I would have to wait for an hour. I bet those people parking their cars had eaten a hearty breakfast: bacon and eggs, porridge, maybe kippers. I ate my last square of chocolate, swigged the last of my bottle of water and walked on. Some neatly made concrete bridges told me I was walking beside the railway again, as it moved towards the loch shore. An elegant double-masted yacht bobbed at anchor and in the distance I could see the clouds lifting and some splashes of sunshine on the mountains of Mull and Morvern.

For a long stretch, I walked beside the Oban road and I smiled to see a rickety, rusty old tubular steel and canvas chair set against a fence. And further up, there was another one. I was tempted, but Benderloch lay ahead, maybe a mile away, and the OS Explorer suggested it was a substantial village. Maybe there would be a cafe, one that was open. When I reached the '30' signs, I came across a surprising piece of technology by the side of the road. Like an electronic standing stone, a tall black structure digitally displayed the temperature, the time and the number of cyclists who had passed it that day (1) and the number so far this year (544). I was not certain who needed that information; perhaps a guide to the local cafés and their opening times would have been more helpful. But even though it was early April, before Easter, these numbers still seemed to me to be disappointing for such a well-made and well-maintained route. People really should get out more.

The path rejoined the line of the railway and led behind the back gardens of the single street that seemed to be Benderloch. After two bridges, an information board told me I was standing in Benderloch Station and a colour photograph as late as 1960 showed a signal box and a large station house. All gone now. But what I could see was a very present café. Glory be. As I ordered coffee that would be made by an approved brand of Italian machines (my coffee snobbery is unreconstructable), I saw and smelled a tray of freshly baked scones: fruit, plain, cheese, raspberry (?) and treacle. Enjoyment of the latter was only slightly marred by the butter and jam: one came in little postage stamp-size foil packets, hard from the fridge, and the other was a sugary red jelly in a plastic container. But the scone was excellent.

Only three miles to go to Connel and the end of the line. The path rejoined it and bright seas views greeted me as the sun flickered in and out. Across the Firth of Lorn I could make out the southern tail of the island of Lismore and somewhere in the haze was the site of its ancient church. The early Christian monks of Ireland and Atlantic Scotland loved these islands because they believed that their literal isolation might bring them closer to God. Their example was a group of ascetics known as the Desert Fathers, men who left the towns of the Near East to seek solitude in remote caves and shelters. There, far from the tumult of the world, and persecution, they could pray, fast and try to bring themselves to a transcendent state. These men sometimes formed small communities, the first monasteries, and they much impressed early Christians in Western Europe. In place of deserts, Irish and Scottish monks chose the wastes of the sea to cut them off from the temporal world. That was what drew Columba to Iona. At about the same time, Moluag came to Lismore.

Sometime around 561 to 564, Moluag founded a *diseart*, a hermitage whose Gaelic name derives directly from desert, and over the centuries it grew in importance, eventually becoming an abbey in the Middle Ages. By 1200, there were Bishops of Lismore and their see received gifts of land from pious lords, powerful men who used their wealth to buy themselves salvation, or at least a shorter term in purgatory. Much of the patrimony given to Lismore was in Appin and that is the origin of the unusual place name. It means 'the lands of the abbey', the *abbatial*, in Latin, and in Gaelic b's are often sounded like p's.

Beyond Benderloch the line crossed the Moss of Achnacree, and according to Duncan Kennedy, this stretch presented problems for the engineers. The ground was so wet and soft that digging down to find bedrock was out of the question. And so on either side of the trackbed an earth blanket was spread. Its weight would stop the peat spewing up as a train crossed the moss. Essentially the engineers floated the track on the bog, but when a train did travel over it, the track visibly sank and rose again.

To the west of the railway, I came across another sort of station. I had no idea that Oban airport existed, but here it was right on the edge of the loch shore where the ground was flat. Two helicopters took off while I watched and I could see a light aircraft parked at the end of a runway. Behind me, in this most scenic and sunlit place, a steep bank was covered with fly-tipped rubbish: television sets, fridges, bit of doors and other disfigurements.

When the path climbed a little, I could make out the grey girders of Connel Bridge up ahead, rather in the way that motorists on the northern approach to the Forth see the profile of the great rail bridge. Duncan Kennedy wrote with passion about the work at Connel. Unlike at Creagan, no central pier could be sunk into the water. The tide-rip was much too strong. When I reached the bridge, I looked a long way down to see what is known as the Falls of Lora. The water does not fall far, but it is very dramatic. Loch Etive is much longer than Loch Creran, and where it meets the open waters of the Firth of Lorn there is a three- or four-foot drop over an underwater shelf where the force of the flow can be tremendous on an ebb tide. I could see it clearly as the sun glinted off the fast-moving falls.

The bottleneck of the narrows added greatly to the power of the tide-rip and all of this meant that Arrol & Co. would have to use a single span to connect North and South Connel across 500 feet of clear water. 'All things are possible, but some are difficult' was the comment of an engineer, reported by Duncan Kennedy. But Arrols achieved it brilliantly. Having prefabricated the steel structure in Glasgow, they shipped it to Connel and began building outwards from two large piers on the landward sides of the narrows. As steel girders were bolted on each side, the two structures crept closer and were eventually linked. When the bridge was finished, its load-bearing was given a severe test when eight locomotives and four wagons slowly inched out over it and then stopped in the middle. A nervous moment.

The Connel Bridge is a stunning achievement, especially given its remote location. For a time, it was the second-longest cantilever span in Europe after the Forth Bridge. Seen from the road below, it is monumental, an entirely fitting end to an epic project built by Scottish workers and Scottish companies. When the line opened to the public on 24 August 1903, the steelwork had all been painted mustard yellow and bunting was strung along each station platform. But when regular services began, there were fatalities. Nothing so fast had ever been seen in Appin, and sheep and cattle did not move quickly enough to avoid trains hurtling along at the recommended average speed of 40 miles an hour.

When I walked across the great bridge to South Connel, I reached journey's end in elegiac mood. Of course, the closure of the railway line was to be regretted. Unlike some, it can never be reopened because of the way the modern road has been re-routed and taken over its bridges. Instead, I reflected on the breezy confidence that built the line, which suffuses every page of Duncan Kennedy's book, and the skills and knowledge that backed it. On my long walk I had seen what these had achieved at first hand. But all of that expertise has gone from Scotland. Without outside help, we could never again build anything like the Connel to Ballachulish line.

As the sun glinted off the water and the gulls called, I was glad to have walked where it once ran and grateful to the builders of the excellent path.

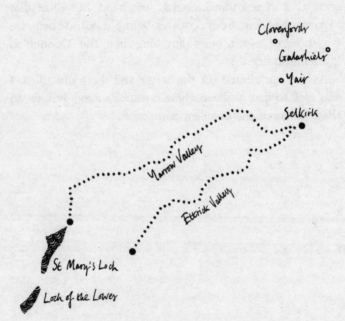

Clovenfords

Galashiels

Mair

Selkirk

Yarrow Valley

Ettrick Valley

St Mary's Loch

Loch of the Lowes

The Summer Roads ⑨

9

The Summer Roads

This is not one hidden way but many. Really it is a description of the arteries of an economy now long lost and of a culture that has all but evaporated. Before the coming of the internal combustion engine, people walked the roads to do business. They could be chapmen or packmen who walked deep into the rural hinterlands to sell thread, thimbles, tobacco, linen, pins and needles . . . almost anything that could be carried and would have required a journey to a distant town to buy.

I also wanted to tell the story of Roger Quin, a poet and musician who appears to have been loved and respected in the Borders. Now, he would be labelled a vagrant, a tramp, but in the late nineteenth and early twentieth century he was only one of many who walked the roads. And, for obvious reasons, they did that mostly in the summer.

Their routes can be found all over Scotland. The Tinker Roads of Caithness, Ross and Sutherland were the subject of a superb Gaelic TV documentary I was involved in. Those who walked the summer roads were also familiar to Bina Moffat, my grandmother, and she sometimes talked to me about the characters who came to knock at her mother's door at Cliftonhill Farm.

I mourn the passing of the summer walkers. They were colourful, unexpected and somehow exotic, people who slept under the stars and heard owls hoot and foxes bark before they

closed their eyes. Nowadays, tramps are rarely seen in the coun-
tryside. And travellers are suspected, sometimes hounded, and
they react defensively. Last summer, some caravans parked on
open ground at Tweedbank in the Borders. Their coloured horses
were tethered on the roadside verges to graze the long grass and
their washing strung out between their vehicles. But when I
went over to talk to them, they were openly aggressive, probably
seeing me as prying officialdom or worse. I was vexed, sad to
think that night might have fallen on the world of the summer
roads.

In the late spring of 1920 Pringle Elliot was unloading a
cartload of fence posts by the side of the road between
Clovenfords and Galashiels. Having survived the horrors of
the trenches, then come home to find that his old job in the
tweed mills had simply disappeared, Pringle had bought a
pony and cart and set up as a fencing contractor.

It was very misty when he began digging out the deep hole
needed for the strainer-post. Perhaps the light would lift when
the sun climbed higher in the sky. Pringle stood up, shoved
his long-bladed spade in the ground, arched his back and
turned to look down the narrow, hedge-lined road. It was
early in the morning, and the mist must have muffled sounds,
but Pringle was sure he could hear low voices and the squeak
and trundle of carts. Then he saw it. Something he never
forgot all his long life. Looming huge out of the mist, plodding
along the single-track road, its trunk swinging, was an
elephant.

Transfixed, Pringle stood stock-still as the great beast
approached. On its shoulders sat a little man carrying a stick.
When the elephant drew abreast, the mahout tapped it
lightly on its flank and it stopped, turning its vast head
towards Pringle, only a foot or so from his face. Behind it

a line of carts stopped. Most were piled high with gear and one was a wheeled cage where two lions slept.

'Are we on the correct road for Galashiels?'

Unable to utter a word, Pringle nodded and the travelling circus moved on, disappearing back into the morning mist.

Many First World War veterans had suffered shell-shock and some had lost their minds, even in the peace of the Scottish Border country. For many years Pringle told no one what he had seen on that spring morning in 1920. Perhaps it had been an apparition, but then there were often strange folk about, and you never knew who or what you would meet as you walked the roads or clicked a pony and cart between the hedgerows.

In only sixty years, the span of two generations, cars have changed life radically and now no one walks the summer roads to go about their business. The country chapmen with their backpacks have disappeared, the woodcutters with their saws and axes, the horseman leading his stallion from farm to farm, the tinkers with their knife-grinders, tin pans and cups, the bards and the musicians – they have all melted into the mist. But the world of the summer roads is not entirely lost: it has not quite outrun living memory.

The winter before Pringle Elliot saw the elephant, his future wife was taking a bowl of soup to an old tramp who had been allowed to overwinter in the grooms' loft at the Yair, an estate near Galashiels. Roger Quin had worked as a clerk in Glasgow but sometime around 1900 he walked out of his job, out of the city and made his way to the Borders to begin life as a tramp, a talented tramp. In the bustle and din of Victorian Glasgow, he longed for the freedoms of the summer roads. Having taught himself to play the flute and the concertina, he also composed poetry for recital, some of it autobiographical, like this fragment about the day he left for a new life.

> I shall leave it in the morning –
> Just slip out without warning,
> Save a hand-clasp to the friend who knows the call
>   that lures me on;
> Into the city's clang and clatter
> One old man the less won't matter;
> And no one here will say me nay, or care that I am
>   gone.

Quin lived on pennies dropped in his cap as he busked in Galashiels and the mill towns, walking the Border country until ill health forced him into care. He died in 1925. Much-loved, he had a street named after him in Gala – Roger Quin Gardens.

More common than bards and musicians were the chapmen and the invisible economy they sustained. Based in the towns, they walked long country rounds in the spring, summer and autumn with their backpacks full of goods needed in nineteenth- and twentieth-century farm-places. At cottage doors, they sold matches, tobacco, thimbles, reels of thread, needles, buttons, scissors, clay pipes, lampwicks, linen, newspapers and some even operated circulating libraries of penny-books. Housewives traded with the chapmen, bartering butter, cheese, honey, bacon and other produce at their cottage doors. And this was carried back in the chapmens' pack into town to be sold or exchanged once more for the goods needed for their next venture into the countryside.

Chapmen often walked far into the hills on their rounds and one who specialised in fine linen fetched up at Tibbie Sheil's tavern at the very top of Yarrow, between St Mary's

Loch and the Loch of the Lowes – where he took a glass or two too many. By St Mary's Kirk his unsteadiness toppled him into the loch and soaked all of his merchandise. But it was a warm summer Saturday night and once the auld chapman had wrung out his linen tablecloths and sheets, he draped them over the headstones in the kirkyard. The following morning was misty, the loch invisible, but a fresh breeze got up just as the first of the congregation was walking to the kirk for the Sunday service. It lifted and wafted the linen sheets like shrouds and stunned the approaching faithful. 'My God,' exclaimed Jock Darling, a local farmer. 'It's the resurrection!'

During the bitter winter months of short days and long nights, the shepherds who worked in the hills at the heads of the valleys of the Borthwick and Tima Waters, the Ettrick, the Yarrow and Eskdalemuir held an annual chess tournament. Fiercely contested, the prize was an impressive silver cup. But contenders had to make more than an effort of the intellect to win it. The shepherds lived within a twenty-mile radius of each other around the heads of the valleys and each had to take turns to walk to his opponent's cottage to play. And there were no roads, only tracks up and down the hillsides and stony fords across burns and sikes. Fixtures generally took place at the full moon so that players could see to walk home. It must have been a long hike for the losers.

There are many of these half-forgotten stories about the world of the summer roads, some very poignant, others very strange, most of them never before told. Sadly I am old enough to remember the very end of it in the 1950s, the time before cars became affordable for ordinary people. Ethel and Doddie were a bad-tempered brother and sister, black as craws, constantly squabbling, who sold hessian sacks of firewood around the doors, bags of twigs they had picked up in the woods and dried. And I remember that they always asked for the hessian sacks back, insisting that we shake out the kindling into our bunker. My mum was sure they had been abandoned as children. They foraged in the woods around Kelso, picking up fallen branches, even twigs, and stooking them like cut corn until they dried. As children, we stole apples, made fires to roast spuds pinched from home, took birds' eggs and were involved in all manner of mischief. But when we came across Ethel and Doddie's stooks in the woods, we left them untouched. I suspect we made an exception not through some vague sort of respect for noble savages, people who had nothing and lived off the land, but because Ethel and Doddie were frightening, feral. In the silent depths of a dark corner of a wood, they might suddenly appear from behind a tree, their lined, wind-worn faces a rictus of rage.

I remember Puzzle Bobby entrancing groups of children by making cat's cradles, corn dollies and little metal puzzles of linked squares and triangles, and Wullie the Troot was a bespoke poacher who lived out all summer tending his snares and traps before wintering in an abandoned roadside smiddy in the foothills of the Cheviots. Once seen at the bus stop in Kelso Square at 9.30 p.m. waiting for the 10 p.m. bus, Wullie replied to jibes that he couldn't read the time with the immortal, 'Aye, mibbe, but it'll no take me long tae wait half an hour.'

Before all is lost, this tale of those who walked the summer roads might recall a sense of the countryside before cars, as a space where people lived and made a living without the need to live in a house. They slept in barns, took shelter behind dykes and on warm nights they made a bracken bed under the stars. Here is Roger Quin's own rationale, one that incidentally does not equate the life of a tramp with ignorance:

> What tho' my wallet's meagre?
> That won't quell my spirit eager –
> Like careless-hearted Goldsmith when he wandered
>   by the Po,
> Which ever way I turn me,
> My simple flute will earn me
> In the kindly Border country, food and shelter as I go.

Roger Quin was an unusual figure, a tramp who was held in high affection by the communities of the Borders. Most vagrants were viewed with deep suspicion, people likely to steal from or dupe the unwary and then vanish into the countryside; but Quin cut a very different figure and is still remembered fondly almost a century after his death.

To the south of the once-bustling mill town, Gala Hill was both a playground for children and a place where Sunday afternoon walkers could enjoy the long views. Now the hill is mostly wooded, but I found a well-signposted path that led to open ground and a pleasing view of the Eildon Hills. By a gate stands a grey granite, tombstone-like memorial to Roger Quin that quotes a line from his most famous poem, 'The Borderland': 'Gazed on Scotland's Eden from the spur of Gala Hill'. And at the foot of the slope is Roger Quin Gardens, a street of new houses named after the man who called himself 'the Tramp Poet'.

By themselves, his verses are not remarkable. They sit squarely in the traditions of pastoral poetry much enjoyed by late Victorians and Edwardians, and because they some-times dealt with local places, also by Borderers. It was more the idea of Quin's life that attracted so much affection. He was clearly a well-read and educated man who rejected the regimented world of work, one inhabited by the bulk of his readers and admirers, and he decided to follow the life of a tramp and all its freedoms – and privations. The image of Quin walking the summer roads composing his verses and playing his music for gatherings of country people summoned up the romance of strolling minstrels and troubadours, the sort of thing Walter Scott occasionally brought to life in his novels. What enhanced the romance was the fact that the tramp poet was not like his fellow travellers, not a miserable creature covered in rags. There exists a photograph of Roger Quin and it shows a handsome man with a full head of well-barbered grey hair and a splendid Edwardian moustache. He is wearing a dark three-piece suit with a white handkerchief in the breast pocket and a neat collar and tie. His hands are folded in his lap as he gazes off camera with a somewhat melancholy expression. Now, Roger Quin clearly did not walk the roads wearing a suit, but even if all was borrowed and got up for the occasion, he was nevertheless a good-looking man.

Quin was by no means unique. Born in Dumfries in 1850, the only son in a family of twelve children, he was named after his father. Roger Quin Snr was himself a published poet and his collection, *The Heather Lintie*, went into a second edition. I have an original copy and its yellowed pages contain seventy poems that range from one addressed to Scottish MPs about to deliberate on the great petition of the Chartists to another that celebrates the beauties of potato flowers. It is not McGonagall, but neither is it Keats, Shelley or Wordsworth.

Roger Quin Snr moved his large family to Galashiels sometime after 1861, when his only son would still have been a schoolboy. Perhaps it was then he fell in love with the Borders landscape. But by 1866, Quin Jnr had returned to Dumfries to work as an assistant in the office of the town clerk before moving on to another position with the Caledonian Railway Company. This led to a move to Glasgow and ultimately to Quin's decision to leave the clang and clatter of the city to return to the Borders. At the age of fifty, he then entered upon a life that followed loosely in a tradition made world famous by the genius of Robert Burns. Hailed as a 'heaven-taught ploughman' by the condescension of the urban elite, he established the notion of poetry coming almost unbidden even to the most humble. James MacFarlane, the Pedlar Poet, built a reputation founded on lowly origins as well as talent, and since around 1700 the writers of chapbooks (of which more later) had helped create an appetite for literature, of a sort, amongst ordinary people.

In 1908, A. Walker & Sons of Galashiels published a collection of Roger Quin's poetry. Entitled *Roger Quin, Poet and Bohemian*, the preface is in places excruciating, some of it about the talents of Roger Quin Snr. However, there are some nuggets of biographical information. Quin was first published by a London-based publication called *T.P.'s Weekly*, founded by the Irish Nationalist MP T.P. O'Connor. Apparently a friend had received a letter from Quin that included the text of a poem and he took an initiative to send it to the newspaper. It was the poem quoted on the memorial on Gala Hill, 'The Borderland', and here are its opening stanzas:

From the moorland and the meadows
To this city of the shadows,
Where I wander old and lonely, comes the call I
  understand;
In clear, soft tones enthralling,

It is calling-calling-calling-
'Tis the Spirit of the Open from the dear old
   Borderland!
Ah that call! who can gainsay it?
To hear is to obey it;
I must leave the bustling city to the busy city men,
Leave behind its feverish madness,
Its scenes of sordid sadness;
And drink the unpolluted air of Yarrow once again!

Two other poems were published, one in the *Glasgow Herald* and another in *T.P.'s Weekly*, and then there appears what may be a quote from Quin himself, something that self-consciously continues the myth and image of the Tramp Poet:

I have never written a line with a view to immediate or ultimate publication. When the idea of a Book was first entertained I had not a scrap of manuscript in my possession. I had consequently to rake the cells of my memory, and furnish my publishers piecemeal (as it were), and at irregular intervals, with such scraps of verse as I could remember. Much of my best work has been frittered away in letters to friends- and-others and is now gone, beyond recall. My publishers found, to their cost and their consternation, that to trap and cage your Tramp Poet is one thing; to get him to sing, when there, is another! No sooner had I entered the door of Convention that my errant Muse left me with a contemptuous flip of her wing, and sailed away in the direction of Yarrow and Moffat. She sometimes pays me a flying visit – jeers at me through the window and taunts me with the memory of the happy days we have spent together in the Open.

The claim that all was composed, retained in memory, however imperfectly, and not written down feeds the image of the troubadour inspired by the glories of the landscape he walks through and inhabits. It is, however, contradicted by a frontispiece photograph of Quin standing on the spur of Gala Hill, where his tombstone-like memorial was planted. He wears a long overcoat and a hat – and he is writing in a notebook. Robert Burns is said to have composed entire poems while working at the manual tasks of farming, but he was careful to commit them to paper later. It is difficult to believe that such a bookish man as Roger Quin did not usually carry the sort of notebook and pencil shown in the photograph, but the simple notion of him making his verses and holding them in memory as he walked the summer roads seems more pleasing. And he knew it.

Quin spent many sunlit summers in the Borders and was genuinely held in great affection. In the otherwise cringeworthy introduction to his collection of poetry, its author (wisely writing under the nom de plume of John North) observed:

> Quin has a bright, buoyant, breezy temperament, and you may understand that he receives so hearty a welcome from the lonely people in quiet country places, to whom his coming means as much as the packman's visit in pre-newspaper days.

In the winter Roger Quin appears to have returned to Glasgow, where he wrote both prose and poetry about the plight of homeless people. It is his best work, an authentic voice, and here is a poem entitled 'Nocturne' that describes what Quin saw in George Square in the shadow of City Chambers.

The City's clamour has now ebb'd away,
And silence settles o'er the dusky square,
Save for a cough, sepulchral, here and there,
From shivering forms, that wait the coming day;
Hunger and Houselessness, without one ray
Of hope to chase the shadow of Despair,
Keep weary vigil in the wintry air,
Each heart to dread Despondency a prey.
Proudly the Civic Palace, over all,
Looms through the night, and, with a sculptur'd frown,
Meets the dull gaze of Want's lackluster eye:
Till slowly, like some vast funeral pall,
The chill, dense curtain of the mist creeps down,
Shrouding the splendour, and – the Misery.

Roger Quin applied for winter jobs as a doorman at the Mitchell Library and at Glasgow University but was not successful. Potential employers probably guessed that when summer came he would be away south. In the depths of one winter in the early 1900s, Quin met an acquaintance in the street, George Eyre Todd, the president of the Glasgow Ballad Club, and told him he was starving. When Todd took him for a meal, the Tramp Poet asked if he could keep on his overcoat at the table. He had no jacket underneath.

Quin seems to have been generally adept at keeping body and soul together in the Borders and there is a casual mention of him in the diary of Dr J.S. Muir, who served the communities around Selkirk for fifty-four years. 'Looking more respectable than I ever saw him, Roger Quin called. Gave him six shillings.' And in 1921 the St Andrew Society of Bradford (probably a group of exiles since the town had strong links with the Borders because of the textile industry) sent Quin ten guineas as 'assistance and encouragement'.

But by that time, the Tramp Poet seems to have been failing and more comfortable accommodation was found for him at the Yair, near Galashiels. He was given the use of a cottage and his many friends and admirers found a few sticks of furniture for him, as well as the occasional gifts of food and other necessities. Later he moved back to Dumfries to a charity home, where he died in 1925.

It was a singular life. However self-conscious and contrived Roger Quin's image and attitudes might have been, the raw rigours of an existence on the summer roads will have been testing. Sometimes it rained, and often he will have been alone in the chill of still, dark nights.

Roger Quin walked along country roads much busier than they are now. He saw the closing years of high farming in Scotland, a time when big places could have sixty or seventy people living in the rows of cottages, a steward or grieve in his house and a farmer in the 'big hoose'. And just as my grandmother did, children helped almost as soon as they could walk. Quin will have met people every day and often enjoyed a bite of something homely at a cottage door, perhaps in payment for a tune or two on his flute or the recital of a poem. In an age before radio and television, such entertainments were valued.

The 1891 census that notes the presence of my one-year-old grannie at Cliftonhill was valedictory, a demographic snapshot taken as high farming was beginning to fade. There were nine labourers' cottages and the enumerator counted sixty-two people living on the farm: twenty-three were working and twenty-five were children, the balance made up by the families of the steward and the farmer. After 1891 the rural workforce began to decline and now it takes only two people, Archie and Maggie Stewart, to run Cliftonhill Farm. What remains of that community is very poignant, a place where only ghosts flit around the arches of the cart-sheds and under the lintels of the cottages, only silence now where twenty-five children shrieked and careered, where four pairs of Clydesdales clattered over the cobbles out to the fields, and where twenty ploughmen and farm hands had a quiet smoke and a blether at the day's end after they had groomed and fed their horses. Cliftonhill is still beautiful and still well farmed, but it is a place where I have sometimes felt the tears prickle for the loss of all that experience in one place.

Farms across Britain used to depend on horsepower and many kept a brood mare that could be put into foal to keep up the supply of muscle power. Heavy horses like Clydesdales carry their foals for eleven to twelve months and early spring was considered the optimum time to put a stallion to a mare. A year later, there would be spring grass to make her milk rich and nourishing, and perhaps warming weather. Now, this is all managed by artificial insemination, but for most of the twentieth century such methods were unknown. Natural covering meant that Roger Quin will have occasion-ally met a Clydesdale stallion as its owner or handler led the horse from farm to farm. It could be a highly lucrative but also dangerous business and because mares had to be in season, timing was crucial.

Perhaps the most famous Clydesdale stallion was Dunure Footprint. He was a breeding phenomenon. At the height of his prodigious powers, he could cover 400 mares in a season, although he was falling off them by the end of the spring. It is reckoned that he sired more than 5,000 foals and consequently his progeny have dominated Clydesdale breeding for generations. As he was led into a farmyard, he must have been a splendid sight for all who gathered to see him.

The reasons for such demand were not aesthetic but practical. Their great power enabled Clydesdales to pull a plough through even the most difficult, wet and clayish land. Dunure Footprint may have been so-called because he was blessed with big feet and strong legs that could generate immense power under well-muscled hindquarters and shoulders. Black with white feathered socks, he had near-perfect conformation and was not only neat with his feet and well-balanced, but also took a good grip of the land. This is important because after the first furrow is ploughed, a Clydesdale walks with one foreleg and one hind leg on unploughed ground and the other two in the furrow he has just ploughed. That makes good balance vital. Daintiness of foot in such a huge animal was also much prized for another reason. It was important to be able to turn tightly at the end of each furrow so that as little land as possible was left unploughed. Well-schooled Clydesdales could do this well by stepping carefully inside each other and changing their leading legs.

Dunure Footprint was also said to stamp his foals with his equable temperament, making them easy to train and manage. A horse of such bulk simply must be obedient. I once led a vast eighteen-hands Clydesdale when he was very unsettled, looking about himself constantly, not watching where he was going. And he stepped on my foot, more than a ton of horse. Mercifully, I was wearing steel-toecapped boots and survived with only black bruising. An old ploughman who kept heavy horses out of sentiment and an unwillingness to see the old skills die allowed me to take the long reins behind a plough pulled by his best horse. A wonderful, emotional experience for me, to do, very approximately, what my great-great-grandfather, William Moffat, had expertly done on the rigs at Cliftonhill. With a complete incompetent hanging onto the plough stilts for dear life, the old horse kept his head down and made a straight furrow no matter what the idiot holding the reins did to impede him. My clear memory of that day was the ploughshare slicing cleanly through the ground like butter.

Dunure Footprint made his owners a fortune. Each covering cost the farmer £60 and even in a slower year that could amount to £2,000 – almost £250,000 in today's values. William Dunlop took his precious stallion all over Lowland Scotland by train and, to conserve his energy, walked him slowly to farms to cover their mares. It could be a dangerous business. Dunure Footprint's sire, a much sought-after stallion called the Baron of Buchlyvie, had his leg broken by a kick from a mare as he covered her and had to be put down when he was only fourteen. But his son carried on until he was twenty-two, dying in 1930. In photographs, the great black stallion stands beautifully, but I would have loved to have seen him in all his glory and power. Perhaps Roger Quin did.

The first line of one of Scotland's most famous poems, 'Tam O' Shanter', is evocative of another sort of man who walked great distances to make a living. 'When chapmen billies leave the street' recalls an old economy – and culture. The word comes from the Old English *ceap* and it meant 'to deal' or 'barter'. In London, Cheapside and Eastcheap are place where deals were made, and 'chap' for a man is cognate. He was a customer, the person with whom to bargain.

In addition to small, portable items like thimbles, needles, pins and thread, most of the items carried by chapmen billies were designed to appeal to women, the people on a cottage doorstep with whom they would strike a bargain.

These transactions gave rise to the phrase 'pin money'. It was originally a small amount of cash women kept back to buy the chapmen's wares when they had little produce to barter.

In the Ettrick and Yarrow Valleys, west of Selkirk, chapmen were known as packmen and almost all of them were indeed men. With one exception. In the late nineteenth century, Jean Dunlop carried bread on her back once a week to supply the farms in Yarrow. The manse at Yarrow Kirk ordered a quartern-loaf (a four-pound wheat loaf) and another went to Whitehope Farmhouse. Cottages could only afford penny rolls, but bread made with wheat used to be a luxury. Most made bannocks with oatmeal, or scones and drop-scones (a variety of pancake cooked on a very hot griddle). My grannie used to talk of shop bread with the faintest trace of a sneer and she herself only ever baked scones, drop-scones and tarts with whatever fruit was available.

Packmen also brought news. No doubt it was often embroidered, supplemented and occasionally little more than rumour, much like what passes now for news on the internet. But it was eagerly devoured by remote communities. When a postal service was established in the middle of the nineteenth century and made affordable, letters could take some time to reach the heads of the Ettrick and Yarrow Valleys. Before they were equipped with bicycles and then vans, postmen walked to make all their deliveries, and it was impossible for them to venture far out of the towns. And so when they saw someone in Selkirk who was about to travel up Ettrick or Yarrow, they asked them to deliver as many letters as they could on their way home. What was left might then be taken on further up the valley by someone going that way. And so the post was delivered in relays. When the Selkirk postmen had letters for Eskdalemuir or Craik, on the farther side of the watershed hills, these were deposited by shepherds at Post Office Knowe. Long scattered now, this was a specially built cairn on the track from the head of Ettrick to Eskdalemuir. Letters were carefully placed under the stones of the cairn in places expertly built by dykers to keep them dry and out of the wind. When someone was passing over the watershed, they would collect them and deliver them on their way down to Eskdalemuir.

The packmen or chapmen also had chapbooks. These were light, usually eight-page fold-ups of a single sheet, and they were cheap, so to speak, often only a penny. And also immensely popular. In Scotland, between 1750 and 1850, it is believed that more than 200,000 chapbooks were sold each year. As a result of the central emphasis placed on mass literacy by the Scottish Reformation (everyone had to be able to read the Bible), even those who lived in remote valleys could read.

Walter Scott noted that he had a collection of 114 chapbooks 'formed by me when a boy from the baskets of pedlars'. He had to keep rescuing them 'from the clutches of servants'. Popular chapbooks usually contained the lyrics of songs or some poetry, and their authors were sometimes also their sellers. An early form of self-publication. John Milne of Aberdeenshire was a chapman–author–publisher with his own signature lines.

> I, Jock Milne of the Glen
> Wrote this poem wi' my ain pen:
> And I'm sure I couldnae sell it cheaper,
> For it'll hardly pay for the price o' the paper.

The contents of chapbooks were sometimes bawdy, even coarse, often amusing. Alexander Wilson was caught relieving himself behind a dyke by the baillie, a local magistrate, and he responded with a poem, of sorts.

> My order, sir, was Nature's laws,
> That was the reason, and because
> Necessity's demands and ca's
> War very gleg,
> I hunkered down 'mang this hard wa's
> To lay my egg.
> And sir, I'm seeking naethin frae ye;
> My offering here I freely leave you,
> Sic presents ilka one won't gie you,
> Take ye my word,
> Ye're richer since I first did see you,
> That reeking turd.

As well as recording his own experiences, however embrassing, Wilson observed the world of the chapmen and wrote this of Old Ralph, who walked the roads in the 1790s. He carried a heavy burden.

> Stooped him half to earth. A goat's rough skin
> Inwrapt the costly stores. Scissors and combs,
> And knives and laces long; sharp-pointed awls,
> And pins, arranged in many a glittering row,
> Strong Shetland hose, and woolen night-caps warm,
> Clasps, bonnets, razors, spectacles and rings.

In various guises, chapmen continued to trade into the twentieth century. Those with packs like Old Ralph's walked up the remote valleys, and in towns and cities door-to-door salesmen were their heirs. As late as the 1980s in Edinburgh, my wife bought dusters, chamois leathers, brushes and cleaning solutions from a salesman who carried a large suitcase rather than a pack as he rang the doorbell every spring. Specialists also drove along the improving country roads and a clothing firm from Eaglesfield in Annandale still sent a tailor up the Ettrick and Yarrow Valleys to measure customers for suits as late as the 1960s. My old friend Walter Elliot still has a suit made for him in 1959 by Sandy Anderson of Eaglesfield. The tweed is so thick 'it could stop bullets'. More than a sentimental keepsake that Walter refuses to cast out as old-fashioned, it recalls a different way of doing business. Anyway, the jacket still fits. Anderson made two trips each year up the Ettrick Valley. He first came to measure customers and be paid a substantial deposit. Then, six months later, he brought back the suit for a fitting. And fifty-eight years later Walter Elliot's bullet-proof suit still hangs in his wardrobe.

On a bleak winter's day, I drove along the back roads to Ettrickbridgend to meet Tommy Wilson, one of the last of the hill shepherds. Now long retired, he used to summer out on the high pasture with his flocks and his dogs, sleeping in shieling huts if there was rain or high wind across the hills. As autumn approached Tommy gathered the fat lambs and drove them to market along the roads. He told me that one of his favourite routes was the one I had just taken to come to him, and part of it was the single-track road half a mile south of our farm.

In the late 1960s there was markedly more traffic and that made the main roads impossible to drive beasts along. Depending absolutely on the bright-eyed intelligence of his Border collies to lead the flock, Tommy walked behind so that he could use his other dogs to return stragglers or strays.

When I asked him what happened when the occasional car appeared ahead of his sheep, he told me that the collies planted themselves in the middle of the road and faced it down, forcing it to stop quickly, holding the driver in their unwavering gaze.

Before the Second World War, there was much less traffic on the roads, and what there was moved much more slowly. Almost all flocks were driven on foot, and from the high valleys to the markets at Hawick and St Boswells it could be a two- or three-day journey. Shepherds from Eskdale, Craik and the Borthwick Water moved their sheep along the ancient Roman road that joins Dere Street at St Boswells. Those bound for Hawick left it at Roberton and turned down the trail by the Borthwick Water. When he was a boy, Pringle Elliot lived at Meadshaw, a farm that sat astride the old road. He can remember his mother feeding the passing shepherds dinners of ham and eggs with bannocks, scones and jam. The dogs were given bowls of warm porridge. And because so many passed the cottage at the end of the summer each shepherd put sixpence on Mrs Elliot's table 'for her trouble'.

So that they kept condition and were up to weight when sold, the flocks were moved on slowly, grazing the hillside by the road as they went, always kept in a pack by the collies. They stopped only when darkness fell, and one of the shepherds always stayed with the sheep while the other men sought to sleep under cover in a barn or an empty loosebox. But as soon as the sun lit the eastern hills all of the shepherds went immediately to see to their flocks. Usually, other farmers were driving their flocks to market at the same time and the great fear was mixing. It could take a great deal of trouble and swearing to disentangle two flocks in open country.

Once the beasts had safely reached the markets and been sold, the shepherds from several up-country farms often hired a sixteen-seater cart drawn by two horses to take them and their dogs home in some comfort. Meadshaw stood at the end of the cart road (not enough of the Roman road remained to make onward travel advisable) and Pringle Elliot recalls the men arriving late in the evening with gifts of kippers, herring, sausages and at least half a bottle of whisky. After supper, some tale-telling and perhaps music, the men bedded down in the hay barn for only a few hours' sleep. They needed to get back to their hirsels before first light so that they could see to the ewes and lambs that had not gone to market.

During the Second World War, shepherding and farming were a reserved occupation, but young men from the valleys nevertheless managed to volunteer. As the war wore on, both Italian and German prisoners of war were drafted to the Border hills to help short-handed farmers. At that time, Walter Elliot was at school in Ettrickbridgend and was taught by a remarkable man, Mr Douglas. Having been badly wounded in the First World War and left for dead in no-man's-land, he was picked up by a German medical team, patched up and eventually freed. During his confinement, Mr Douglas had learned to speak German and when the Second World War broke out he took a more measured, less hostile view of the enemy. At Christmas, the schoolteacher insisted that the prisoners of war be invited to the celebrations since they were far from home. Walter remembers a very young German soldier, a boy of only seventeen, being asked by Mr Douglas to sing a carol. There is a catch in Walter's voice when he casts his mind back to hearing a pure tenor voice beginning the words of

'*Stille Nacht*' ('Silent Night'), as the snow fell in the Ettrick Valley.

Both before and after the Second World War other Europeans came voluntarily to Scotland to travel the summer roads, and I remember them well. Onion Johnnies, or as we called them in Scots, Ingan Johnnies, cycled all over the countryside with long strings of onions draped over the handlebars and the back wheels of their tall bikes. Most wore black berets and spoke Scots with a strong French accent. Onions could be grown at home, but it was the quality of what the Ingan Johnnies sold that sustained this surprising trade. My grannie always bought a string, even though they were more expensive than what the local greengrocer sold. 'You could peel them and eat them like an apple' – although I never saw her do that.

The onions came from Brittany and they were large and pink. And while it may have looked hand-to-mouth, the onion trade was well organised. String sacks of onions were loaded onto a cargo ship at Roscoff, and once it docked at Leith they were stored and strung. An Ingan Johnny could carry 350 onions on his bike and he was not encouraged to come back with unsold stock. They started very early to catch domestic customers before they went out to work and then sold to butcher's shops in particular. Strings of garlic, very exotic in the 1950s, were also sold, but I never saw them, and they probably went to the butcher's or specialist shops in the cities. I remember a tall, cadaverous Ingan Johnny cycling down our street in Kelso, his big, black bike laden with onions, and, along with my grannie, many of the neighbours came out to buy some. He bowed when the women handed over the cash. By the 1960s the Johnnies gradually stopped coming. In Brittany, young people simply did not think all that effort worth the trouble.

The summer roads are much less travelled now. The gypsies and their horse-drawn caravans have disappeared except at the occasional country show, and seasonal workers like the squads of Irish potato pickers, the tattie howkers, have been replaced by machinery. Not even tramps tramp the roads any longer, although in the towns and cities there seems to be no shortage of beggars and homeless people. Those few who do still roam the countryside are held in deep suspicion and in 1999 a remarkable story surfaced in Scotland that showed how much attitudes have changed.

In the summer of that year, the police were called to a barn near Denny in Stirlingshire. People passing had heard 'noises' and some sort of activity inside but had been too timid to go in. Without a struggle, the police arrested Robert Sinclair. Their investigation uncovered a life described as 'feral'. For twenty-three years, Rab had lived the life of a tramp, stealing milk off doorsteps, sometimes food from shops (but never money), occasionally guddling fish from rivers and streams, eating summer berries or old turnips left in fields. In the winters, he had sometimes starved: '[I] might stay huddled up for five or six days without eating because it was too cold to go out. I didn't know what day it was except by looking at a paper and guessing how old it was.' He was essentially harmless, but was nevertheless charged.

While on remand, awaiting trial for petty theft, Rab was kept in a tiny cell. One night he pulled the string out of his prison issue tracksuit bottoms and tried to hang himself. Eventually he was given a room in a council house by a fellow inmate after they had both been freed. But Rab still felt confined 'looking at walls and rows of houses', and later he found himself in Barlinnie Prison.

I searched for more recent news of Rab Sinclair online but could find nothing. Perhaps he has taken to the summer roads again, or perhaps he has simply faded into everyday life.

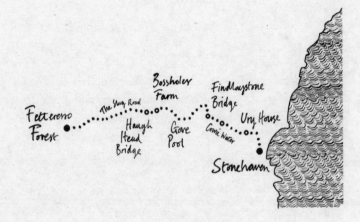

Fetteresso Forest — The Slug Road — Haugh Head Bridge — Bossholes Farm — Gove Pool — FindMaystone Bridge — Cowie Water — Ury House — Stonehaven

The Road Block ⑩

10

The Road Block

Stonehaven to the Edge of the Grampians

The abandoned debris of panic can be found all over Scotland, amongst sand dunes, on moorland hilltops and rural roadsides. When Hitler's armies overran Poland in 1939 and France fell the following year, it seemed only a matter of time before the panzers rumbled onshore somewhere along Britain's coastline.

The evacuation from Dunkirk in May 1940 rescued many soldiers but left most of the British army's equipment on the beaches. This meant invasion had to be made difficult not by installing artillery batteries (there was very little artillery at that time) or deploying units at strategic points, but by putting up obstacles, mostly made out of concrete. I came across the Cowie Stop Line by accident while commissioning a TV documentary series called Scotland's War *and it fascinated me.*

The line is short and the road that linked its anti-tank cubes and pillboxes is lost in places, but it is poignant. It was built by my parents' generation and, even though it seemed almost futile in the face of the German war machine, they did it to prevent the triumph of evil. When I was a boy, the memory of the Nazis, Hitler and the Second World War dominated British cultural life and, as one of its most fascinating relics, the Cowie Stop Line brought back memories of games with wooden rifles, comics, television documentaries and films, as well as the black-and-white realities of war and the simple heroism of those who fought both at home and abroad.

When the panzers rumbled across the Polish border in September 1939 and the Luftwaffe spat destruction from the skies, the world was shocked by the awesome, murderous power of Blitzkrieg, of total, ruthless combat. And when Britain and France declared war, it was clear that Adolf Hitler's ambition would flare across other frontiers.

Colonel Birger Eriksen was an experienced soldier and he felt certain that Norway's neutrality would not be respected. It was only a matter of time before an attack came. Conscription was revived and thousands of raw recruits were quickly added to the armed forces. More than 400 young men were posted to Eriksen's command for training and the colonel must have shaken his head in despair – these men would form the front line of Norway's defences. They had been sent to the Oscarsborg Fortress, an island (and some islets) in the Oslofjord which housed artillery batteries and sat astride the narrow Drobak Sound, the sea lane that led to Oslo and the heart of the country. Hidden below the waterline, even at the lowest of tides, there was a secret weapon of devastating power. But Eriksen had no one who knew how to operate it. The officer in charge of it was on sick leave, not likely to return soon.

By late March 1940 tension in Europe had intensified and Colonel Eriksen was forced to take desperate measures. His secret weapon was a land-based torpedo battery located below the ramparts of the island fortress. The Germans were mobilising on the Danish frontier and Eriksen feared a simultaneous attack on Norway, almost certainly seaborne up the Oslofjord, aimed at the capture of the capital, the king, the government and the national gold reserves. He sent an urgent message to an old comrade, pleading for his help.

Andreas Anderssen had been involved in the installation of the torpedo battery and he lived at Drobak, on the shores of the fjord, not far from the fortress. A boat carried a message imploring Anderssen to take his old uniform out of the wardrobe, dust it down and get into the boat immediately. Having retired in 1927, Andreas had not worn it for some time. He was seventy-eight years old.

Delighted, and mightily relieved to see the old man, Eriksen asked him to take command of the battery. Anderssen ordered an inspection and quickly began to instruct the raw recruits on how to load torpedoes into the elevators that took them down to the underwater launch tubes. The old man reckoned they would be able to fire nine – if they were needed.

Two days later, in the late evening of 8 April 1940, Colonel Eriksen received a series of very disturbing radio signals from the fortress at the wide mouth of the Oslofjord. Observers had made out the dark outlines of six ships steaming northwards. None showed any lights or means of identification and they did not respond to radio signals. The defenders fired warning shots across the bow of the leading ship, but there was no response and, ploughing on through the gloaming, the black shapes of the flotilla did not slow or make to turn about.

Norway was formally neutral and there had been no clear direction from the government or the king on what to do if the Germans invaded. Eriksen was not certain the ships were part of the Kriegsmarine, and they might even have been Allied vessels on a clandestine mission he knew nothing about, but as darkness fell he realised the flotilla, whoever it was, would reach the Oscarsborg in an hour, maybe two. He decided to attack.

The artillery crews on the conventional gun batteries were ordered to stand to and Anderssen hurried to assemble his crew for the torpedo launchers. Anyone with any sort of experience at all was woken and given orders, even the cooks. Raw recruits manned the great guns and loaded the torpedoes. And they waited. And waited.

A few minutes after 4 a.m. on 9 April 1940, lookouts on the ramparts of the fortress sent an urgent message to Colonel Eriksen. They could make out the looming bulk of a large battleship steaming up the fjord, making straight for them and the narrow Drobak Sound. Behind it was a flotilla of five smaller vessels and at least one appeared to be heavily armed. They would be alongside the walls of the Oscarsborg in minutes. Eriksen did not hesitate. All batteries were alerted, the breaches of the huge guns loaded with shells and the torpedoes lowered into their launch tubes. Eriksen stood on the ramparts, waiting, peering into the darkness. Once he judged the leading ship was in range, he gave the order: 'Either I will be decorated or I will be court-martialled. Fire!'

At such short range, shells could scarcely miss. They slammed into the battleship and it quickly caught fire. Anderssen's deadly torpedoes slid silently under the waters of the fjord and scored direct hits. Blazing, listing, doomed, the battleship slewed out of control and passed very close to the ramparts of the Oscarsborg. The Norwegian defenders swore that they heard something strange, disconcerting; men on the stricken ship were singing: 'Deutschland, Deutschland über alles'. The rest of the flotilla turned about and steamed back the way it had come. And a few minutes after that Eriksen received a message that the ships were indeed

German. The battleship so badly hit was the *Blucher* and it sank quickly with all hands only a short distance to the north of Andreas Anderssen's deadly torpedo battery.

These remarkable events were the first action of the war in Western Europe and they signalled the end of eight months of uncertainty, the so-called Phoney War. In reality, all that Eriksen and Anderssen achieved was delay, but it was enough to allow the evacuation of the Norwegian government, the king and the gold reserves from Oslo. Resistance continued until June 1940 and the inevitable surrender followed. What the Dad's Army at the Oscarsborg did was nevertheless all the more admirable precisely because it knew that Norway could not resist the might of the Wehrmacht for long.

For the Germans, the invasion had a vital strategic aspect. Not only did it facilitate direct access to Sweden's iron-ore reserves, but, in the words of the directive authorising the invasion, there was another, very specific purpose: 'to give our navy and air force a wider start-line against Britain'.

Not even the wildest optimists in German High Command or the most fanatical Nazis could have imagined the speed of events that followed the invasion of Norway and Denmark. In a matter of days, Holland and Belgium were overrun and France had fallen. The lightning-fast panzer strikes and the all-out onslaught of Blitzkrieg tore apart resistance, and the entrapment of the British Expeditionary Force at Dunkirk was a disaster. While the rescue of so many men was hailed as a miracle, the loss of vital equipment was catastrophic. Divisions left at home had been stripped of much of their transport and armament so that it could be given to the BEF, and when the panzers cut off retreat and the Luftwaffe bombed and strafed the beaches almost all of it was abandoned. More than 1,000 field guns,

850 anti-tank guns and 600 tanks were lost. Britain was suddenly almost defenceless. And Scotland lay open to a seaborne or airborne invasion.

All that stood in the way of a series of German landings were nine battalions of infantry and their strength was unclear. Historians put the number of available defenders at between 5,000 and 8,000 men. They lacked field artillery and armour, and in any case were heavily concentrated on individual military priorities. One battalion was based on Orkney, where Scapa Flow needed land-based protection, and another was stationed on Shetland, now suddenly much closer to enemy-held territory. Three battalions guarded the Royal Navy base at Invergordon on the Moray Firth and there were three in Fife to defend attacks on the Royal Naval Dockyard at Rosyth and RAF Leuchars. Covering the entire coastline from Alness in Easter Ross down to Grangemouth on the Firth of Forth was precisely one battalion. At full strength, 800 soldiers to defend against landings along approximately 400 miles of coastline. Eastern Scotland was essentially defenceless. As many of my parents' generation remarked, in 1940 the Germans could have walked in.

North of the Tay there were only forty single-wing fighter aircraft and the bombers based at Lossiemouth, Kinloss and Wick were not designed to resist the squadrons of Luftwaffe aircraft that would carry an airborne invasion force that would attempt to capture airfields. Those at Wick and Thurso could be overwhelmed by parachutists flown across the North Sea. As early as May 1940, a month before the Norwegian surrender and the disastrous events on the beaches around Dunkirk, the Germans had taken the aerodrome at Sola, near Stavanger on the southwestern coast. It lay only 300 miles from the Home Fleet base at Scapa Flow on Orkney, less than two hours' flying time. On 10 May, the Admiralty was warning of a concentration of flat-bottomed boats along the Norwegian coast, and a week later there were reports of troop-carrying aircraft assembling at Sola.

After their spectacular successes in France, achieved at dizzying speed, it seemed that the boldness of the German war machine made almost anything possible. The Commander in Chief of naval forces at the Nore, the extravagantly named Sir Reginald Plunkett Ernle-Erle Drax, believed that an attack on Scotland was not only possible, but that it would also succeed and give the Germans tremendous strategic advantages. With an invasion force of only 30,000 troops, parachutists followed by airborne and possibly seaborne detachments, the Germans could secure the aerodromes near Wick. There was no garrison of any size to stop them. From Wick, they could then launch devastating air attacks on Scapa Flow. Forced to scatter, the Home Fleet would sail into a lethal trap set by a ring of waiting U-boats. Drax reckoned that northern Scotland could be overrun in weeks, if not days. There was nothing to stop the Germans.

The mood in Britain in the summer of 1940 was desperate, on the edge of panic. The war cabinet met to discuss options, among them the wisdom of continuing resistance after France had fallen. Would it not be prudent to seek a ceasefire and a discussion of what the terms of a peace with the Germans might be? If a significant part of the British mainland had fallen into German hands, how would the Cabinet have responded to Hitler's offer of a settlement? Would there still have been the will to fight the Battle of Britain and suffer significant losses of men and aircraft? If Hitler's troops had occupied the north of Scotland, a large area of the British landmass from where they could launch air strikes to the south, and many soldiers and civilians had died in the fighting, it must have been doubtful. The German offer to allow Britain to keep the Empire in return for a free hand in Europe would have seemed very tempting.

On the same day as Winston Churchill made his memorable speech about fighting on the beaches, frantic efforts were being made to make that less likely. Large concrete cubes were being set up and cast along Scotland's shorelines. Many still survive and they usually stand five feet apart and are arranged so that they funnel tanks into killing lanes. Very simple devices were used. Long wooden posts were hammered into wide beaches where low tide would have allowed gliders to land. Several stretches of these are still visible on the south coast of Fife. Eighty miles of beaches with direct access inland were identified along Scotland's east coast and one of the most vulnerable stretches was between Fraserburgh and Aberdeen. There were about thirty miles of open beaches suitable for landings. General Sir Robert Carrington, Commander in Chief, Scotland, reported, 'Aberdeen, if captured, would be capable of maintaining a large force.' Its harbour would allow big ships to dock and land thousands of infantry, field artillery – and Germany's most potent weapon of the war. The speed of the panzer thrusts through northern France had astounded military strategists and, if a landing in the north-east of Britain had been successful, then the Germans might have overrun Scotland very quickly.

Most of the coastline south of Aberdeen is rocky, often guarded by high cliffs. The first beach that has access inland is at Stonehaven, with more cliffs to the south of the town. This is also the point on the coast where the Grampian massif reaches closest to the sea. It was decided that great and immediate efforts needed to be made to slam the door on advancing panzer divisions and the line of the little Cowie Water was chosen as a defensive barrier, a stop line, a makeshift rampart to prevent a disaster: the overrunning of Scotland and Britain.

It was a soot-black, moonless March morning, drizzling and miserable. When I set my rucksack and hazel crook on the back seats of my ancient Range Rover at 5 a.m., I looked up to see if there was any light at all in the sky. Nothing, not even the heads of the western hills could be made out in the thick darkness. The lights of the lambing shed up at Brownmoor were only a dim, yellow twinkle. No ewes and their newborns would be going anywhere this morning – all would be staying snug in the straw under the heat lamps.

I felt like joining them, but repeated checks on the forecast had insisted that my day to walk the Cowie Stop Line would be bright and clear. Stonehaven lay 160 miles due north, and often the weather changes on the way up the east coast, sometimes radically. Or not. When I crossed the Forth, the morning mist meant that I could barely make out the elegant new bridge only a few hundred metres upstream and, an hour later, the placid waters of the Tay looked dull and grey. But at least it had stopped raining when I turned north towards Forfar and the Angus coast. Perhaps the day would brighten. Huge cumulus clouds billowed out over the Howe of the Mearns, driven towards the mountains by the wind off the sea. And over its grey horizon I could see some blue breaks in the cloud. It was after 8 a.m. when at last I turned off the A90 and wound my way down through the wooded deans to Stonehaven, where the sun was shining.

Like many Scottish coastal towns, Stonehaven turns its back to the sea and the bitter winds that whistle off it. Those who built houses as the town expanded did not need sea views, they saw enough of it every day. I parked on the town square. Laid out in 1824, it is pleasingly proportioned and gives Stonehaven a genuine centre rather than an accidental concentration of shops along a single street or at a cross-roads. And parking was free for the first half-hour! Not what I expected in Aberdeenshire. I set off to find a takeaway coffee and make a quick tour of this well-set little town.

In June 1940, military planners saw Stonehaven differently. The 9th Divisional Operation Instruction reckoned that the first and best option was to 'strengthen the defence of the line STONEHAVEN – COWIE WATER in the event of an enemy tank landing North of that line in MORAY or ABERDEENSHIRE with no landing south of it'. If this sequence of events took place – and after the drama of the Fall of France and the overrunning of Belgium, Luxembourg and the Netherlands, nothing seemed impossible – then the panzers would rumble south from Aberdeen, detachments of their grenadiers following in their motorised transports. The first resistance they would meet would be the Cowie Stop Line. And if the panzers followed the line of the old A90 (once they had broken through the French army, they followed the main roads of northern France, refuelling at roadside petrol stations), the first sight of them for the defenders of Stonehaven would have been on the northern horizon as they roared over the Hill of Megray, only a mile away.

The divisional instructions included orders for the bridge over the Cowie to be blown and a long string of anti-tank cubes were set beside it; they ran down to the beach where the little river flowed into the sea. From all of the surviving documentation, it is clear what would happen next. Street fighting was likely, as German infantry were expected to find places where they could cross the Cowie, and facing them would be detachments of the Home Guard, stiffened by such regular troops as could be brought up to the front in time. It was clear that Stonehaven itself was seen as a barrier, a giant anti-tank cube and, to smash through into the straths of Angus and Tayside beyond it, the panzers would have to reduce the town to rubble. Surely no senior officer at general headquarters thought that the Cowie Line could be held indefinitely; its role must have been to slow down an enemy advance, buy time to regroup.

Having found a cheery coffee shop, and armed myself with enough caffeine, I walked down to the shore. From the narrow promenade, I could see a horned bay with high cliffs at either side. Behind me, enjoying glorious sea views, were modern houses, most of them grey and uniform. It was as though a 1960s low-rise council estate had been strung out in a line and each modest house given epic views. I liked that. Two surprises struck me as I walked along the promenade. Stonehaven must be so called because of its stony, shingle beach, and to prevent panzers from outflanking the defences along the banks of the Cowie Water, the concrete cubes must have extended by some distance, probably as far as the low tidemark. But where was the outfall of the little river? I asked a passer-by if the narrow stream I could see in the distance was it. Indeed it was. And if it was, surely this could have presented no barrier at all to the Germans. They had the concentrated firepower to blast a path through a line of concrete cubes. But what I first saw turned out to be deceptive. I climbed onto a platform that was certainly new and saw that behind it the Cowie had been partly dammed to create a wider and deeper stretch downstream from the bridge. What trickled into the North Sea seemed like a controlled outfall. Perhaps it was more of a barrier in 1940.

I reparked my car outside the Co-op, did my usual checks and set off. The plan was to walk the southern banks of the Cowie Water, where there was a path, and see what remained of the stop line. In 2005 Gordon Barclay of Historic Scotland did an excellent survey, but he did the journey in reverse, beginning in Fetteresso Forest in the foothills of the Grampian massif, ending where I was proposing to begin. Perhaps a different viewpoint would discover more. And it turned out that it did, not always in a positive sense.

The sun shone, it was bright and early, there were cheese sandwiches in my rucksack, what could go wrong? At the undemolished Cowie Bridge, it appeared that all the concrete cubes had been removed and for the first few hundred metres a tarmac path made life easy, pleasant. Immediately after I turned left at the parapet of the bridge, the banks on the south side rose up steeply and had been retained by what looked like an old concrete wall. Perhaps that was all that was needed to make it a formidable barrier for tanks. And when the ground eventually dropped away beyond it, flat enough to be used as primary school playing fields, the northern bank rose higher, too high for the caterpillar tracks of a panzer to negotiate. And then I saw the first evidence of the stop line. Even in a leafless March a pillbox built into the north bank was very difficult to see. It blended in with the dark earth. The logic of its location seemed to be that it offered a field of fire that covered the flat ground of the playing fields opposite. Perhaps if panzer grenadiers had left their motorised, armoured vehicles and scrambled down the steep slopes to cross the shallow Cowie, they could have been fired on from behind. Suddenly the sunny morning darkened a little.

Up ahead rose the tall piers of the railway viaduct that still carries the main line from Aberdeen to Edinburgh across the river. The divisional reports of 1940 did not plan demolition but instead solid blocking at either end. I was not about to climb up the steep embankment to check. The banks of the Cowie were less formidable here, and if there had been cubes placed here, they had long gone. The tarmac path stopped abruptly as I made my way under the arches of the viaduct and into a wide strip of sitka spruce. On the floor of the wood, particularly where fallen trees offered places to sit, litter had been widely strewn: the Siporex trays now used by chip shops, the empty plastic bottles of sugary drinks. I looked at my map and there was indeed a school nearby.

My collection of Pathfinders for Scotland is full of gaps and Stonehaven is one of them. I had tried to find second-hand copies online without success and was forced to content myself with a much smaller scale Landranger. It was maddening. Not only did it carry little detail, the damned thing was too big and too stiff to fold well enough to show the Stonehaven and Cowie segments unless I held it in my hand all the time, or put it in my rucksack, which I would have to take off and put on again every time I needed to check something. This sounds like a grumpy detail, but it is important. Looking too often at a map, because it is in your hand, means that you can look too little at what is around you: the shape of the land, its detail, how others might have seen it, pillboxes hidden in riverbanks. In the end, I tore out the bit I needed and folded it so that it fitted in my pocket. Sorted. I needed both hands because after I had left the litter behind me there was only the vaguest suggestion of a path through the sitka wood.

The banks of the Cowie became suddenly steep and I climbed uphill on a wet slope, grabbing at branches and saplings to avoid slithering backwards. It was not dangerous, but I did not want a dunking in the river. At the top of the bank I could see a fence and a green field beyond it. It was the playing fields of Mackie Academy, the local secondary school. Around the fringes of a wide area of grassland, enough for half a dozen rugby pitches rather than the one whose posts I could see, ran a path. In the distance a man was walking with two golden Labradors, and I caught up with him where the path took us both downhill towards what had become the gorge of the Cowie. Close by, a bridge carried the dual carriageway of the A90 over it and the dog walker and I fell into conversational step. In 1940, he told me he had been four years old and remembered the tall radar masts being built above Stonehaven. But even though he had seen concrete cubes and pillboxes on his daily walks, he knew nothing of the frantic work on the stop line. All he could recall were lorry loads of soldiers leaving the market square. As he talked to me, the old man pointed out the route he usually took, and other things, all the while holding a transparent plastic bag. It only slowly dawned on me that it was full of dog poop. Something of a distraction.

The work on the defences along the banks of the Cowie was carried out by two companies of Royal Engineers, one following the other, and they were supported by detachments of the Pioneer Corps. Armed with shovels, sledgehammers, axes and wirecutters, these men tended to be reservists anxious to do their bit. And the Pioneers were the only units in the British army that would accept men who were technically enemy aliens, Germans and Austrians. Usually these were Jews or political opponents of the Nazis who had fled to escape persecution and they were dubbed the King's Most Loyal Enemy Aliens. The notorious newspaper publisher Robert Maxwell was in the Pioneers. Their knowledge of the German language and German ways of thinking were thought very useful.

After I left the old man and his loyal dogs (one of them growled at me), I set off through another strip of woodland, this time on a good and hard path. Down to my right, the banks of the Cowie seemed too steep to need any defences and the road looked old to me (behind me, it stopped dead at the line of the dual carriageway) and might have been used by the lorries carrying Royal Engineers, Pioneers and their kit. About a mile ahead, I could see Ury House, a vast mansion on the slopes of the north bank of the river. In black-and-white photographs I had looked at while I was researching, it had been roofless, deserted, but now the house was encrusted with scaffolding. The road dipped down to the Cowie and at a low metal bridge I found the first elaborate defence works. On either side of its southern approach there were cubes with slots in them. These were probably used to accommodate iron rails so that a strong roadblock could be set up. The banks on either side of the Cowie were very overgrown, but they seemed passable by panzers.

On a knoll above the bridge stood a pillbox. Shrouded in gorse and with grass growing on the roof, it glowered, menacing. The small window-like gaps, the gun loops, covered the bridge and the flat ground beyond. Built from blocks of granite, the pillbox looked indestructible, its walls very thick and solidly bedded into the ground. These squat little structures are named after an everyday item that echoed their shape: the pillboxes people used to keep pills in. At the back, the narrow doorway had a massive lintel, fringed by yellow gorse, and I stooped low to avoid it. Inside was very dark, very cramped, but dry. It surprised me that nothing had made its home there in the winter just past.

Even to my untrained eye, the banks of the Cowie at Ury House looked vulnerable, with stretches of relatively flat ground on either side. It seemed that in response the south bank had been made much steeper, and as I walked along what I guessed had been a service road I came across another pillbox, positioned to cover more of the flatter ground. Almost completely enveloped by gorse, I would not have noticed it without the help of Gordon Barclay's survey. Below it was a cluster of concrete cubes, and some improvised agricultural fencing offered a clue to other defences. This was a line of angle iron fence posts, russet with corrosion, through which barbed wire had been threaded, and it ran along the top of the ridge along the south bank of the river. Originally, they almost certainly formed the basis of a barbed-wire obstacle. So many trees and so much gorse has grown up in the space of seventy years that it has obscured what must have been a clear and forbidding rampart. And the new growth also hides the point of the siting of pillboxes and cubes because it is difficult to see what they saw when the landscape was much more open and had been cleared for better visibility. Across the river, Ury House stood on the wrong side of history: if the panzer commanders had chosen to strike at this vulnerable point, they would have left it in ruins, unwilling to take the risk of snipers or machine-gun nests having been concealed on the upper floors.

By the late summer of 1940, work on the stop line was intensifying. While the Battle of Britain had beaten back the Luftwaffe, invasion in the south was still thought to be imminent. What threatened the north of Scotland was the possibility of a diversionary attack, a bold stroke from a German High Command whose forces had seen spectacular, unprecedented success. By February 1941, British military intelligence had come to the view that the Wehrmacht would commit two infantry divisions, about 12,000 men, two light panzer battalions, about 400 tanks and an airborne brigade of 2,000 parachutists. It was anticipated that about half of this invasion force would attack the long stretches of beaches with access inland that lie between Findhorn on the Moray Firth round to Aberdeen. And if these landings were successful, this small army would likely swing south to punch a hole through the defences at the Stonehaven Gap.

Three battalions of the 51st Division were ordered to be ready to reinforce the Home Guard along about a hundred miles of coastline from Findhorn to Buchan Ness, and another battalion was to cover the beaches west of Findhorn to Lossiemouth. In all, about 3,000 regular soldiers would join the Home Guard to resist an invasion force that might outnumber them four to one and were far better equipped. There could be little doubt that if the Germans landed units on the southern shore of the Moray Firth, only a miracle could prevent them from reaching the Cowie Stop Line a few days later. British senior officers cannot have been unaware of this, nor indeed many of the men working on the defences, but what else could they do? It makes the building of the pillboxes and the back-breaking work of converting the banks of the little river into a tank trap an admirable act of defiance – against what were likely to be overwhelming odds.

As I made my way upriver on the service road, I could see the ground beginning to rise and the contours beginning to bunch on my cut-down Landranger. I came to a splendid bridge, a high crossing over the Cowie that seemed to be an appropriately grand approach to Ury House. On either side of the southern approach lay slotted concrete cubes that would have bookended a road block made with iron rails. And below this beautiful viaduct was another, much smaller, much older bridge and the Barclay survey noted that it had been protected by cubes. I could see no evidence of them. But most impressive was a pillbox on the slightly higher ground to the west of the high bridge. Unlike all of the others I had seen, this one was not covered by gorse or half-hidden behind a tangle of young trees and scrub. It looked very much as it would have done in 1940.

Close to the approach to the stately viaduct was the entrance to a driveway that swept down to a very attractive house. Its older, sandstone core had been sympathetically added to, and beyond lay a paddock, some grazing horses and a stables complex. I decided to ignore a 'Keep Out' sign tacked to a tree and walked down the drive to knock on the door. To my surprise, an American answered and he told me that he had lived in the house for twenty years. When I asked if I could walk along the banks of the Cowie that lay on his land, he said no. There was no path and little to see. Instead he advised me to cross the bridge and take a farm track to the north of the river. I asked him about the pillbox by the entrance to his drive and he was very informative. Having looked after it, apart from the time his children used it in a game of paintball, he had done some research on its origins. His curiosity had been further stirred when he found a great deal of tangled galvanised wire along the riverbank. At first he blamed it on an untidy farmer but later learned that the wire was used to tie together timber posts which were rammed in to keep the heightened south bank of the Cowie from collapsing into the water.

On the night of Saturday 7 September 1940, all of the church bells in Stonehaven suddenly began to ring to rouse the population. Cromwell was the code word for the start of an invasion and it had been issued when many squadrons of German bombers flew over London on what turned out to be the first night of the Blitz. It appears that this huge raid was thought to be the prelude to invasion. The towns-people spilled onto the streets, no doubt searching the skies and looking out to sea. But no parachutists floated downwards, no warships were seen in the bay, and when a false alarm was declared, calm was restored. Nevertheless, the incident brought the realities of war much closer, and when news of the Blitz came, no doubt work on the stop line restarted with some urgency.

The helpful American had looked at my boots and wondered if I would not have been better with wellingtons. And although they do not give as much support as good boots, it turned out that he was right. The farm track was very wet, even on its crest, and I almost lost my left boot in sucking mud. I wanted to rejoin the course of the Cowie and that meant crossing a tussocky, trackless haugh, and it too turned out to be sodden, parts of it moving up and down like a quaking bog. There was nothing much to see where I was squelching: the ground was flat but the southern bank much too high for tanks to attempt a crossing. When at long last I reached a metalled track that was relatively dry, I saw a near-complete section of defensive improvisation. The south bank had been planted with an avenue of beech trees, old enough to have been mature in 1940, and between them the engineers and pioneers had placed fifteen concrete cubes. Nature and man-made objects combining to repel fascism.

By the time I reached Findlaystone Bridge my feet were soaking and if I could have found somewhere dry to sit down, I would have got a spare, dry pair of socks out of my rucksack. But I could find nowhere, and did not fancy the bridge parapet. It was much too close to the road. At least the weather was warm and the hard-going had worked up a sweat. I always wore a good cotton shirt under a woolly pullover and I had a spare if I needed it.

Findlaystone Bridge was fascinating. A squat little struc-ture, it carried the Slug Road, a local name for the A957 to

Banchory and a memory of Aberdeenshire Gaelic. It comes from *sloc* for a hollow. The Slug Road travels through a narrow pass as it climbs into the Grampian Mountains. The bridge was guarded by elaborate defence works, perhaps the most complete to survive along the line. Now surrounded by tall sitka spruce and in near-permanent shade, a pillbox sits in a commanding position above the south approach. And further into the wood, below what looked like a decent track, were the clear remains of slit trenches, firing positions for machine gunners, mortar launchers and riflemen. Nearby was a pit surrounded by rusted angle iron fence posts of the sort I had seen at Ury. It lay some distance from the slit trenches, perhaps a store of some kind.

The track led me into the half-light of old, unmanaged, dripping woodland. It must have rained recently because the ground was so wet in places that it could be treacherous. Even a modest incline required care and in one place I slipped badly, only staying upright by grabbing a sapling. In doing so, I wrenched my left shoulder.

The banks of the Cowie were so steep that no defence work was needed. The river may look small and insignificant on a map, but it was an excellent choice as a barrier. From the sketchy information on the bit of the Landranger in my pocket, I reckoned I had a one-and-a-half mile forest walk until I could see any more of the stop line. I had no idea that I would come close to not seeing any more of anything.

The track I had taken was much obstructed by fallen trees, many of them velvet green with moss, some of them bent over like low archways. I came to a fork. To the left a track led uphill and away from the river, but to the right it seemed to stay much closer to its course. Perhaps I might see something Gordon Barclay had missed (unlikely) and so I chose to go right. After a time, the track narrowed and then completely disappeared amongst the fallen trees and rocky outcrops. And the course of the Cowie deepened into a gorge. The prudent option would, of course, have been to turn around and carefully retrace my steps back to the fork. But being thrawn, male, Scottish and tired, I was not about to take the prudent option. Oh no. And so I started to climb the bank. It was by no means sheer, but very steep and slippery. Hand over hand, kicking at outcrops of rock to check if they were earthfast and grabbing thick branches, tugging them before committing, I made my way slowly upwards. The lush green shoots of wild garlic were very slippery. My shoulder was aching badly. When I wrapped my left hand around what I thought was a well-rooted sapling and then gritted my teeth to lever myself upwards, it came ripping out of the ground.

I fell backwards, my momentum making me swing around, and a moment before I started to tumble down towards the rocky river I was able to grab another branch. And it held. The expletives echoed up and down the gorge. They probably heard me in Stonehaven.

When I finally dragged myself up to level ground, I found I was on what must have been the other track, the left fork, the sensible option. My hands were covered in mud, my jeans were wet and filthy, and I had managed to tear most of the nails on my left hand. But I was now left in no doubt that the Cowie had been an excellent choice as a barrier.

After a few moments to catch my breath, gripping my knees, I started to walk downhill, back towards the course of the Cowie. I washed most of the mud off my hands in a tiny trickle by the side of the track. To my right, barbed wire had been wrapped around the trees with shards of white plastic attached to make it obvious and it barred access to the path, or the lack of a path that I had been on. I wondered if someone had actually fallen in the river, and also why there was no barbed wire at the other bloody end. I was tired, grumpy and hungry, and in these dripping woods was unable to find anywhere dry to sit down. I prayed for a bench or a flat surface of any kind that was not soaked. And around a rocky corner, like some sort of miracle, one appeared. Hooray!

A brass plate on the back of the bench read 'The Gove Pool', and below it the Cowie was much deeper for a few metres. A small sandbank had built up opposite. Perhaps people used to swim here in an age before swimming pools. I gratefully eased off my rucksack and rummaged for my spare shirt and socks – and my cheese sandwiches. When I took off my woolly pullover, it was damp with sweat and my shirt was wringing. So were my socks. Since there was no wind and it was very warm for March, I thought I might cool down if I sat down on the bench for a bit without a top on and with bare feet. A heartbeat later, around the rocky corner came two ladies with their dogs. The sight of a half-naked man eating a cheese sandwich did not cause either to break their stride.

'Yes,' said one, 'so difficult to know what to wear when it's so variable.'

My mouth full of sandwich, I nodded. And wondered if I would meet the local police at the end of the track.

I dressed quickly. Perhaps this path was popular. I drank most of my water and decided to press on. Even though I had walked only five miles or so, I was becoming very tired. Enough drama. After a time, I came to a strange place, a grove of very tall beech trees that had been planted in a wide circle. Slung from one of the topmost branches was a rope, and over the river another had been attached to one of the trees. The only way these could have been securely attached was by climbing the trees. For some reason, that cheered me.

What made me less cheerful after the beechgrove was the gradient of the path as it climbed out of the shaded gorge. It was so steep that I had to pause and rest two or three times. All the walking I had done in the previous few months had made me fitter than I had been for years, but I suspect my earlier acrobatics had tipped me over the edge in more than one sense. Beech turned to birch as I trudged on and finally cleared the treeline. Looking back east towards the sea, it was clear how narrow the Stonehaven Gap was. To the west, the path traversed the flank of a ridge and it was so wet underfoot that a substantial burn was flowing down it. Which was a help. By that time both of my feet were soaked again and it made sense to splash up through it because the wash of the water had left a hard base of pebbles and gravel. And then I arrived at another decision.

The Landranger showed the dotted line of a path, I thought, that continued north-west above the Cowie, but there was no sign of it. Instead the wet path I was on doubled back on itself and would take me the way I had just come. Ahead was a newly ploughed field enclosed by a rickety barbed-wire fence, not its only means of keeping animals and people off it, as I discovered. I waded through a thick patch of bracken, somehow lifted my legs high enough to swing over safely, and staggered down into a deep drain cut around the margin of the field. It would have worked well as a slit trench. Very weary by this time, I plodded up the side of the field, cloying, clarty mud making my boots even heavier, until I reached a B road. Having wiped my boots on roadside tussocks, I leaned against a gatepost to rummage in my rucksack for the last few squares of chocolate and the last of my water.

The sun came out. The sugar rushed and I realised that I had only two more miles to walk and all of it on a road. Hallelujah!

I was in the Fetteresso Forest, a huge Forestry Commission plantation that reaches west into the mountains, up the water-shed of the Cowie and beyond. It almost fringes the Cairn o' Mount road, a scenic if switchback route from the Howe of the Mearns to Banchory and Deeside. It seems on a map to cut a substantial corner, avoiding both Stonehaven and Aberdeen, but the road is winding and slow and the temp-tation to stop for the views is constant. Nevertheless, an 'Appreciation Paper' of 1940 was anxious 'to prevent any enemy turning movement' that is an effort to get around the Cowie Stop Line to the west. And panzers and troop transports could certainly have rumbled south on the Cairn o' Mount road. At Bridge of Dye, where a high viaduct crosses the gorge of the little river, two pillboxes were placed on the north side, the direction the Germans would come. They covered the narrow bridge. Further west, the road through Glenshee from Blairgowrie to Braemar was blocked at a double hairpin bend known as the Devil's Elbow. Long lines of cubes can still be seen crossing part of the glen and two pillboxes were sited to cover the road in both directions. Beyond Glenshee, the road and rail links with Inverness were considered easy to block at the Drumochter Pass.

From the welcome B road (downhill too), I could see some distance to the north, across the valley of the Cowie, and partly screened by a shelter belt the grassy remains of the fortifications of a much earlier invasion force. Raedykes Roman camp was dug on Garrison Hill, surely a later memory of its construction, and it lay about a mile and a half north of where I was walking. The camp was built in the summer of 84 AD on the orders of Gnaeus Julius Agricola, the

Governor of Britannia, the man who had led an army over the Cheviot Hills and marched his men along the line of Dere Street.

Raedykes was vast, almost a hundred acres, able to accommodate the leather tents of 16,000 soldiers: three legions and the Batavian and Tungrian auxiliaries from the Rhine Estuary. It was one of a chain of marching camps that trace Agricola's advance north into Caledonia, and like the German panzers might have been, he was forced to pass through the Stonehaven Gap. For the short time the legions occupied the camp, they will have been busy making preparations for battle. Tacitus recorded that Agricola received news, perhaps at Raedykes, that the native kindred had massed an army and would fight a pitched battle. Exactly what the great general had hoped and planned for. He expected that the discipline and superior equipment of his men would bring victory over a host of Celtic warriors even if it was much larger.

Knowing I would pass close to Raedykes, I had Tony Birley's excellent translation of Tacitus with me: 'And so he [Agricola] came to the Graupian Mountain. It had already been occupied by the enemy.' In the classical tradition of speeches from generals before battles, Tacitus put famous words in the mouth of Calgacus, the leader of the Caledonian Confederacy. Those used to explain why they were forced to fight a pitched battle are both surprisingly critical and wonderfully concise:

It is no use trying to escape their arrogance by submission or good behavior. They have pillaged the world: when the land has nothing left for men who ravage everything, they scour the sea. If an enemy is rich, they are greedy, if he is poor, they crave glory. Neither East nor West can sate their appetite. They are the only people on earth to covet wealth and poverty with equal craving. They plunder, they butcher, they ravish, and call it by the lying name of 'empire'. They make a desert and call it peace.

Unlike the Germans, the Roman legions marched from the south and the Battle of the Graupian Mountain was probably fought on the slopes of Bennachie near Inverurie, about twenty miles north of Raedykes. When Tacitus' manuscript was first printed in Italy between 1475 and 1480 by Francesco dal Pozzo, a mistake was made. Instead of the Graupian Mountain, the Italian editors rendered it as the Grampian Mountain and the mistaken name has stuck.

When I emerged from the forest, I reached Bossholes Farm and a large equestrian centre that had been built next to it. Horses grazed in the fields around its barns and arena, and when I put down my rucksack on a bank at the entrance to look for more chocolate, a friendly mare ambled over to greet me. Horses have soulful, liquid eyes and this big lass liked having her muzzle rubbed and her neck patted. For some reason, she perked me up. The banks of the Cowie at Bossholes were high enough, but where the Burn o' Day joins the river, I found a group of four cubes. More stood by the southern approach to Haugh Head bridge, the last crossing of the Cowie before it plunged into the forest. The banks of the river had been raised, although it looked to me that a good deal of erosion had taken place over the last seventy years.

Two pillboxes covered the Haugh Head bridge (it had been listed for demolition if the Germans invaded). One lies a little way downstream and could fire on any movement on the road, as it turns downhill towards the river. The other was the most spectacularly sited of all that I had seen along the line. Now almost completely enveloped by gorse, it stands on a steep rise in a sheep pasture south of the bridge. What is gained in height, it may have lost in range, for it stands at least 200 metres from the river. It was a good end to a difficult day and I sat down on the parapet of the bridge, praying that my phone would have a signal so that I could call a taxi from Stonehaven to come and collect me.

After I changed my socks, bought some more chocolate and had eaten my last cheese sandwich, I set off on the long drive home to the Borders. Born in 1950, I was raised in the shadow of the Second World War. Like all of my contemporaries in Kelso, we were obsessed with the drama, the scale and the detail of the greatest conflict the world had ever seen. On a ridge above the council estate we lived in, there was a long stretch of scrubland and woods we called the Meadows. Like POWs trying to escape the clutches of our captors in Stalag Luft whatever, we dug tunnels into the hillside. With wooden sticks for rifles, we played a game called Japs and British, although no one was ever very sure of the rules and there were plenty of arguments over who had been shot and who had not. Men still wore bits of their old uniforms to work: short battledress jackets and berets, and we were all dazzled by films that gloried in British victories: *The Dam Busters*, *The Longest Day* and many more. One of the most popular early TV comedies was set in an army camp: *Bootsie and Snudge* starred Bill Fraser and Alfie Bass. And the title of the first *Carry On* film was based on a military order. *Carry on Sergeant* was the first in a long series. Kids' comics featured improbable heroes like Battler Britton, and even men's haircuts took years to change from a short back and sides, what military barbers did for all soldiers. The war was everywhere, an enormous influence on a generation of children who had not directly experienced it.

Our parents had. And therein lay confusion, and for my part the origin of some shameful attitudes about my dad's service in the army. He was an electrician and in early 1940 had joined the Royal Engineers, spending four-and-a-half years on overseas service. Fixing things. Other dads had shot people, been brave, been a bit like Battler Britton. My dad had made the light go on.

He died in 1986, a few days after his 70th birthday and twelve years after a very debilitating stroke. In 2012, my older sister wrote to the Army Personnel Centre in Glasgow to ask for the war records of John Lauder Moffat. There was much that I could not make out on poor photocopies, but his discharge papers of January 1946 made me sit up. At the top of a page of flowing copperplate it said that my dad had been mentioned in dispatches in the *London Gazette*, 'in recognition of gallant and distinguished service in Italy'. There were no more details, but some research told me that in their fighting retreat up Italy, the Germans were in the habit of cutting electricity supplies as they abandoned towns and cities. Transformers and other installations were often booby-trapped and it was the role of the Royal Engineers to reconnect the supply. I do not know if my dad did this or not, but there is no doubt that it was extremely risky. No other campaign in Western Europe cost more lives than the fighting in Italy.

Even though the crassness of youth might supply an excuse, I was ashamed of the way in which I had relegated my dad's service on behalf of his country, of unborn generations, for me, my mum and my sisters. There was of course nothing I could do to make it right with him, but I decided to go to the Cowie Stop Line as a sort of muddled homage, an incoherent mixture of atonement and curiosity. My dad had spent all his service overseas, but it had been built by the Royal Engineers, men from the same corps. In its way, the line was a statement of defiance and stubbornness, of making the best in the face of adversity, and a work of some ingenuity. And it turned out to be very difficult to get to know. These were all elements of the character of John Lauder Moffat, and the reason this book is dedicated to him.

Envoi

The Snow Road

Like tiny parachutes, flakes of snow began to fall at moonset, sometime around 6.30 a.m. There was no whisper of wind and the big flakes seemed to tilt and sway as they floated out of the darkness of the January sky. My puppy jumped up at them, snapping and trying to catch them, puzzled at their evanescence. Entirely distracted, the wee Westie refused to pee or poop and eventually, like me, she settled and stood watching the gentle snowfall, following the flakes as they fell into the light from the kitchen window. It was hypnotic, the first flurry of snow that winter, the landscape becoming silent, the trees and hedges veiled, the fields covered white.

By midday about three inches had fallen and as we crunched up the track with the older dogs, it was clear that it would lie, maybe freeze. There would be no point in putting out the younger horses stabled for the winter. All they would do was snuffle at the snow and perhaps even do themselves injury as boredom persuaded them to play and gallop around on the slippery ground. By the time gloaming gathered, about three o'clock, it had begun to freeze and a snell, stiff wind was blowing out of the north west. I doubted if even the four-wheel-drive vehicles would get up our steep track, and if we tried and failed there would be a vehicle blocking access or exit for anyone else.

Eight of our older horses live out over the winter, well rugged and kept going by big hay bales and bowls of hard feed given to them in the morning. Two Shetland ponies have one of the outbye fields to themselves; hardy little creatures with thick, two-ply coats, they need nothing, having stored fat in the summer. But the snow was too deep, preventing them from getting at the bitter winter grass, and they would need some hay. In a big net slung over my shoulders I reckoned I could manage to carry four kilos and walk the half mile through the snow to feed them.

The outbye is a long meadow on the gently sloping banks of a tiny stream that the horses drink from. It was still running and the snow had stopped falling. At the top of the ridge to the south stands a sheltering plantation of sitka spruce and in the moonlight I could see the Shelties standing under the branches of the evergreens, out of the worst of the wind. As I shook the hay out into two clumps, I noticed that the ponies had football-size lumps of snow on the ends of their tails. As they had brushed the surface of the snow-covered field, it must have frozen onto them. Although they are half-wild and will kick out to protect their food, they stood quietly as I bashed off the clods with my boots.

When I had rolled up the net and turned for the trudge back down to the farmhouse, I was struck by how brightly the full moonlight shone, picking out detail in a monochrome landscape. A buzzard glided low over the sitka wood, its wingspread scarcely moving, but when it called piou-piou, the Shelties looked up from their hay as the silence was broken.

On the hills to the north, about a mile and a half away on the other side of our little valley, the wind had drifted the snow against the dykes that climb straight up to the top of the watershed ridge, leaving most of the ground barely covered. It was then I noticed something different, strange, something I had never seen before. Running diagonally along the flanks of the hills were thick, arrow-straight parallel white lines. It looked as though the snow had been caught by the kerbs and ditches of a road. No dyke would run in that direction and indeed two of them appeared to cut right across its line. I have looked across at those hillsides most days for the last seventeen years and had never noticed the outline of what seemed to be a ghost road.

Two days later, after the melt had turned every track and field entry to mud and slush, I drove over to the other side of the valley. The line of this road, if it was a road, was not marked on the Pathfinder map and despite walking up to several points where I thought I had seen it run I could find nothing, no trace. It was as though the snow road had melted back into the grass. I liked that. Perhaps I might see it again in another seventeen years.

Further Steps

This book marks the beginning of a long-term project to open up the hidden ways and, where possible, to make them accessible to walkers. I enjoyed these journeys enormously, learned a great deal about my country and plan to walk in more of the footsteps of our ancestors.

If funding can be found, we will begin the work of mapping and securing permissions from landowners. Once that is achieved, volunteers will be recruited and, with the cooperation of local authorities and other relevant bodies, we hope to begin the work of making them passable and safe. Signage, especially precise information about mileage (I really appreciated this on the Ballachulish to Connel walk), information boards, perhaps some public sculpture and certainly some treasure will be installed. Along the ways we plan to hide pilgrim badges, waymerks and Roman phalerae or medals, and clues to their whereabouts will be found on a comprehensive interactive website.

Work is being done on enhancing the experience of the walks through the use of augmented reality. From an app downloaded to any mobile phone, walkers will be able to listen to the story of the hidden way as they walk along its line. And video footage shot on phones or stills snapped with these or other cameras will be uploaded to our website as knowledge and experience grows.

Over years, it is hoped that the faded map of roads no longer travelled in Scotland will come alive, and as that happens, a different and richer way of seeing our past will emerge, making a vast and varied archive of the feet.

Acknowledgements

Walter Elliot is a quietly inspirational figure. Having spent many summers and long winters fencing the Borders countryside, he has come to understand the lie of the land better than anyone. Allied to great scholarship, common sense and a willingness to share the vast store of what he knows, Walter's instinct for the shape of the land and its secrets, and his love for it, has been a gift to me. More than anyone, he set me off down these hidden ways and I will always be grateful for his kindness.

Nat Edwards walked the Herring Road with me and is my partner in the wider project beyond this book. He is articulate, can-do and thoughtful and his observations have been illuminating.

Gordon Barclay's work on the Cowie Stop Line was invaluable and his excellent *If Hitler Comes: Preparing for Invasion, Scotland 1940* is a store of fascinating material, and thoroughly to be recommended. I was very glad to follow in, most of, Gordon's footsteps.

Richard Buccleuch and Christopher Thomson of DC Thomson were early supporters of the Hidden Ways project and their enthusiasm has been a vital encouragement, allowing the first steps to be taken.

Simon Thorogood and the team at Canongate have been patient, forebearing and supremely professional and positive. Thanks to them and Debs Warner for making this book a lot better. And Andy Lovell's cover is superb.

And finally a thank you to those landowners who might have seen a forlorn figure trudging across their property, stopping to look at a map, taking photographs, scribbling notes, looking for the ghost roads that are no longer travelled.

Index

321

Index